TIFFANY FRANCIS-BAKER

DARK SKIES
BRITAIN · IRELAND

A STARGAZER'S GUIDE

Bradt Guides Ltd, UK
Globe Pequot Press Inc, USA

First edition published September 2021
Bradt Guides Ltd
31a High Street, Chesham, Buckinghamshire, HP5 1BW, England
www.bradtguides.com
Print edition published in the USA by The Globe Pequot Press Inc,
PO Box 480, Guilford, Connecticut 06437-0480

Text copyright © 2021 Bradt Guides
Maps copyright © 2021 Bradt Guides Ltd; includes map data © OpenStreetMap contributors
Photographs copyright © 2021 Individual photographers (see below)
Project Manager: Anna Moores & Laura Pidgley
Cover research: Ian Spick

ISBN: 9781784778354

British Library Cataloguing in Publication Data
A catalogue record for this book is available from the British Library

Photographs
Photographers & picture libraries all credited alongside individual photos; photographers
for Wikimedia Commons (WC) images are: Ken Crawford (KC/WC), ESO/PESSTO/S.
Smartt (ESO/PESSTO/SS/WC), Fryns (F/WC), JochenK2002 (J/WC), NASA, ESA, A.
Simon (Goddard Space Flight Center), and M.H. Wong (University of California, Berkeley)
(NASA/ESA/AS/MHW/WC), NASA, ESA and the Hubble Heritage Team (STScI/AURA)
(NASA/ESA/HHT/WC), Nathanial Bradford (NB/WC), Olie Nielsen (ON/WC), Pablo
Carlos Budassi (PCB/WC), Stephen Rahn (SR/WC), Sid Leach/Adam Block/Mount
Lemmon Sky Center (SL/AB/MLSC/WC), Sloan Digital Sky Survey (SDSS/WC), Starhopper
(S/WC)

Front cover Valve Tower, Kielder Water (Mike Ridley)
Back cover Stargazing at Dartmoor (Arthur Cauty/Shutterstock)
Title page The Milky Way over Somerset (Phil Kieran/Shutterstock)

Map David McCutcheon FBCart.S

Typeset by Ian Spick, Bradt Guides
Production managed by Zenith Media, printed in the UK
Digital conversion by www.dataworks.co.in

AUTHOR

Tiffany Francis-Baker is a nature writer and illustrator from the South Downs in Hampshire. Her third book *Dark Skies* was published by Bloomsbury in 2019, a nature memoir exploring our relationship with the landscape at night. As part of her research, she travelled to various dark sky sites around the UK and Europe. She watched wild beavers in Devon, hiked through a haunted yew forest in Sussex, listened to migratory birds on an autumn night, stood beneath the northern lights in Norway and swam wild under the midnight sun in Finland. In 2019, she was also a writer-in-residence for Forestry England's centenary project, where she wrote and illustrated a poem about the human connection with forests. She has written for a number of national publications and appeared on BBC Radio 4 and Channel 4.

ACKNOWLEDGEMENTS

Many thanks to Nazanin Jahanshahi and Catherine Johns from Kielder Observatory, Neill Sanders at Go Stargazing and Georgia MacMillan from Friends of Mayo Dark Skies for their expertise and help in writing this book.

A NOTE ON POSTCODES

Many of the Discovery Sites listed in this book are very remote, meaning that postcodes listed should be used for guidance only. In some instances they cover large areas, so it is best to always consult an OS map before setting off. OS map numbers are given for each site listed, and in some instances specific references are also given.

CONTENTS

INTRODUCTION

The night sky has ignited our imaginations for thousands of years, which is perhaps why the late cosmologist Stephen Hawking advised us to 'look up at the stars and not down at our feet'. All around the world, communities have woven stories into the patterns they've found in the stars, from hunters and beasts to wrathful gods and goddesses. Through science and careful observation we have learnt to understand the night sky and our place within it, but up until the last century it still remained just out of reach – a sea of lights beyond the veil of our atmosphere. Then, in 1969, three men became the first to land on another celestial body and walk on the surface of the earth's moon, 384,400km (240,000 miles) away from where the world of humans sat watching on black and white television sets. It is considered to be one of the most remarkable achievements in our species' history, but the sequence of events that got us there started with one thing: stargazing.

Astronomy is the scientific name for stargazing, a Greek-rooted word that literally means the science that studies the law of the stars. Astronomers use mathematics, physics and chemistry to explain the origin and evolution of celestial objects and phenomena, including, of course, the origin and evolution of our own planet. It is thanks to early astronomers that we understand how the earth travels around the sun, and that everything we know and love came from a single cosmic explosion over 13 billion years ago. Astronomy allows us to know the

↑ Stargazing at the Scottish Dark Sky Observatory, which was sadly forced to close in 2021 after a serious fire (Scottish Dark Sky Observatory)

unknowable, and in pushing the boundaries of this knowledge we can begin to unearth the wider mysteries of life and the universe. We can understand time, explore new worlds and even search for other forms of life. But the vast nature of the universe also means that we will never fully understand it, never visit every planet or map out every star. The magic is in the mystery, and for humans, who are a little too accustomed to knowing everything, the universe will always have the upper hand.

In our anthropocentric, pressurised world, gazing at the night sky can help our daily problems and worries feel insignificant. At the same time, it's a reminder that a precise cluster of atoms came together to form our exact minds and bodies, living beings on a living earth. When the *Voyager 1* space probe took the famous *Pale Blue Dot* photograph in 1990, we saw our planet for what it really was – a single pixel against the vastness of outer space. If nothing else, looking up at

↑ The Milky Way over Broadhaven South Beach, Wales (Allan Trow/Dark Sky Wales)

the night sky reminds us how precious our planet is, and how important it is to protect our only home.

Time spent in nature has been proven to benefit our minds and bodies, and while getting enough good-quality sleep is also vital for our wellbeing, studies suggest that being out in nature after dark can offer further ways to feel more mindful and alleviate stress. A recent study in the *European Journal of Ecopsychology* indicated that stargazing and nocturnal wildlife watching led to a heightened sense of participants' personal growth and increased positive emotions. Long-term advocates of stargazing claim it can combat overthinking and help place our problems into a wider perspective. As the months pass and seasons change, we can observe the shifting hours of sunsets and sunrises, become more in tune with our circadian rhythm and appreciate the joy of first light and nightfall. In summer, the evening air is balmy and sweet, full of churring nightjars, hunting owls and sparkling glowworms in the long grass. And in winter, when the days are short and cold, the nights draw in early and allow us to catch a glimpse of the stars before bed.

Of the 18 **International Dark Sky Reserves** in the world, the British Isles are home to eight, which means there are eight places possessing an exceptional or distinguished quality of starry nights and nocturnal environment that is specifically protected for its scientific, natural, educational, cultural, heritage or recreational value. These sites are the Brecon Beacons and Snowdonia national parks in Wales, Kerry in Ireland, Cranborne Chase in southern England, the North York Moors and Yorkshire Dales national parks in northern England, and the South Downs and Exmoor national parks.

As well as these eight Dark Sky Reserves, there are also seven **Dark Sky Parks** and two **Dark Sky Communities**, making a total of 17 **Dark Sky Places** in the UK. Beyond these, there are also over two hundred Dark Sky Discovery Sites around the UK, classified as having low levels of light pollution, offering good sightlines of the sky, and with good public access. This list evolves regularly as new sites are classified and light pollution levels change, so we have included in this guide a comprehensive selection across Britain and Ireland. For an updated list of sites, readers can visit ⊘ darkskydiscovery.org.uk or ⊘ gostargazing.co.uk (see ad, inside back cover), where you can also nominate good stargazing sites in your area.

Stargazing is a simple way to escape the chaos of modern life. It's a chance to break out of our comfort zones and liberate ourselves from the idea that the nightscape is a place for other creatures to enjoy without us. When the daylight fades and darkness creeps over the sky, we can turn to the stars for joy, wonder and inspiration, just as our ancestors had done for thousands of years before us. For as the poet Lord Byron wrote in his poem *Manfred*, at night we can learn 'the language of another world'.

Under the stars at Dunkery Beacon, Exmoor National Park (Laurence Liddy)

GENERAL INFORMATION

01 BACKGROUND INFORMATION

A HISTORY OF STARGAZING

If the art of science is to pursue knowledge through observation and experimentation, then we could consider astronomy to be the most primitive form of scientific thought. It provides the earliest evidence, as far as we know, of man's desire to observe and record the world around him. The first humans cultivated a close relationship with the natural world, being more attuned with nature's rhythms and cycles, and paying closer attention to seasonal changes. Because of this, they were able to recognise patterns in the night sky and try to attribute meaning to them. One of the earliest examples of astronomical study is thought to be the **Nebra sky disc**, a bronze disc around 30cm (11.8") in diameter inlaid with gold symbols, believed to originate from the European Bronze Age. The symbols are generally interpreted as the sun or full moon, a lunar crescent, three solar arcs and a scattering of stars, seven of which are thought to be the Pleiades cluster. The Nebra sky disc is the oldest known concrete depiction of the cosmos and, whether it was an astronomical instrument, a religious item or simply a picture of the night sky, it shows that prehistoric people were celebrating the patterns and rhythms they found in nature.

Before the invention of the telescope in the early 17th century, only seven objects were visible to a human being looking up from the earth. These were the sun and moon, Mercury, Venus, Mars, Jupiter and Saturn. Around 1600BC, the **early Babylonians** produced what would be the earliest written records of astronomical observations, including the positions of planets and the times and dates of eclipses. Similar evidence has been found in early Chinese, Central American and European cultures. Stonehenge, for example, an ancient monument in Wiltshire dating back to the Mesolithic period, was built so the entrance faces the rising sun on the day of the summer solstice, suggesting it was used as a kind of solar calendar to mark the changing seasons.

In the Far East, ancient Chinese astronomy was centered on the correlation between man and the universe. For thousands of years, the emperors of various dynasties tasked special officers with observing the stars. There were two main reasons for this: first, for astrological and political purposes. They believed, for example, that eclipses were caused by a celestial dog devouring the sun, which they saw as a bad omen whose appearance they wanted to be able to predict. Secondly, they wanted to use astronomical data to create reliable calendars and systems to run their dynasties. Ancient Chinese astronomers made huge contributions to the science, inventing various astronomical instruments and maintaining the longest continuous data record of astronomical phenomena.

When the **ancient Greeks** inherited the Babylonians' astronomical records, they used the data to start delving further into the question of the earth's place within the universe. This branch of thinking was known as natural philosophy,

← Stargazing at The Sill, Northumberland National Park (Alasdair Mackenzie)

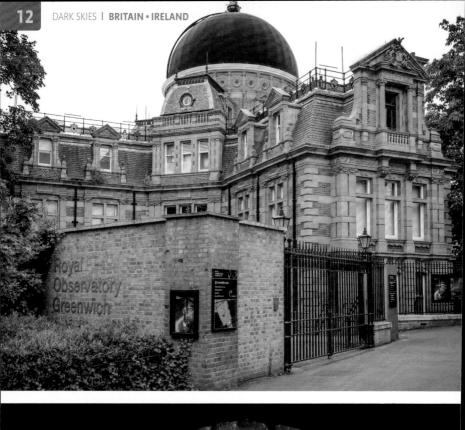

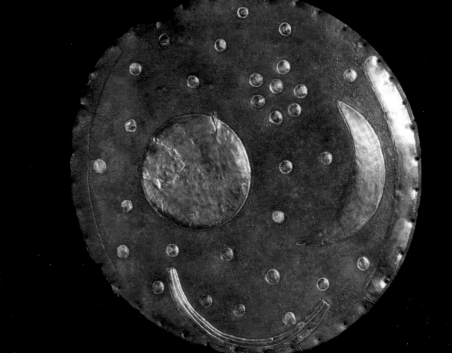

and became the predecessor to modern science. Around 480BC, a man named Thales used maths to predict eclipses, while it was Plato who first proposed that the planets follow circular orbits around the earth. It wasn't until 270BC that Aristarchus suggested an alternative model that placed the sun at the centre, rather than the earth, which became known as the heliocentric model. The idea that the universe revolved around the sun, and not the earth, remained a subject of contention into the **early modern age**, particularly as it contradicted some religious teachings. It was far more appealing to imagine the earth at the centre of all life, and it was also difficult for people to imagine the earth being in motion when they were unable to 'feel' it moving. From the late 16th century onwards, however, with the weakening of the Church in northern Europe, the invention of the telescope and the work of astronomers like Copernicus, Galileo and Kepler, a sun-centred solar system model became gradually accepted. This change was monumental in man's relationship with the universe, as it challenged the idea that the world was designed for us alone.

By the **17th century**, Sir Isaac Newton had developed further ties between astronomy and physics, including his law of universal gravitation. Around the same time, the first Astronomer Royal was appointed by King Charles II when he founded the Royal Observatory in Greenwich, London. The role of the first Astronomer Royal was given to John Flamsteed, who was tasked with 'rectifying the tables of the motions of the heavens, and the places of the fixed stars, so as to find out the so much-desired longitude of places for perfecting the art of navigation'. In other words, he was challenged to improve navigation at sea, a major concern for the newly formed Royal Society. At the time, large portions of the rest of the world were controlled by the European empires, and although trading with other countries was becoming more lucrative, the astronomical information needed to navigate across the sea was lacking. Captains could easily measure their latitude at sea, but it was almost impossible to find their longitude once out of sight of land. In 1714, the government passed the Longitude Act, offering large rewards to anyone who could solve the problem.

It took another 50 years, but it was Nevil Maskelyne, the first person to measure the weight of the planet scientifically, who also made the longitude breakthrough in the **1760s**. He recognised how the moon, being a fixed point in the sky, could be used as a reference point for ships, and went on to devise a calculation known as the lunar distance method. The lunar distance is measured using the angle between the moon and another celestial body (usually a star) and, by comparing this angle with a set of data tables called the nautical almanac, navigators were finally able to approximate their position.

Advances in astronomy continued through the centuries, particularly with the invention of photography in 1826 and the spectroscope in 1859, a device that

← **Top:** Royal Observatory, Greenwich (Lukasz Pajor/Shutterstock); **Bottom:** The Nebra sky disc is thought to be one of the earliest examples of astronomical study (SuperStock)

measures the spectrum of light. A handful of women also started working their way into the male-dominated scientific world. German astronomer Caroline Herschel (1750–1848), for example, discovered eight comets and became the first paid female astronomer in history. American astronomer Annie Jump Cannon (1863–1941) revolutionised the way scientists classified the stars, not only developing the important Harvard spectral system, but classifying approximately 350,000 stars herself. And in the 1920s, Anglo-American astronomer Cecilia Payne-Gaposchkin (1900–79) was the first to propose that stars were made up of hydrogen and helium.

The **20th century** continued to see rapid advances in the scientific study of stars, particularly as photography and quantum physics became more valuable astronomical tools. In 1910, Williamina Fleming discovered the first white dwarf, while in 1912, Henrietta Swan made discoveries in star luminosity that would later enable Edwin Hubble to measure the distance to the great nebula in Andromeda, the first measurement of distance for a galaxy outside the Milky Way. Shortly before his death in 1916, German physicist Karl Schwarzschild used Einstein's theory of relativity to lay the groundwork for black hole theory, suggesting that if any star collapses to a small enough size, its gravitational force will be so strong that no form of radiation will be able to escape it.

In **1929**, Edwin Hubble made a discovery that changed the way we see the world around us. He showed that galaxies are moving away from us with a speed proportional to their distance, which means that the universe is expanding. The theory was devised, once again, using Einstein's theory of relativity, and concluded that the entire universe had originated in what would come to be known as the Big Bang, an expansion caused by an extremely high temperature and density around 13.8 billion years in the past. With this discovery, the science of cosmology was born, a branch of astronomy that involves the origin and evolution of the universe. Hubble made his observations through the best telescope in the world at that time, located on Mount Wilson in southern California. In 1990, the Hubble Space Telescope was named in his honour, a large, space-based observatory which has since been used to observe some of the most distant stars, galaxies and planets.

Less than a decade after Hubble's discovery, German-American physicist Hans Bethe calculated how stars generate energy by turning hydrogen into helium, a reaction that happens so slowly that they are able to burn for billions of years. His work on the production of energy in stars earned him the Nobel Prize for Physics in 1967, although he is also remembered for being an advocate for the social responsibility of science. His work in atomic processes, for example, helped pave the way to the creation of the hydrogen fusion bomb in 1952. But he only agreed to take part in the development of fusion bombs because he believed them to be immoral, and wanted to prove they were unfeasible to build. He later joined the campaign against the nuclear arms race.

→ Edwin Hubble, Albert Einstein and other scientists at the Mount Wilson Observatory, California (SuperStock)

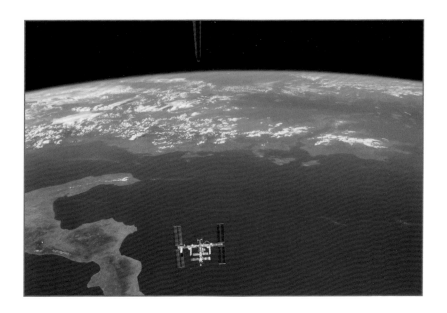

In **1957**, the Soviet Union launched the first artificial earth satellite into a low orbit, triggering the Space Race between the US and USSR to prove who was supposedly 'superior' in technology, military firepower, politics and economics. The satellite was called *Sputnik*, which is Russian for 'traveller'. A year later, the US launched its own satellite, *Explorer I*, in response and President Eisenhower signed a public order to create the National Aeronautics and Space Administration (NASA), a government agency dedicated to space exploration. Twelve years later, after numerous launches of space probes and shuttles from either side, Neil Armstrong became the first man to walk on the moon's surface and, with the Space Race unofficially 'won' by the US, government interest in lunar missions waned.

Further probes were, however, still launched throughout the following decades to learn more about space, and in **1998** the International Space Station (ISS) was collaboratively launched by five space agencies from the US, Russia, Japan, Europe and Canada. The ISS is a modular space station serving as a microgravity laboratory in which research is conducted in the fields of astrobiology, astronomy, meteorology, physics, human health and other studies. It is also used to test commercial products like espresso machines and 3D printers, to grow plants and breed small mammals, and to test systems and equipment required for possible future missions to the moon and Mars. The ISS flies at a distance of 400km (249 miles) above the earth at speeds of around 28,800km/h, and it takes just 92 minutes for the weightless laboratory to make a complete circuit of the earth. This means that astronauts who live and work on the ISS experience 16 sunrises and sunsets every single day.

↑ The International Space Station overlooking the Mediterranean (SuperStock)

So now that we have ventured into space itself, what of the future of stargazing? Modern astronomers are now divided into the observational and the theoretical, with the former focused on physical bodies like stars and planets, and the latter using data to analyse how the universe has evolved. Unlike other fields of science, no astronomer can observe their subject in its entirety. Nobody can study a galactic system from birth to death, as even the tiniest star will exist for millions of years at least, so instead they must rely on snapshots of the universe in various stages of its evolution, in order to work out how different objects form and when they will die.

For the first time in human history, we are seriously entertaining the idea of leaving our planet to take up permanent residence on another. In **October 2020**, NASA announced that scientists had identified water on the sunny side of the moon. They also found the moon's water sources were more widespread than previously thought, with pockets of ice hiding in some of its darker, more shadowy regions. This has excited the scientific community because water is such an essential resource for space exploration, and if water can be extracted from the moon, it means space shuttles can carry less water and make room for more equipment. It also means that we can more easily return astronauts to the moon, and create long-term habitats on the lunar surface to use as a base for exploring Mars.

What does the future hold for our earth-dwelling species? Will we soon be living on the lunar surface, with anti-gravity hotels and moon rock gift shops? Space agencies and private investors have already begun looking at how the moon can be mined for resources, while commercial space tourism is becoming more of a reality owing to investments from business magnates like Jeff Bezos and Elon Musk. It is exciting to imagine what our future relationship with space might look like, but there are also concerns about how other planets and celestial forms might be colonised. Who will control cosmic territories? Will resources be used for good or bad purposes? Can humans be trusted to settle in new worlds when we are struggling to look after the one we already have? For thousands, if not millions, of years, we have looked up at the bright lights of the night sky and been enchanted by their mystery, the allure of the unknowable. But how long will it be until, instead of looking up from the earth, we are looking back down at it from a second home planet? And who – or what – might we meet along the way?

UNDERSTANDING OUR SKIES

CONSTELLATIONS The **first star catalogue** was created by Hipparchus around 100BC, when he wrote down and recorded the names of all the known constellations. Simply put, a constellation is a group of stars that appears to form a pattern or picture. Not only do they help us distinguish between the mass of twinkling lights in the night sky, they also provide an archive of stories, mythology and folklore from around the world and across the breadth of human history. The **International Astronomical Union (IAU)** recognises 88 constellations in the night sky, over half of which originate from ancient Greek, Babylonian, Egyptian and Assyrian cultures. The rest were mostly added between the 16th and 17th centuries, when European astronomers and celestial cartographers 'discovered' new star patterns when they colonised the southern hemisphere. One of these was the Italian navigator Amerigo Vespucci, from whose name the word 'America' is derived.

The collection of stars within a **constellation** is not necessarily close together, as constellations are only interpreted as a pattern from our view on earth. The stars are distributed in space in three dimensions, and vary greatly in their size, temperature and distance from earth, so dimmer stars may be smaller, cooler or further away than brighter stars, but the brightest stars are not necessarily the closest either. In the swan constellation Cygnus, for example, the faintest star is the closest, while the brightest is the furthest away.

If you look long enough (or take a long exposure photograph) most stars and constellations appear to move across the sky. As the earth spins, the stars move from east to west, just as the sun appears to 'rise' and 'set'. If a star is close to the celestial poles (imaginary points in space where the earth's north and south poles extend upwards), it has a small circle of spin, so the further a star is from Polaris, the North Star, the wider the circle the stars trace. With the exception of the sun, the nearest star to earth is Proxima Centauri, which is more than four light years away. A light year is a unit of astronomical distance equivalent to the distance light travels in one year – approximately 6 million miles.

Other star patterns that do not fall under the formal definition of constellation are known as **asterisms**. These are also used by astronomers to navigate the night sky and may include a cluster of stars within a constellation, or a cluster that shares stars with more than one constellation. An example of an asterism like this is the Pleiades, also known as the Seven Sisters, which lies within the constellation Taurus. When the IAU formally accepted the modern list of 88 constellations, they also designated constellation boundaries to cover the entire celestial sphere. This means that any given point in a celestial co-ordinate system lies within one of the modern constellations, and some astronomical naming systems even include constellations to approximate the locations of celestial objects in the sky. Interestingly, the IAU defines a constellation by its boundary rather than the shapes and patterns that give a constellation its name.

All constellations are given a Latin name made up of two forms. The first is the nominative, used to talk about the constellation itself, and the second is the genitive, which is used in star names. For example, **Sirius**, the brightest star in the night sky and in the constellation Canis Major (nominative form), is also

called Alpha Canis Majoris (genitive form), literally 'the superior star of Canis Major'. Most of the constellation names we are familiar with come from ancient Middle Eastern, Greek and Roman cultures, but they were not the only ones to give names to pictures they found in the stars. Native American, Asian and African civilisations have their own astronomical stories and myths, sometimes with ceremonial or religious significance, or sometimes to help mark the seasons or the passage of time between planting and harvesting.

Many **constellation stories** are centered on animals, gods and divine figures. One of the most recognisable is **Orion the Hunter**, which is visible in both the northern and southern hemispheres. In the UK, Orion appears in the winter sky with his bow, star-studded belt and two hunting dogs, Canis Major and Canis Minor, following behind him. Greek mythology tells the story of how Orion once boasted that he could rid the earth of all its wild animals, but when the earth goddess Gaia heard his plans, she was so furious that she sent a scorpion to stop him. Unable to pierce its armour, Orion was defeated and placed in the sky with the scorpion, which became the constellation Scorpius. The middle star in Orion's sword isn't a star at all, but the Orion Nebula, which is a giant cloud of dust and gas in space. Today, Orion is used by UK charity CPRE as part of the 'Star Count' citizen science project to measure light pollution. Each February, stargazers are invited to count the stars they can see in Orion's belt and submit their data at ⊘ cpre.org.uk.

↑ Sirius (top right) is the brightest star in the night sky (SuperStock)

The constellation **Ursa Major**, or the Great Bear, contains a smaller group of stars known as the Plough or Big Dipper, which is one of the easiest patterns to spot in the night sky because it looks like a saucepan. In Roman mythology, the goddess Juno transforms a nymph named Callisto into a bear to stop her husband Jupiter falling in love with her. Callisto is almost shot by her son after he encounters her in the woods so, to avoid such a tragedy, Jupiter turns her son into a bear too and places them both in the sky to form Ursa Major and Ursa Minor – the Great Bear and Little Bear.

Another northern hemisphere constellation, **Lyra**, has roots in Greek mythology. Lyra is thought to be a small harp belonging to Orpheus, a heroic poet and musician. The harp was made out of tortoise shell by the messenger of the gods, Hermes, and the music played upon it was said to be so beautiful that it could charm mortals, gods, animals, trees and even rocks. He was even able to charm Hades, the god of the Underworld, into letting him take his lover Eurydice back to the world of the living, but only on the condition that he never looked back when he left. At the last moment, Orpheus faltered and looked back, and Eurydice was condemned to the Underworld forever. Within Lyra, the star Vega is one of the brightest stars in the night sky, and in 1850 became the first star other than the sun to be photographed.

Taurus is one of the oldest identified constellations, and was particularly important to the ancient Celts as it marked the location of the rising sun in spring. In ancient Egypt, the sacred bull was associated with the renewal of life in spring, while in Greek mythology, the god Zeus transformed himself into a bull to kidnap a beautiful princess. In the ancient stories of Mesopotamia, Taurus was known as the Bull of Heaven, and was sent by the goddess Ishtar to destroy her enemies.

The constellation **Leo** is thought to have been named after the ancient Greek story of the Nemean lion killed by the mythical hero Heracles, or Hercules to the Romans, as one of his 12 labours. It remains one of the easiest to recognise because, unlike some other constellations, its shape actually resembles its namesake of a crouching lion. Leo's mane and shoulders also make up an asterism known as the Sickle, which looks like a backwards question mark. Historians suggest that in ancient Mesopotamia, Leo may have also been interpreted as the monster Humbaba, who was killed by Gilgamesh.

OTHER GALAXIES Outside the Milky Way (which contains our solar system) our nearest large galaxy is **Andromeda**, which can be seen in the constellation of the same name. Andromeda is a circumpolar constellation, which means it is always visible above the horizon. The galaxy itself is so far away that its light takes 2 million years to reach us, and it is the most distant object visible to the naked eye. In the darkest winter skies, it appears as an elongated, fuzzy blob within the Andromeda constellation. To find it, locate the constellation Cassiopeia by following the line formed by the two stars at the edge of Ursa Major, up and through the North Star until you reach a 'W' shape on the other side. The right-hand half of this 'W' points like an arrow towards Andromeda. The galaxy will be extremely faint, but with a pair of binoculars it looks like a pale cloud.

THE GREAT RIFT
Aside from regular constellations, there is also a series of dark patches within the Milky Way known as the **Great Rift**. Most visible and striking in the southern hemisphere, the Rift is a swathe of dark nebulae several thousand light years from the earth. It stretches lengthwise through the galaxy from the constellation Cygnus, through Aquila and Sagittarius, to Centaurus. Throughout history, some cultures have discerned shapes in the Rift's patches and given names to them, known as 'dark cloud constellations'. The Inca civilisation believed a number of animals lived in the Milky Way, which they called the Mayu, meaning 'celestial river'. Within the Rift they saw Mach'acuay the serpent, Hanp'atu the toad, Urcuchillay the llama and Kantur the condor, among others.

WHAT IS ASTROLOGY?
Although astrology is generally refuted by the scientific community, the subject itself still plays an important role in our historical relationship with the stars. Astrology is the idea that the movements of stars and celestial bodies can help observers find answers and meaning in their day-to-day lives, as well as offering signs and predictions for the future. For centuries, astronomy and astrology were considered to be the same thing. The word astrology was originally derived from the Latin and Greek for 'study of the stars', and it was only later that it shifted to mean 'star divination' instead. This was around the beginning of the Enlightenment in the late 17th century, when Sir Isaac Newton mathemetised the motion of the planets and realised that gravity controlled everything. Throughout most of its history, astrology was studied in close relation to alchemy, meteorology and medicine. It was also present in political circles and mentioned in various works of art and literature, including Dante, Chaucer and Shakespeare.

Divining meaning from the stars might date back as far as the Stone Age. A number of cave drawings indicate the belief that animals and objects – even celestial ones – could be imbued with some kind of spirit, so if you could appease that spirit it may have a positive influence on your life. In ancient China, eclipses and sunspots were interpreted as omens of either prosperity or hardship for the land and its people, while the Sumerians and Babylonians were known to watch the planets and stars as a way of keeping track of the gods in the sky. This idea can be traced back to the Venus tablet of Ammisaduqa from the Neo-Assyrian period, around 911–612BC. The tablet tracks the rising and setting times of Venus for a period of 21 years, and was part of a longer text dealing with Babylonian astrology, which mostly consisted of omens and interpretations of celestial phenomena.

By 1500BC, the Babylonians had divided the sky into the 12 **signs of the zodiac**. These were later incorporated into Greek divination, and when Ptolemy wrote the *Tetrabiblos*, a core book in the history of western astrology, the 12 signs became popularised. Each of these signs are matched with dates based on the apparent relationship between their placement in the sky and the sun. According to astrology, an individual's zodiac or 'star' sign is based on their date of birth, and can reveal certain traits of their personality, such as creativity, ambition or cynicism. The 12 signs and their approximate dates are Aries (21 March–19 April), Taurus (20 April–20 May), Gemini (21 May– 21 June), Cancer (22 June– 22 July), Leo (23 July–22 August), Virgo (23 August–22 September), Libra (23 September–23 October), Scorpio (24 October–21 November), Sagittarius (22 November–21 December), Capricorn (22 December–19 January), Aquarius (20 January–18 February) and Pisces (19 February–20 March).

Interestingly, the earth actually travels through 13 signs as it moves around the sun. It is believed the 13th sign, Opiuchus, was excluded from the zodiac by the Babylonians as it didn't fit as neatly into their 12-month calendar year. According to NASA, the line from earth through the sun points to Virgo for 45 days, but it points to Scorpio for only seven days. The Babylonians ignored the fact that the sun moves through 13 constellations instead of 12, and chose to assign equal amounts of time to the remaining constellations. Consequently, the sign Opiuchus is not included in most western interpretations of the zodiac.

THE MOON   The **moon** also plays a part in the art of astrology, especially with regard to the lunar cycles and the energy 'emitted' by the moon at different times of the month. A new moon is said to be a time for new starts and intentions; a waxing moon is a chance to take action; a full moon is a time to fulfil projects and plans; and a waning moon encourages inward reflection and gratitude. The lunar cycle has also long been associated with madness, and although the scientific evidence behind this theory is still unclear, a 2021 study in *Science Advances* suggests there is a link between human sleep patterns and the moon. In the past, both the Greek philosopher Aristotle and Roman historian Pliny the Elder suggested that the brain was the 'moistest' organ in the body and therefore, like the oceans, most susceptible to the influence of the moon. Today, many people believe the powers of the full moon induce erratic behaviour, and at one point in 2007, several police departments in the UK added extra officers during the full moon to help cope with presumed higher crime rates. As Shakespeare writes in *Othello*: 'It is the very error of the moon. She comes more near the earth than she was wont. And makes men mad.'

HOROSCOPES A **horoscope** is the name for an astrological chart that represents the positions of the sun, moon, planets, stars and other celestial data at the time of a specific event, such as a birthday. The word is derived from the Greek for 'marker of the hour'. Like most aspects of astrology, the accuracy of horoscope predictions is not supported by conventional science, but for many psychologists they offer an insight into the human mind. Theories suggest our brains are wired to look for patterns, even when none exist, and horoscopes are often used as an example of what is known as the Barnum effect. Simply put, this is where individuals are presented with personality descriptions and predictions that are so generic, they satisfy most of the members of the group. The effect was named after the businessman, hoaxman and 'Greatest Showman' P T Barnum, to whom is attributed the infamous aphorism: 'There's a sucker born every minute.'

Within the modern scientific framework, astrology is considered to be a pseudoscience. Despite this, it is still hugely popular in the western world, and was even used by MI5 during World War II. According to files released in 2008, the Special Operations Executive recruited astrologer Louis De Wohl after he persuaded intelligence officers that he could use horoscopes to influence Adolf Hitler and his advisors. Nancy Reagan is also believed to have hired a secret astrologer for the White House to help plan her husband's schedule around 'lucky' and 'unlucky' dates. Her belief in the stars led one local church leader to call astrologers 'agents of Satan'. Today, the stars retain a powerful hold over the popular imagination, with one National Science Foundation poll in 2014 revealing that more than half of millennials think astrology is a science. Psychologists suggest that one of the reasons behind a new resurgence in astrology among young people is due to anxiety, stress and rising mental health issues. For those who believe in it, astrology can offer a wider meaning to the chaos of modern life, and encourage people to feel like their lives, relationships and choices have more purpose.

So is there any scientific credibility behind astrology? The significance of the zodiac stems from the fact that the narrow path in the sky that the sun, moon and planets appear to follow, known as the ecliptic, travels directly through these constellations. But as far as we know, astrology has not demonstrated any significance or effectiveness in controlled studies, and therefore has no validity in the eyes of the scientific community. According to NASA astronomer Sten Odenwald, however, theories suggest that even if astrology isn't based on scientific study, there is a reason people continue to look to the sky for answers. He says it comes down to a psychological phenomenon called 'self-selection', which is similar to confirmation bias. Under this influence, an individual will search for evidence to match what they already hope to be true, magnifying the positives and forgetting the negatives.

Astrology may not have much basis in scientific fact, but for many it's a source of wonder and a reason to believe in something beyond human comprehension. Whether you believe in celestial powers or not, stargazers can still use astrology to understand the stories our ancestors told, see the world through different eyes, and allow ourselves to have a little fun with the mystery of the universe. Because who doesn't love reading their horoscope at the hairdresser's once in a while?

FOLLOW US

Tag us in your posts to share your adventures using this guide with us – we'd love to hear from you.

f BradtGuides
🐦 BradtGuides & tfrancisbaker
📷 bradtguides & tiffany.francis

02 PRACTICAL INFORMATION

WHERE TO GO STARGAZING

DARK SKY PLACES The **International Dark Sky Places** (IDSP) programme was founded in 2001 to encourage communities, parks and protected areas around the world to preserve dark sites through responsible lighting policies and public education. As of May 2021, there are over 160 certified IDSPs in the world. The UK and Ireland are home to 17 Dark Sky Places across three of the five types of designation offered by the IDSP programme: two Communities, seven Parks and eight Reserves.

International Dark Sky Communities are legally organised cities and towns that adopt quality outdoor lighting ordinances and educate their residents about the importance of dark skies. **International Dark Sky Parks** are spaces protected for natural conservation that implement good outdoor lighting and provide dark sky programmes for visitors. **International Dark Sky Reserves** consist of a dark 'core' zone surrounded by a populated periphery where policy is put in place to protect the darkness of the core. The remaining two designation types are International Dark Sky Sanctuaries and Urban Night Sky Places, although neither of these have officially been recognised anywhere in the UK. For more information visit ⭗ darksky.org.

DISCOVERY SITES The UK Dark Sky Discovery Partnership is a network of national and local astronomy and environmental organisations. Their aim is to map out the best dark sky areas in the UK, known as Dark Sky Discovery Sites, as well as promoting astronomy and supporting the development of Dark Sky Places and astrotourism. Dark Sky Discovery Sites are places that are away from the worst of any local light pollution, provide good sightlines of the sky, and have good public access, including firm ground for wheelchairs. There are two darkness ratings: Orion sites and Milky Way sites, both of which are referenced in each listing within this book. The listings also include an **SQM reading**, which stands for Sky Quality Meter. The higher the SQM reading, the darker the sky. At **Orion sites**, the seven main stars in the winter constellation Orion are visible to the naked eye, and at **Milky Way sites**, the Milky Way galaxy is visible to the naked eye. These tend to be much darker sites found in more rural spaces.

All International Dark Sky Parks and Reserves are further divided into **gold, silver and bronze tiers**, depending on the quality of the night sky. To achieve gold status, a site must have a complete lack of lighting on towers or buildings within the area boundary, with the ability to see the aurora, Milky Way, zodiacal light and faint meteors. Silver tier means the Milky Way must be visible in summer and winter, with minor to moderate artificial skyglow allowed. Bronze is awarded to areas that don't meet the silver standard but still provide good views of the night sky.

← Bringing a camera stargazing is another way to enjoy the magnificence of the night sky
(Realstock/Shutterstock)

There are currently over two hundred Dark Sky Discovery Sites around the UK, classified as having low levels of light pollution, but this list evolves regularly as new sites are classified and light pollution levels change, so we have included in this guide a comprehensive selection across Britain and Ireland. For an updated list and more information on Dark Sky Discovery Sites, including an interactive map, visit ⊘ www.darkskydiscovery.org.uk.

INSIDE AN OBSERVATORY Astronomical research facilities like observatories are designed to maximise their ability to obtain as much data from the skies as possible, sometimes by collecting light, and sometimes through radio waves. The telescopes at these facilities are fine-tuned to perfection to enable this, although the designs of the telescopes themselves aren't always drastically different from the ones you can buy at home. They are simply on a much larger scale with some additional equipment. The telescopes themselves are made using either lenses or mirrors, and research telescopes can track objects as they move across the sky at night, meaning one object can be observed for an extremely long time, and more light can be collected. This produces incredibly detailed and clear images that astrophysicists can analyse. They also use different light filters and combine multiple images together to obtain as much detail as possible.

↑ Durdham Down, one of over two hundred Dark Sky Discovery Sites around the UK (Martin Fowler/Shutterstock)

Modern telescopes have become so large that their mirrors have had to be split into several smaller mirrors to stop them from warping under their own weight while still allowing researchers to collect more light. The measurements of a telescope refer to the diameter of the telescope's lens or mirror, and are usually expressed as inches or millimetres. A larger lens or mirror is capable of collecting more light than a smaller lens or mirror. Since objects in the night sky are faint, collecting as much light as possible allows viewers to see them more clearly, so the bigger the telescope measures, the better. Observatories will have a range of telescopes to show their visitors, including older designs that were used by pioneering astronomers. They may also have pieces of space rock from

DARK SKIES FESTIVALS AROUND THE COUNTRY

Most of the Dark Sky Places around the UK celebrate their starry skies through annual Dark Sky Festivals (⊘ darkskiesnationalparks.org.uk). Taking place in the autumn and winter months, when the nights are at their longest, these festivals are all about discovering, learning and enjoying the darker side of the landscape. Events include night walks, runs and bike rides, caving, stargazing parties, making rockets, talks, workshops and discussions with night sky experts. These events are perfect for families, new stargazers, and anyone wishing to expand their knowledge or astrophotography skills. Annual Dark Sky Festivals take place across the country, including the South Downs, North York Moors, Yorkshire Dales, Cumbria, Northumberland and Exmoor.

↑ Stargazing events take place at observatories and discovery centres up and down the country
(Alasdair Mackenzie)

the Moon or Mars on display, as well as planetarium software to share more about what interesting objects you can observe in space. Many observatories also offer hands-on, educational activities like learning to make your own rocket or looking at meteors under microscopes.

GETTING STARTED

Stargazing is a wonderfully versatile activity. Whether you simply want to be able to recognise constellations, or go all out and photograph deep sky objects, you can choose how much you wish to invest, and the rewards are always spectacular.

The most important piece of stargazing equipment is **your own eyes**, adapted for night vision. It can take your eyes up to 30 minutes to fully adjust to the dark, especially if you have recently been exposed to bright lights, so the first thing to do is find a spot that's as far away from light pollution as possible. You may have already scouted out some dark sky sites, and getting as far from artificial lighting as you can will dramatically increase the visibility of fainter objects in the sky. One thing to also remember is the moon, which can act as another source of light pollution and drown out the details of fainter stars of the Milky Way. It's important to check the phases of the moon, as the closest you can get to a new moon, the better the conditions for stargazing. Make sure to check when the moon is rising and setting that day so you can make the most of the darker skies.

↑ The 26" telescope at the Observatory Science Centre at Herstmonceux Castle, East Sussex (page 55) (David Dennis/Shutterstock)

Once you arrive at your chosen location, try to reduce the amount of artificial light around you as much as possible, and as soon as you can. Turn off any car headlights, torches or screens and allow your eyes to unlock their natural ability to detect the faint light of the stars.

The best way to begin stargazing is to simply look up and absorb the wonder of the cosmos. However, if you want to start learning how to identify the constellations, you may need a few aides. There are lots of useful books that can show you the constellation lines and give you more information about the stars within them. You could use an app – most of them have a feature that allows you to point your phone at the sky and your display will show which constellations you're pointing at. However, be aware that if you are using your phone while stargazing you may lose your night-adapted vision, so try to lower the brightness of your screen or find an app that uses night mode to turn your display red. For a list of useful stargazing apps, see page 189.

If you want to take a closer look, you might want to invest in a pair of binoculars or a telescope. **Binoculars** are a great place to start to practise navigating the night sky, especially if you require something portable or don't have the space for a telescope. Astronomers find deep sky objects, some of which are too faint to see with the naked eye, using a method called star hopping. They hop from star to star, drawing familiar patterns in the sky and using them as a guide to lead them to the object they are looking for. Binoculars allow you to see these objects in far greater detail than your eyes alone can detect. As well as deep sky objects, such as galaxies or star clusters, they are also fantastic for looking at planets and the moon. All binocular brands will provide enhanced views of the night sky, but good recommendations include Celestron (see ad, inside-front cover), Opticron, Vortex, Nikon and Meade.

You can also take your exploration of the stars even further by using a **telescope**. While they can provide you with a slightly better view of nearby objects like the moon and the planets, telescopes are most useful when looking at galaxies, star

WHEN TO GO STARGAZING

Late autumn, winter and early spring are the best seasons to go stargazing, as the nights are at their longest and there are more hours of true darkness to enjoy. A good rule of thumb is what astronomers refer to as 'observing season', which is the time from when clocks go back in October to the time they go forward in March. Keep an eye on the weather as cloudless nights are ideal for observing, and make sure to check the moon phases too, as a full moon will light up the sky. The days around a new moon are perfect for enjoying the darkness.

A DAY IN THE LIFE OF AN ASTRONOMER

Nazanin Jahanshahi
Kielder Observatory, Northumberland

Hello! I'm Naz, an astronomer at Kielder Observatory. Our days as astronomers can be quite different from a regular person's, who is mostly active in the daylight hours. It's the opposite for us! Unless we're observing the sun, the busiest part of our day is at night. As astronomers, we are forever at the mercy of the weather, so we usually begin our days by checking the forecast. The excitement builds as soon as we find out we're in for a clear night. Then we check the sun and moon's rise and set times. If the moon is out that night, it is usually one of our main targets along with bright stars, or even binary stars. The ever-changing face of the moon makes it something we never get tired of observing, although we love the nights when it's not around even more, as it allows us to see the fainter, more distant objects that are harder to spot.

After the sun sets we wait until astronomical darkness, when the sun has dipped far below the horizon. Even though it appears dark once the sun has gone down, the trace amounts of light still lingering makes a huge difference to the sky's visibility. As we wait, we may begin to plan what we wish to observe that night. The skies change considerably between the seasons here in the UK, so objects that we want to observe may be too low in the sky or even below the horizon completely. We never choose to observe objects

clusters and nebulae. They are designed to collect as much light as possible and bring it all to a focus, allowing viewers to see the faintest or furthest away objects in space. If you are travelling to darker skies, portability may be something to consider when picking the right telescope. Recommended telescopes for beginner astronomers include the Celestron NexStar 5SE, the Astronomers without Borders OneSky Reflector, and the Sky-Watcher Traditional Dobsonian. Many dark sky reserves have local telescope hire available for those who would like to try before buying.

Be sure to keep warm, as Dark Sky Parks are often much colder than people expect, even in summer. Wear thermals, a hat, gloves and plenty of layers – layers help trap air between them which increases insulation, and they can also be discarded if you're too warm. It's important to carry a torch for safety, although avoid turning it on if possible, or consider buying a red torch as the red light does not affect eyesight as much. A big flask of something warm is never a bad idea, either, as well as a chunk of cake or packet of biscuits. You could also bring a heated dog blanket to wrap yourself in or to lie on while you're gazing skywards. Always remember to check the weather before leaving, as nobody wants to get that are too close to the horizon as we would be looking through more atmosphere than if we were to choose something higher overhead. The atmosphere distorts the light coming from space, making it hard to get a clear, detailed view. Aside from all the usual suspects, we make sure to keep an eye out for any special events, such as lunar eclipses, meteor showers, International Space Station sightings or even comets. We fire up our telescopes, turn on all our red lights and make sure we're wrapped up and ready to go. Then we turn on our radio mast, which can detect when a meteor has entered the atmosphere anywhere between us and France, and we make sure to keep an eye out for the possibility for any Aurora Borealis appearances.

Our evenings (and sometimes early mornings!) are spent sharing our knowledge of the cosmos with the general public and inspiring them to look up and wonder about our place in the universe. Special evenings are never hard to come by at the observatory, and most nights are filled with 'Ooo!'s and 'Woah!'s as visitors catch a glimpse of a bright shooting star, or find out that you could fit the earth inside the sun around a million times. Once our guests' brains are ready to explode and the night is coming to an end, we look through the telescopes. I and most of the astronomers at Kielder Observatory are avid astrophotographers, so we also get out our cameras and try to capture the beauty of our dark skies as fully as possible. We even use our astroimaging suite to take photographs of deep sky objects. Astrophotography can take hours, but once we've had our fill, we all head home through the winding darkness of Kielder Forest.

↑ Stargazing in the Elan Valley International Dark Sky Park (Portia Jones/Dafydd Wyn Morgan/Cambrian Mountains Initiative)

caught out in the rain when you were expecting a dazzling night of stargazing. A star chart is also useful for beginner astronomers, either in pocket book or almanac form, or through a smartphone app. And last but certainly not least, depending on the area, insect repellent could be essential.

Most importantly of all, remember to bring your sense of adventure, as stargazing can take you to some interesting places. The dark sky sites around the UK are located in some of the most stunning countryside landscapes on offer, so be sure to take in your surroundings if you're out on the hunt for those darker skies. And if you're in a more urban location, there is still plenty to see in the night sky. Try heading to an area with less light pollution and as high up as possible. Use a pair of basic binoculars to study the moon up close. A loft window, rooftop or a park on the outskirts of a city can work well as vantage points.

↑ The best way to develop your astrophotography skills is to get outside and start experimenting
(Marti Bug Catcher/Shutterstock)

Once you're set up, allow 10 to 15 minutes for your eyes to adjust to the dark, and try to avoid looking at phone screens or torches if possible. Wherever you are, it's always worth researching any rare events that might be happening, too, such as meteor showers or lunar eclipses. You don't want to miss out!

ASTROPHOTOGRAPHY

Bringing a camera stargazing is another way to enjoy the magnificence of the night sky. Taking photographs of the night sky requires you to be able to take long-exposure photographs, as your camera sensor needs to collect more light in order to detect the faintest stars. Generally speaking, astrophotography is divided into two distinct styles: long-exposure shots, which show stars streaking across the sky as the earth moves, and short-exposure shots, which are great for

more glamorous photos of objects like the Milky Way. Both types of photograph require a **digital single-lens reflex (DSLR)** camera with interchangeable lenses and manual controls, although this doesn't mean you need to spend thousands on a new piece of equipment. An entry-level DSLR camera and lens will be perfect for beginner astrophotographers, and if you are willing to spend extra on a wide angle lens with a wide aperture, you can shoot even better quality photographs. To get started with equipment, try contacting your local astronomy group for advice or get in touch with the **British Astronomical Association** (⊘britastro.org).

Another essential piece of equipment is a **tripod**, as creating long-exposure photographs is a slow and steady business. If your camera moves even an inch during an exposure, the composition of your photo will be ruined. There is a range of cheap tripods available for beginners, but bear in mind that you might like a more lightweight option if you're planning to hike around in the dark for hours on end. A headlamp on a low setting is also useful, as it will help you see the dials and buttons on your camera while leaving your hands free. You can also use a flashlight to illuminate or 'light paint' parts of the landscape to add interesting focal points to your photos that would naturally be too dark to see. To do this, experiment with flashing the light on foreground objects like trees, people or buildings while your long-exposure photograph is being taken.

The best way to develop your astrophotography skills is to get outside and start experimenting. Remember to check the weather and moon phases before heading out in order to avoid disappointing conditions and, for details on how to make the most of your camera settings, there are thousands of videos on YouTube to get you started.

LIGHT POLLUTION

A recent report by the Mental Health Foundation suggests that nearly a third of the UK population suffers from insomnia or other sleep-related problems. One of the reasons for this is chronic exposure to blue light from our computer screens and phones. When our eyes are exposed to too much blue light at night, our bodies produce a lower amount of melatonin, the hormone that regulates sleep and our circadian rhythms. Studies suggest that the combination of long working days, exposure to blue light and failure to get enough sleep is disrupting our natural sleeping patterns.

Humans are not the only species to have their circadian rhythms disrupted by artificial illumination. Light pollution is broadly described as the presence of anthropogenic and artificial light within the nocturnal environment, exacerbated by the poor use or misdirection of lighting, and it has been proven to affect the habits and behaviours of various species of wildlife. Some animals, like snakes, salamanders and frogs, restrict their movements when the moon is full to avoid

predators being able to spot them in the moonlight. This means they tend to hunt more on moonless nights, but as artificial light pollution is spreading further across the habitats of these species, they are spending less time hunting and more time waiting for the light to dim away which, not being a natural light with natural rhythms, it never does.

In cities, wild birds are shifting the start of their early morning dawn chorus to avoid light pollution from urban developments, although researchers suspect this could also be due to noise pollution. One study conducted at five airports in the UK found that birds had started to anticipate the morning rush of planes on the runway, changing their song times in order to avoid the noise and make themselves more audible to other birds. As the dawn chorus usually takes place just before it is light enough for the birds to navigate and forage for food, this means that by singing earlier they are increasing their efforts without the opportunity to replenish their energy stores immediately afterwards. It also makes them more susceptible to nocturnal predators whose active hours are more likely to overlap with those of the birds.

To combat increasing levels of light pollution, the **International Dark-Sky Association** was founded in 1988 to preserve and protect the night time environment through education and quality outdoor lighting. In the UK, the Commission for Dark Skies is now the largest anti-light pollution campaigning

↑ Light pollution is an increasing problem for wildlife in built-up areas like central London (ExFlow/Shutterstock)

group, and their work has contributed to the certification of several dark sky spaces. Light pollution may not make the headlines as much as ocean plastic, rainforest deforestation or melting glaciers, but South Downs Ranger Dan Oakley believes dark skies are just as important an issue for life on earth. 'Under a really dark sky like the South Downs,' says Dan, 'we can see over a thousand stars. We can even see our own galaxy, the Milky Way, stretching across the sky. The Milky Way is our home and without dark skies we just can't see it.'

As well as causing problems for human and animal health, excessive outdoor lighting wastes energy and contributes to greenhouse gas emissions, while glare from bad lighting can also lead to unsafe driving conditions and cause accidents. And for stargazers, or anyone who enjoys standing beneath the dark night sky, light pollution robs us all of a visual connection with the universe.

To help combat light pollution, start by switching outdoor lights off where possible, and try using motion sensors for essential outdoor lamps. Not only will they light up porches and walkways when needed, but you'll also save on the electricity bill. You could also consider replacing outdoor lights with more intelligently designed, low-glare fixtures. The International Dark-Sky Association evaluates fixtures for low glare and efficiency, and also provides an IDA seal of approval on low-pollution lighting. Lastly, get in touch with your local council and ask what they are doing to combat light pollution in your area.

WILDLIFE AT NIGHT

Exploring the landscape at night isn't just about watching the stars. We share our rural and urban spaces with thousands of wild species who, for reasons of safety, convenience or opportunity, carry out most of their routine behaviours at night.

One of the UK's most recognisable and popular mammals, the **European badger** has existed in Britain for at least half a million years, meaning it once co-existed with the wolves, brown bears and wolverines that also lived in the British Isles. They are short, stout and powerful animals that live in large underground networks called setts. A social group living together in the same sett is called a 'clan', and research has shown that a badger's powerful sense of smell is used to tighten bonds between social groups, as studies suggest that members of the same clan have similar scents. Badgers are nocturnal and rarely seen in the day, but during warm summer weather they may emerge from their sett just before sunset.

Foxes also live underground, in a space known as a den or an earth, and while they are most active at night, they are generally less worried about being seen in the day, particularly in more urban settings. It is not uncommon to find a fox sunbathing on a shed roof or snoozing under a garden shrub. Their hearing is so advanced that they can hear a watch ticking 35m away, and they communicate with each other using 28 different types of call. They will eat almost anything,

→ **From top to bottom:** Foxes, hedgehogs, badgers and bats are some of the UK's most recognisable nocturnal creatures (Jamie Hall; colin robert varndell; Rudmer Zwerver; Agami Photo Agency – all Shutterstock)

including berries, worms, spiders and jam sandwiches, and can sometimes be found scouting for fallen seeds underneath bird feeders. Listen out on winter nights for the blood curdling screams of vixens and the *hup-hup-hup* triple barks of dog foxes, as mating season begins and foxes roam far and wide to meet each other.

Together with bats and dormice, **hedgehogs** are one of only three mammals that hibernate in the UK. They hunt mainly using their excellent hearing and sense of smell, travelling up to 3km (1.8 miles) each night to forage for berries, fruit, beetles, caterpillars and slugs. Although small and elusive, one of the best ways to meet a hedgehog is to listen out for the snuffling sound that gives it its name. The 'hog' part originates from the pig-like snorting and grunting sounds they make, while the 'hedge' comes from their habit of building their nests in hedgerows and bushes. Hedgehogs make excellent natural pest controllers if given access to the garden through small holes in fences, particularly if there is also a water source and hidden corners to hide themselves in.

Of the five species of **owl** in the UK, the two most commonly encountered are the barn owl and tawny owl, although because tawny owls don't like flying over water, they are absent from Ireland and many of our small islands, including the isles of Man and Wight, the Outer Hebrides, Orkney and Shetland. Both barn and tawny owls are nocturnal and prey mostly on small mammals, using specially adapted characteristics to help them hunt in the dark, like super-sensitive hearing and the ability to see movement from a fair distance and with very little light. According to folklore, the barn owl has also been known as the ghost, church or demon owl, due to its habit of gliding silently across churchyards. The tawny owl is often associated with the generic *twit-twoo* call owls are said to make, but this sound actually comes from two different owls, not one. The female tawny owl lets out a high-pitched *keewik*, and is met with the male's reassuring *huhuhuhooo*.

There are 18 species of **bat** in the UK, 17 of which are known to breed here, which means that bats represent almost a quarter of all native mammals in the UK. They are entirely nocturnal, very fast and very quiet, which means it is not always possible to know if they are in your midst. The most common species is the common pipistrelle, a tiny bat weighing the same as a 20p piece but still managing to consume around 3,000 small flies in one night. Around 75% of all bat sightings are thought to be common pipistrelles, but other common species include the noctule, brown long-eared and Daubenton's. The noctule is a large bat that will often be one of the first to emerge, just before sunset, but to the untrained eye they can easily be mistaken for a swift with their narrow wings and elevated flight. The brown long-eared bat is sometimes the hardest to spot as they emerge after dark and stick close to the tree canopy while hunting for food.

→ **Top left:** Redwing (Glenn R Gregory/Shutterstock); **Top right:** Tawny owl (David Oldham); **Middle:** A male blackbird feeding its young (SuperStock); **Bottom:** Nightjar (Martin Pelanek/Shutterstock)

Daubenton's bats are the most common species found around water, as they tend to skim the surface of rivers or lakes in search of aquatic insects, which they take from the water using their feet.

On summer evenings, a quiet walk on a lowland heath may lead to an encounter with a **nightjar**, although they are far easier to hear than to see. The word 'churr' is normally used to describe a nightjar call, a mechanical, gyrating gurgle that falls between notes, a higher and a lower, as the bird turns its head to project in a different direction. This eerie shift in tone, together with its narrow, black eyes and bristled beak, are perhaps what has contributed to the nightjar's mysterious reputation. The scientific name for the bird is *Caprimulgus europaeus*, which translates roughly as 'goat sucker'. The name originates from an ancient belief that they stole the milk from goats' udders, and for centuries they were disliked and persecuted. With its beautiful feather patterns that look like dead leaves and tree bark, it is almost impossible to find a nightjar in daylight, but if the churring suddenly stops, be sure to look to the sky. The bird will be on the move, and after a bubbling trill combined with a sharp wing clap, it may appear as if from nowhere, silhouetted against the dusky sky.

Another heathland species is the **glow-worm**, which is not technically a worm at all but a species of beetle, the female of which glows greeny-orange on summer nights. In order to be seen by the males' photosensitive eyes, they climb up plant stems to ensure their light spreads as far as possible, like a beacon. In daylight they appear as many other beetles do to the untrained eye – light brown with grey larvae, but with yellow triangular markings along their body.

Moths are one of the most misunderstood invertebrate species in the UK, sometimes jokingly referred to as the butterfly's boring cousin. But moths are some of the most beautiful and fascinating species in the country, with over 2,500 species to be found in a rainbow of colours. Moths and their caterpillars play an important role in our ecosystems as a food source for many other species, including amphibians, small mammals, bats and birds. The UK's blue tit population alone needs an estimated 35 billion moths a year to feed and raise their chicks.

Contrary to popular belief, not all moths are nocturnal, but the best way to get to know the ones that are is to set a moth trap. The word 'trap' might sound cruel, but moth traps are completely harmless and allow conservationists to record which species are in abundance. It's also a great way for beginners and families to learn more about moths, as you don't need any expensive equipment. Visit the **Wildlife Trust** website (⌀ wildlifetrusts.org/actions/how-attract-moths-and-bats-your-garden) to learn how to make a moth trap using everyday items like a white sheet, torch, bottle of wine and strips of old cloth.

The smallest true thrush in Britain, the **redwing** is a distinctive autumn and winter migrant bird, with a creamy stripe above their eye and a rusty red

→ **Top:** Elephant hawk moth (poidl/Shutterstock); **Bottom:** Glow-worm (Igor Krasilov/Shutterstock)

smear under each wing. Most of the UK population arrives around October and November, after gathering in their thousands along the Scandinavian coastlines and launching into the sky for a single 800km (500 mile) flight across the North Sea. It was only in the last century that scientists started to understand the complexities of bird migration, as for years it was thought that birds either hibernated in trees, hid at the bottom of ponds or turned into something else completely. For centuries, robins were thought to be winter redstarts, and barnacle geese were thought to hatch from actual barnacles. Some redwings migrate from the birch forests of Russia and Iceland, all the way down to Portugal, Greece and even Iran, travelling mostly at night to avoid detection by predators. If you step out into an autumn or winter night, it is possible to hear the redwings overhead as they travel across the country under cover of darkness. Their soft *seep seep seep* call is a wonderful accompaniment to a night of stargazing.

After a long night under the stars, there is nothing more welcoming than the slow greeting of a new day. One of the loveliest ways to enjoy the sunrise is to wake up early – very early – and listen in on one of nature's greatest spectacles: the spring dawn chorus. The night is still pitch black when the first bird wakes up, the ripe, velvety notes of a male blackbird bursting out the first symphony of the morning. Soon he is joined by the bold melodies of the wren and robin, the wheezing greenfinch, pat-a-cake song thrush, whistling starling, dunnock, goldfinch and sparrow, until the air is filled with the beautiful chaos of birdsong chiming like a thousand silver bells. From 04.00 onwards our gardens, hedgerows and woodlands erupt into a cacophony of song as every male bird attempts to charm a female, aligning their breeding season with the warmest times of year, when food is plentiful and any eggs laid will have a greater chance of survival.

It's not just the 'early bird' attitude that encourages birds to sing so promptly. This early in the day there is less background noise from the human world, the air is of a different quality and can carry birdsong up to 20 times further. The males will sing both to defend their territory and to find a mate, and females will be eager to find a partner with a strong voice, as he is more likely to have the stamina to raise chicks and protect his territory. The breeding season for most garden birds can last until late July. A typical blackbird's nest will hold a clutch of three to five eggs, and the chicks will hatch a couple of weeks later, after which they are fed on a diet of earthworms and caterpillars. At two weeks old, they are ready to leave the nest, and it is at this point that gardeners may find baby birds in the grass who appear to have fallen. As long as there are no immediate predators around, like cats or cars, it is always best to leave baby birds where you find them; they are still finding their feet and may simply be building up the confidence and strength to try flying again.

The award-winning Slow Travel series from Bradt Guides

Over 20 regional guides across Britain.
See the full list at bradtguides.com/slowtravel.

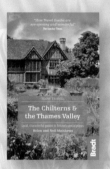
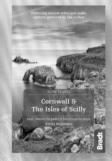

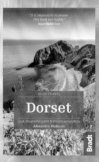
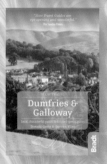
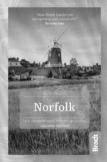
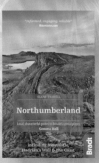

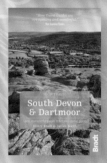

The Milky Way over Dartmoor (Arthur Cauty/Shutterstock)

DARK SKY PLACES

✱ Certified Sites (from page 50)

1   Moore's Reserve
      (South Downs National Park)
2   Bodmin Moor
3   Cranborne Chase
4   Exmoor National Park
5   Brecon Beacons National Park
6   Elan Valley Estate
7   Snowdonia National Park
8   Yorkshire Dales National Park
9   North York Moors National Park
10   Northumberland National Park
      & Kielder Water & Forest Park
11   Galloway Forest Park
12   Moffat
13   Tomintoul & Glenlivet
14   Coll
15   Davagh Forest Park &
      Beaghmore Stone Circles
16   Mayo Dark Sky Park
17   Kerry

✱ Discovery Sites (from page 130)

03 CERTIFIED SITES

The International Dark Sky Places (IDSP) programme was founded in 2001 to encourage communities, parks and protected areas around the world to preserve dark sites through responsible lighting policies and public education. The UK and Ireland are home to 17 certified sites across three of the five types of designation offered by the IDSP programme: two Communities, seven Parks and eight Reserves.

MOORE'S RESERVE
(INTERNATIONAL DARK SKY RESERVE)

South Downs Centre, North St, Midhurst, West Sussex GU29 9DH ☎ 01730 814810
e info@southdowns.gov.uk ⊘ southdowns.gov.uk ♀ OS Explorer Maps OL3, OL8, OL10, OL11, OL25, OL32 & OL33.

Standing at dusk on the summit of Old Winchester Hill in Hampshire, you would never know you were an hour's drive from London. Wildflowers flourish in hillside meadows, a haven for butterflies on summer afternoons, while Bronze Age burial mounds protrude gently out of the earth. It is easy to visualise the ancient people who once walked here, standing in exactly the same place thousands of years before, gazing up at the same veil of stars drifting across the darkness. The sky is almost pitch black – diluted only by the skyglow of the cities by the Solent, over to the west.

Officially established in 2010, the **South Downs** is the UK's newest national park, stretching from the valley of the River Itchen near Winchester in Hampshire, down to Beachy Head on the Sussex coast. The Downs take the form of a long chalk escarpment extending for 110km (68 miles), intersected by the rivers Arun, Adur, Ouse and Cuckmere. The boundaries of the national park and the dark sky reserve are the same, although the latter was given its own name when it earned its Dark Sky Status. Moore's Reserve is, however, unlikely to appear on general maps in print or online, so searching for the South Downs National Park is the easiest way to find the area.

Some 2 million people live within 5km (3 miles) of the boundaries of the park, while the southeast in general is rapidly expanding owing to ongoing development in both urban and rural areas. Despite this, and the light pollution radiating from Portsmouth, Southampton and the surrounding area, the average darkness in the South Downs has been classified by the International Dark-Sky Association as 'Bronze Level'. To earn this status, the South Downs Dark Skies Officer Dan Oakley worked with a team of volunteers over three years, taking 30,000 measurements with sky-quality meters and working with local authorities to switch the area to more efficient and sensitive lighting. In 2016, the park was officially granted Dark Sky Status, after which the reserve was named after

← The world-renowned Kielder Observatory first opened in 2008 (Mike Ridley)

Sir Patrick Moore. The English amateur astronomer, writer, researcher, radio commentator and television personality was best known for presenting the BBC's *The Sky at Night* for over 50 years, and lived in nearby Selsey on the West Sussex coast until his death in 2012.

The night sky is dark enough in the South Downs that, from the most popular spots, stargazers are able to see the Milky Way with the naked eye. In places like **Butser Hill** and **Black Down**, thought to be two of the darkest and highest points in the park, the surrounding views are spectacular and easily accessible. The rolling Downs themselves offer extraordinary panoramas of the night sky in all directions, but it isn't just the stars that make the South Downs a great destination for nocturnal trips. The natural habitats here are so varied that, for wildlife lovers especially, a night walk is a unique experience. Chalk grassland provides a rich mosaic of food and habitat for insects and small mammals, which in turn attracts **barn owls** and **tawny owls**, as well as almost every UK species of **bat**. The UK is also home to approximately 20% of Europe's **lowland heath**, a habitat that is globally rarer than rainforest. The South Downs contain much of this heathland, which comes alive after dark with the sound of **nightjars** churring in the bracken, along with the mesmerising **glow-worm**, a bioluminescent beetle that emits a greeny-orange light at night.

The Hampshire and Sussex landscapes at night have inspired numerous writers, artists and creatives over the centuries, including *fin de siècle* science fiction writer H G Wells. Wells spent some of his youth at Uppark House near South Harting, now managed by the National Trust, after his mother became the housekeeper in 1880. He spent his days reading in the library, and his nights stargazing through a telescope in the attic, experiences that may have sparked what would become his space-inspired novels *The War of the Worlds* and *The Time Machine*.

Not long afterwards, the writer Edward Thomas moved to the village of Steep in Hampshire, where he was encouraged by American poet and friend Robert Frost to begin writing poetry. In the two years that followed he completed around 140 poems, before his early death in World War I. Thomas and Frost would regularly walk through the downs at night, discussing everything from marriage and war to poetry and wildlife. One night in the summer of 1914, Thomas wrote in his notebook how he had imagined his countrymen fighting under the same moon as he and his friend were now standing:

> A sky of dark rough horizontal masses in N.W. with a ⅓ moon bright and almost orange low down clear of cloud and I thought of men east-ward seeing it at the same moment. It seems foolish to have loved England up to now without knowing it could perhaps be ravaged and I could and perhaps would do nothing to prevent it.

In 1937, 20 years after his death on the Western Front, Thomas had his own commemorative Poet Stone placed at the top of the Ashford Hangers nature reserve in Steep, just outside Petersfield. For him, the landscape was a constant in a life plagued by depression, with nature providing such a restorative power for him that he pledged to live a pastoral life, there in the foothills of the Downs. In 2002, another creative, environmental artist Andy Goldsworthy, designed the **Chalk Stones Trail**. The trail is a collection of giant balls made of chalk, a material originating from the skeletal remains of marine creatures deposited 70 to 100 million years ago, when a warm sea covered most of southern England. The South Downs are based on chalky soil, giving them their rich abundance in wildlife, and the Chalk Stones Trail takes ramblers along an 8km (5 mile) route into the heart of West Sussex. At night, the stones are said to glow in the moonlight, marking out the way ahead.

The South Downs National Park is the perfect location for city dwellers to escape the urban glow and find truly dark skies on their doorstep. From undulating hills to chalk streams, yew forests and bright, white cliffs overlooking the sea, the diversity of the park landscape makes it more than worthy of a weekend visit. Food and accommodation are plentiful, particularly along the South Downs Way, a 160km (100 mile) trail running from Winchester to Eastbourne. Most of the reserve is also dog-friendly, except for signposted areas where livestock or ground-nesting birds require dogs to be on leads.

GETTING THERE Regular trains run through the area to gateway stations like Winchester, Petersfield, Lewes and Eastbourne. The South Downs Discovery Ticket offers transport by bus. The park can be accessed from the A3 at Petersfield, various exits along the M3 near Winchester, or the A27 between Emsworth and Eastbourne. The South Downs Way is suitable for hiking, cycling and horseriding. Other major towns and cities include Midhurst, Petworth and Arundel.

DARK SKIES HIGHLIGHTS In the Hampshire end of the national park, both **Old Winchester Hill** (page 135) and **Butser Hill** (page 135) offer beautiful evening views as the sky darkens, as well as having interesting Bronze and Iron Age earthworks. **Buriton Recreation Ground** (page 134), on the outskirts of Petersfield, is great for stargazing after a drink at the Five Bells pub. In West Sussex, both **Harting Down** (page 135) and **Iping Common** (page 136) are good for nocturnal wildlife under the stars – Iping is a hotspot for glow-worms and nightjars on summer nights – while **Bignor Hill** (page 136) is said to have a dragon sleeping at the top. **Devil's Dyke** (page 136) near Brighton is semi-rural, so best enjoyed when the moon is less full. **Ditchling Beacon** (page

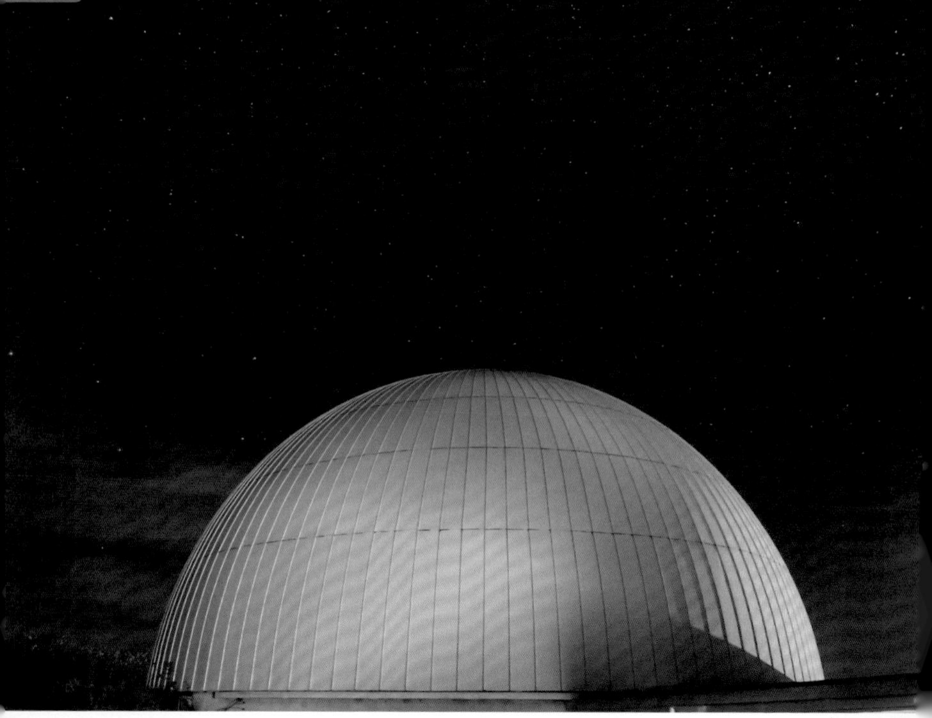

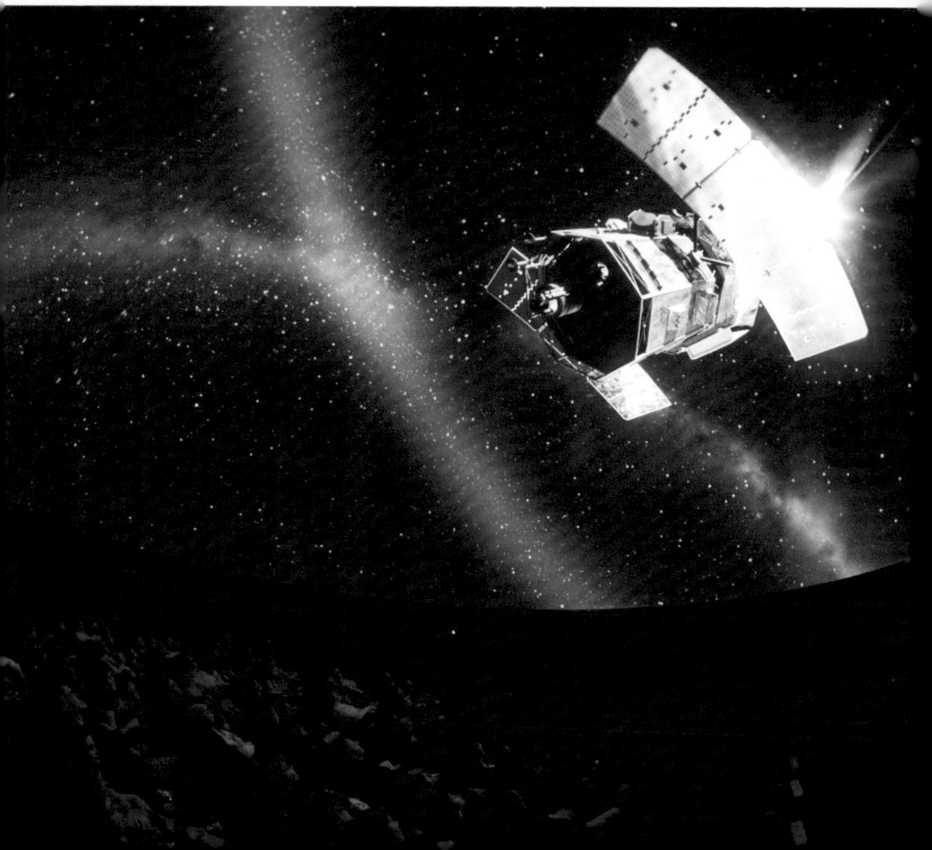

136) offers 360-degree views of the surrounding countryside and sky above, and **Birling Gap** (page 136) is perfect for stargazing over the Seven Sisters cliffs and the sea beyond.

OBSERVATORIES AND ACTIVITIES A trip to Winchester Science

Centre & Planetarium (∅ winchestersciencecentre.org) is recommended for families who love science and space. Located on the eastern edge of Winchester, the planetarium is the largest of its kind in the UK, while their interactive exhibits, varied events programme and café make this a well-rounded day out. Just outside the national park boundary, the **South Downs Planetarium & Science Centre** (∅ www.southdowns.org.uk) in southern Chichester was officially opened by Sir Patrick Moore in 2002. Their star theatre offers public shows on everything space themed, from the moon landing to the northern lights. On the southern edge of the park, the **Observatory Science Centre** (∅ the-observatory.org) in the grounds of Herstmonceux Castle, a 15-minute drive east of Hailsham, provides hands-on science among the domes and telescopes of a world famous astronomical observatory. The South Downs area is also home to a number of astronomical groups who welcome new members and guest visitors, including the Hampshire Astronomical Group (∅ hantsastro.org.uk) which offer tours and talks at the privately owned **Clanfield Observatory** just north of Waterlooville. The **South Downs National Park Authority** (∅ southdowns.gov.uk) hosts several astronomy events across the park throughout the year, culminating in their annual **Dark Skies Festival** in February.

DAYTIME ACTIVITIES For history lovers, **Arundel Castle**

(∅ arundelcastle.org) in West Sussex is a 20-minute walk north of Arundel train station, dating back to the Battle of Hastings and featuring beautiful gardens and interactive exhibits. Experimental archaeology centre **Butser Ancient Farm** (∅ butserancientfarm.co.uk), 8km (5 miles) south of Petersfield, offers Stone Age to Saxon buildings, rare breed animals and crackling fires, while **Gilbert White's House & Garden** (∅ gilbertwhiteshouse.org.uk) in Selborne, a 10-minute drive south of Alton, is a peaceful spot for fans of natural history and fresh scones. **Monk's House** (∅ nationaltrust.org.uk/monks-house) was home to writer Virginia Woolf and is now managed by the National Trust, an 8-minute drive from Lewes train station. For wildlife seekers, **Kingley Vale**, just north of Chichester, boasts an ancient yew forest said to be haunted by Viking ghosts, while **RSPB Pulborough Brooks** is home to peregrine falcons, lapwings and nightingales, a 17-minute drive east of Petworth, West Sussex.

← The Planetarium at Winchester Science Centre is the largest of its kind in the UK (**top:** Harvey Mills Photography; **bottom:** Winchester Science Centre)

BODMIN MOOR (INTERNATIONAL DARK SKY PARK)

Bodmin Information Centre, Shire Hall, Mount Folly, Bodmin, Cornwall PL31 2DQ ✐ 01208 76616 **e** info@bodmin.gov.uk ♂ bodmin.gov.uk ♀ OS Explorer Map 109.

Welcome to deepest, darkest Cornwall, the land of smugglers, ghost stories and ancient stone circles. Located in the heart of the county, Bodmin Moor measures nearly 200km^2 (77 square miles) of grassland and heather, punctuated by granite outcrops and strewn with boulders. Owing to the endless expanse of exposed boggy ground and susceptibility to fog, Bodmin has gained a reputation for the macabre and mysterious, despite being one of the most beautiful and evocative stretches of the Cornish landscape. In fact, one of the best reasons to visit Bodmin is that it doesn't attract as many tourists as the more coastal hotspots, which means much of the moorland still feels untouched and unexplored.

Cornwall is where the novelist Daphne du Maurier called home, once writing that she had finally found freedom, 'long sought for, not yet known. Freedom to write, to walk, to wander. Freedom to climb hills, to pull a boat, to be alone.' In this hidden corner of England it is easy to see why she loved Cornwall so much, and why she set so many of her stories here. Bodmin Moor, in particular, is home to the **Jamaica Inn**, first built in 1750 as a coaching house for changing horses. Du Maurier's famous novel of the same name was first published in 1930, after she had been lost on the moors while out riding her horse. Disorientated in the fog, she sought refuge at the inn, where she was entertained by the local rector with tales of ghosts and smugglers. She would later be inspired to write her own story about a band of criminals who lure ships into the rocks using false lights, before looting the wrecked ruins and drowning any survivors. "'Have you ever seen a moth flutter to a candle, and singe his wings?'" says Jem Merlyn to the heroine Mary, before she witnesses the wrecking herself on the shingle beaches of north Cornwall.

The nature of the Bodmin moorland makes it easy to imagine getting lost or disappearing altogether, even more so with the countless tales of ghosts, hauntings, wandering souls and unhallowed corpses. The most famous ghost to roam the area is Charlotte Dymond, whose murdered body was found on Rough Tor on 14 April 1844. Dressed in her Sunday best, the crime was attributed to her boyfriend and he was hanged. It is said that the ghost of Charlotte Dymond roams the moor on the same date every year, wearing the clothes she was killed in. It doesn't help the moor's sinister reputation that it is also home to **Bodmin Jail**, a former prison built in 1779 using 20,000 tonnes of local De Lank granite, and stone from the adjacent Coocoo Quarry. At least 55 executions took place within the formidable walls of the jail, many of which were viewed by the public, who would travel especially to witness the hangings.

→ **Top:** Rough Tor, one of Bodmin Moor's many tors (Matt Jessop, VisitCornwall); **Bottom:** The observatory at Eddington Lodge, not far from the seaside town of Bude (Jonathan Davey)

It isn't just the supernatural that makes Bodmin such a unique place to visit. Inhabited since the Neolithic period, the moor is home to a number of ancient sites and there is plenty of evidence to suggest that it was once a bustling hub of civilisation. One of the most impressive sites is **Trevethy Quoit**, one of only 20 examples in the world of a Neolithic portal tomb. This type of structure was later used to deposit the ash from a cremation during the Bronze Age, and in this one a small and mysterious rectangular opening has been cut into the front. Elsewhere, a collection of three stone circles known as The Hurlers date back to around 1500BC, so called after a local tradition that the stones were once men who committed the crime of playing a game of hurling on a Sunday. And just south of the A30, a large Bronze Age settlement known as **Black Tor** consists of a huge complex of 94 huts and enclosures, with several upright stones still visible.

And as for the present day, have you heard of the **Beast of Bodmin Moor**? This legendary creature is said to resemble a huge, black, panther-like cat with yellow eyes, and in 1995 there had been so many sightings of the Beast that the government ordered an official investigation to confirm its existence. The ensuing report concluded there was no verifiable evidence of a big cat on Bodmin Moor, although it also claimed there was no evidence against it, either.

But despite its eerie reputation, Bodmin Moor is a place rich in life, nature and beauty. Many local rivers have their roots here, and the moor is also the only place in the world where you can find the rare **Cornish Path Moss**. A haven for wildlife, it is home to numerous plants and protected species such as **otters**, **marsh fritillary butterflies** and songbirds like the **stonechat** and **wheatear**, as well as 1,000 or so **Bodmin Moor ponies** who are allowed to graze freely. Although it is largely privately owned, in the last two decades much of the moor has been designated as open access land, which means that members of the public have the right to walk freely within specific areas without having to stick to the paths. For those hikers who wish to take in as much of the moor as possible, try following the newly devised **Copper Trail** ($\mathscr{O}$ visitcornwall.com/things-to-do/copper-trail-bodmin-moor), so called because of the abundance of disused copper mines seen along the route.

In 2017, following a bid by Cornwall Council and Caradon Observatory, the International Dark-Sky Association awarded the designation of Dark Sky Landscape to Bodmin Moor in recognition of the exceptional quality of its night sky and commitments to reduce light pollution. This included new covers being placed over street lights and guidance being produced for homeowners on how to minimise light pollution. The designation covers an area of 207km^2 (80 square miles), which also makes it the first International Dark Sky Place in an Area of Outstanding Natural Beauty.

Bodmin Moor is a stunning and atmospheric location for new and experienced astronomers, easily accessible and less crowded than other areas of the county. And – best of all – where better than Cornwall to treat yourself to a post-gazing pint of sparkling West Country cider?

GETTING THERE The area is easily accessible from the A30, a trunk road from London to Land's End that was once a major coaching route. Nearby towns include Bodmin, Launceston and Liskeard inland, Fowey and Par on the south coast, and the port of Boscastle on the north coast. Private transport is recommended due to the rugged and remote nature of the area and the abundance of free parking, but local bus services are available. Main line train services run to Bodmin Parkway station, where visitors can interchange to ride the Bodmin & Wenford Railway, Cornwall's only full-size railway still operated by steam locomotives.

DARK SKIES HIGHLIGHTS Just to the south of the Jamaica Inn, **Colliford Lake** (Liskeard PL14 6PZ) is Cornwall's largest body of inland water, with lots of parking, picnic areas and lakeside walks. As a nature reserve, it is an important site for birdlife including overwintering wildfowl, and the quiet conditions make for a peaceful spot to stargaze. Another popular spot for birders, **Crowdy Reservoir** (Camelford PL32 9XJ) is well worth a visit on winter evenings to see the starling murmurations rise above the water, before settling down for a night beneath Bodmin's dark skies. On the eastern flank of the moor, the **Hurlers Stone Circles** (Minions PL14 5LE) are managed by the Cornwall Heritage Trust, and consist of three late Neolithic or early Bronze Age stone circles arranged in a line. A great spot to try your hand at astrophotography, the close grouping of stones like these is extremely rare in England, and a grouping of three such regular circles is unique. For family stargazing adventures, **Siblyback Lake** (Liskeard PL14 6ER) offers lakeside walks, a play area and café during the day, and huge open skies at night with plenty of nocturnal wildlife.

OBSERVATORIES AND ACTIVITIES On the eastern edge of Bodmin Moor, **Caradon Observatory** (⊘ caradonobservatory.com) is an amateur-run facility and home to the XTR-C 4.5m radio telescope, an educational and outreach tool run primarily by students from the University of Exeter. The observatory has four individual domes with different types of telescope in each, offering a variety of views. Nearby, just northeast of the seaside town of Bude, **Eddington Lodge** (⊘ eddington-lodge.co.uk/astronomy) offer self-catering log cabins for astronomy holidays. They have a fully equipped and automated 2.7m motorised observatory dome housing a Williams Optics triplet refracting APO telescope, used for both planetary photography and imaging deeper objects in the night sky. They also have observation pods and offer courses as part of your stay. Just southwest of Bodmin, near the town of St Austell, the **Roseland Observatory** (⌂ roselandobservatory.com) is set in a holiday campsite, with the observatory itself open to the public every Tuesday evening throughout the observing season, whether they are staying guests or not. Facilities include an activity room, binoculars, weather instrument and several telescopes.

DAYTIME ACTIVITIES The Jamaica Inn (⌂ jamaicainn.co.uk) is the perfect place to stop for a cream tea, pub lunch or pint of cider. It became a coaching inn in 1750 when coaches first started crossing the moor, being exactly halfway along the desolate road from Launceston to Bodmin, now the A30. For horrible history lovers, **Bodmin Jail** (⌂ bodminjail.org) is located just a couple of minutes' drive north of Bodmin town centre, and has recently opened a new immersive visitor experience called the Dark Walk which promises theatrical tales of smuggling, mining and prison life. Around 10 minutes' drive south of the town centre is **Lanhydrock** (⌂ nationaltrust.org.uk/lanhydrock), a Victorian country house with beautiful gardens and a tearoom, all managed by the National Trust. On the southern edge of Bodmin Moor, 10 minutes' drive north of Liskeard, the **Golitha Falls** (⌂ woodlandtrust.org.uk/visiting-woods/woods/golitha-falls) are a series of spectacular cascades and waterfalls along a section of the River Fowey as it makes its way through the ancient oak woodland of Draynes Wood. Further out of the Bodmin area, the **Eden Project** (⌂ edenproject.com) is a 10-minute drive from St Austell, famous for its giant greenhouse biomes filled with exotic plants. On the north coast between Tintagel and Bude, a 20-minute drive north of the moor, **Boscastle Witchcraft Museum** (⌂ museumofwitchcraftandmagic.co.uk) is a charming independent museum exploring the practice of magic in Britain.

CRANBORNE CHASE (INTERNATIONAL DARK SKY RESERVE)

Cranborne Chase AONB Office, Rushmore Farm, Tinkley Bottom, Tollard Royal, Wiltshire SP5 5QA ☏ 01725 517417 **e** info@cranbornechase.org.uk ⌂ cranbornechase.org.uk ♥ OS Explorer Map 118.

Overlapping the boundaries of Wiltshire, Dorset, Hampshire and Somerset, Cranborne Chase is a unique and diverse landscape, rich in rare flora and fauna. Fans of the Wessex writer Thomas Hardy might recognise it from early scenes in his 1891 novel *Tess of the d'Urbervilles*, where he describes the chase as:

A truly venerable tract of forest land, one of the few remaining woodlands in England of undoubted primeval date, wherein Druidical mistletoe was still found on aged oaks, and where enormous yew trees, not planted by the hand of man, grew as they had grown when they were pollarded for bows.

As an Area of Outstanding Natural Beauty, this 984km^2 (380 square mile) Dark Sky Reserve offers a variety of different habitats, including rolling chalk grassland, ancient woodland, chalk escarpment, downland hillside and chalk river valleys. In total, there are around 7,200ha (17,800 acres) of ancient woodland within Cranborne Chase, 451 of which are also designated as Sites of Special Scientific Interest (SSSIs), and the reserve has also been identified as an Ancient Woodland Priority Area by the Forestry Commission. As an officially recognised Dark Sky Place, Cranborne Chase is known for its tranquillity and excellent night sky conditions, making it one of the best destinations for stargazing in the south of England.

Around 100 million years ago, the area that is now Cranborne Chase was covered by a shallow sea. As the skeletons of invertebrates fell to the seabed and accreted over time, they formed layers of chalk which would later determine the character of this unique landscape. During this time, the silicate skeletons of sea sponges also fell to the seabed and formed flint, a hard but frangible rock that was valued by early humans who used them as tools and building materials. Human settlement in the area dates back at least 8,000 years to the Neolithic period, when communities first started to manage the land for farming, as well as building burial mounds and other earthworks that still exist today. The **Dorset Cursus**, for example, is possibly Britain's largest Neolithic site, originally consisting of a pair of parallel banks running for 10km (6 miles) and 90m apart through the chalk downs of Cranborne Chase. A walk along the Cursus is available from the village of Gussage Saint Michael, although few remains are still visible due to years of plough damage. During the Bronze and Iron ages, the area became settled by more people who created large areas of pasture and arable farmland.

One of the most beautiful aspects of the chase are the remnants of unimproved **chalk grassland** held within its dramatic scarp slopes. Chalk grassland is a rare and precious habitat, often protecting a huge variety of plant and invertebrate species. The chalk streams are also rich in wildlife and nutrients, and the arable fields surrounding them are home to a number of rare plants and declining bird species such as turtle doves, grey partridge, corn bunting and lapwing. The area is also one of the richest in southern England for species of lichen.

By the Anglo Saxon period, the area had become a royal hunting ground, from which the name Cranborne Chase originates. Owing to restrictions imposed by royal decree, it was preserved for hundreds of years for kings and their noble relatives. William the Conqueror gave it to Queen Matilda, their son William Rufus gave it to a cousin, an illegitimate son of Henry I acquired it by marriage, and King John was known to have made at least 14 hunting visits. Centuries later, the echoes of its hunting past still reverberate around the chase in the form of **roe deer**, usually found in ones and twos, and herds of **fallow deer** which roam through the heart of the forest in the winter months. Patient stargazers are likely to meet these herds as they wait for the sky to darken, so please keep dogs on leads and remain still for the best views of the deer feeding and socialising in the woods.

In 1880, archaeologist and army officer Augustus Pitt Rivers inherited the Rushmore Estate on the Wiltshire–Dorset border of Cranborne Chase. Because of its hunting history, it had been forbidden to harm the deer and the vegetation on which they grazed for centuries, which meant the estate was incredibly well preserved. Pitt Rivers uncovered a vast number of monuments and settlements dating from prehistoric times to the medieval period, many artefacts from which would later form the founding collection of the Pitt Rivers Museum at the University of Oxford. He became the country's first official inspector of ancient monuments, after the passing of Sir John Lubbock's 1882 Ancient Monuments Act, as well as taking a keen interest in public education, publishing his archaeological research in the four-volume *Excavations in Cranborne Chase*.

The undulating landscape of Cranborne Chase offers dramatic scenery and stunning panoramic views of the night sky, including the prominent summits of Breeze Hill (262m), Win Green (277m) and Melbury Hill (263m). On the southwestern corner of the chase, visitors can climb **Hambledon Hill** and take in views across the three counties of Dorset, Somerset and Wiltshire. Hambledon is widely considered to be one of the finest Iron Age hill forts in Dorset, and at dusk is also a great spot for watching **hares** and finding **glow-worms** in the long grass. The chase is also home to the rare **barbastelle bat**, an elusive species that roosts in tree crevices and feeds on midges, moths and other flying insects they find using echolocation. They mate in autumn and hibernate underground over the winter, but keen wildlife lovers may be able to hear them on spring and summer evenings using a bat detector.

First designated in October 2019, Cranborne Chase was the 14th International Dark Sky Reserve to be recognised in the world. More than 50% of the Area of Outstanding Natural Beauty has the lowest levels of light pollution found in England, and staff are still working to make the rest of the reserve as dark as possible. Their 'Chasing Stars' campaign is focused on educating local people about the importance of reducing light pollution, protecting wildlife and landscapes, and keeping the skies dark. They also host stargazing events throughout the year, culminating in their annual Dark Skies Festival in February.

→ The Milky Way over Anvil Point Lighthouse, close to Durlston, Swanage (Tony Cowburn/Shutterstock)

GETTING THERE The village of Cranborne at the heart of the chase can be accessed from either the A338 or A354, both of which lead out of the nearest city of Salisbury. Nearby towns include Blandford Forum and Shaftesbury to the west, Warminster to the north, and Ringwood and Wimborne Minster to the south. Private transport is recommended due to the rural nature of the area and the abundance of free parking, but local bus services are available. Main line train services run to Salisbury, Warminster, Bruton, Tisbury, Gillingham and Poole.

DARK SKIES HIGHLIGHTS Built in 1772, **King Alfred's Tower** (Bruton BA10 0LB) is a striking 49m folly 3km (2 miles) northwest of the town of Mere, believed to mark the site where King Alfred rallied his troops in AD878. It is now designated as a Grade I-Listed building and although closed at night, the surrounding grounds make a great spot for stargazing. A 10-minute drive north of Cranborne village, **Martin Down Nature Reserve** (Salisbury SP5 5RH) is home to an exceptional collection of wildlife associated with chalk downland and scrub, including a number of rare species. It is easy to feel connected to the ancient people who once lived here and gazed at the same stars. At **Win Green** (Ludwell SP7 0ES), a 15-minute drive east from Shaftesbury, visitors can enjoy extensive views from the highest point in the chase, while the medieval church ruins at **Knowlton** (Wimborne BH21 5AE) southwest of Cranborne are a perfect spot for reading up on the constellation myths or trying astrophotography. **Badbury Rings** (Wimborne BH21 4DZ) northwest of Wimborne Minster is an Iron Age hill fort with majestic open skies, while **Cley Hill** (Warminster BA12 7QU) is another ancient hill fort that has been popular with UFO spotters for the last 40 years. Nearby Warminster even has a designated National Reporting Centre for UFOs so you won't have to go far if you get a lucky sighting!

OBSERVATORIES AND ACTIVITIES Although there are no observatories within the Cranborne Chase boundaries, there are two relatively close by in Swanage and Southampton. The **Durlston Astronomy Centre** (⊘ durlston.co.uk/visit-astronomy.aspx) at Durlston Country Park in Swanage consists of a 14" Meade telescope housed in its own observatory, together with supporting facilities for talks and lectures in the nearby Learning Centre. The centre is supported by the ranger staff at the country park and by members of the Wessex Astronomical Society. A number of public events are run at Durlston throughout the year, and are open to everyone, and private bookings for clubs or societies can be arranged by contacting Durlston. The **Toothill Observatory** (⊘ solentastro.org) is located just north of Southampton in the quiet village of Toothill, and is run by the Solent Amateur Astronomers. The facility uses a range of equipment including a 14" Meade telescope, which is accessible to wheelchair users. The observatory is made accessible to the public during regular open evenings that take place throughout the observing season from August through to May each year. The Cranborne 'Chasing Stars' project also hosts their own **Dark Skies Festival** (⊘ chasingstars.org.uk).

DAYTIME ACTIVITIES For a taste of ancient history, **Rockbourne Roman Villa** (⊘ hampshireculture.org.uk/rockbourne-roman-villa) and the **Ancient Technology Centre** (⊘ ancienttechnologycentre.com) are both within a 15-minute drive of Fordingbridge on the western edge of the New Forest. The former displays the remains of the largest known Roman villa complex in the area, and the latter is a hub of reconstructed historical buildings dating back to the Stone Age, open to the public three times a year. The **Museum of East Dorset** in the centre of Wimborne Minster (⊘ museumofeastdorset. co.uk) dates back to the 1500s, and is a must-see for anyone interested in local history. The heritage-planted walled garden is a highlight, containing traditional fruit trees like quince, medlar, walnut and black mulberry, and visitors can also enjoy a slice of cake in the Garden Tea Room. Nearby, **Salisbury Cathedral** (⊘ salisburycathedral.org.uk) in Salisbury city centre is home to one of the original copies of the Magna Carta, as well as a pair of peregrine falcons nesting 68m up on the cathedral tower. Lovers of rural traditions should head to the **Dorset Heavy Horse Farm Park** (⊘ dorset-heavy-horse-centre.co.uk) located an 8km (5 mile) drive north of Verwood; the farm park is fantastic for animal-loving families. Meanwhile, the **Cranborne Chase Cider** farm (⊘ cranbornechasecider.co.uk) offers local produce in their on-site shop and tours of the orchard and cider shed.

EXMOOR NATIONAL PARK (INTERNATIONAL DARK SKY RESERVE)

Dulverton National Park Centre, 7–9 Fore St, Dulverton, Somerset TA22 9EX ✆ 01398 323841 **e** info@exmoor-nationalpark.gov.uk ⊘ www.exmoor-nationalpark.gov.uk ♥ OS Explorer Map OL9.

Historians believe that it was in a marshy copse in the wilds of Exmoor that the poets Samuel Taylor Coleridge and William Wordsworth, together with Wordsworth's sister Dorothy, took one of their favourite night walking routes that would later lead to Coleridge writing his poem *The Nightingale*. 'All is still', he wrote:

> A balmy night! and though the stars be dim,
> Yet let us think upon the vernal showers
> That gladden the green earth, and we shall find
> A pleasure in the dimness of the stars.
> And hark! the Nightingale begins its song

Nightingales were more abundant when Coleridge wrote these lines, but they are still passage visitors through the Exmoor landscape, and their distinctive song, although rare, can still be heard across the south of England. The name originates from the Old English for 'Night Songstress', and its song features heavily in literary history as one of love and passion. In fact, it was such a beautiful song that in the 19th century bird catchers tried to capture large numbers of nightingales for the caged songbird trade. Most of the birds captured died quickly in captivity, but some survived until autumn, when they killed themselves by dashing their bodies against the cage bars in an attempt to follow their migration instinct.

At the time Coleridge and the Wordsworths were taking night walks through Exmoor in the 18th century, rural, working-class people would have been more accustomed to low levels of light, and without modern light pollution it would have been even more dense and black than it is today. On cloudless nights they would have used the night sky to navigate their way across the land, but what about when the sky wasn't so clear? One theory is that they carried little white stones with them, dropping them like breadcrumbs as they walked to help them find their return journey home.

Although nightingales no longer breed on Exmoor, its rich mosaic of different habitats means that numerous wild species are still drawn here. After a successful introduction programme, one of the UK's rarest butterflies, the **heath fritillary**, has seen increased numbers on Exmoor, along with a wide variety of other butterfly and insect species that thrive on the mixture of open moorland, deep wooded valleys, high sea cliffs, wildflower meadows and fast-flowing streams. **Exmoor ponies** also roam the land, adapted to survive on low-quality moorland grazing. Their thick winter coat, mane and tail helps to keep them warm and dry, and their brown, bay or dun colouring helps them blend into their surroundings. The Domesday Book records the existence of these ponies on Exmoor as far back as 1086, although some believe the breed has been purebred since the ice age.

Exmoor is also home to a population of around 3,000 **red deer** that have survived since prehistoric times, primarily because the area was once a Royal Forest and the law protected the deer in order to keep a healthy supply available for the king to hunt. Stargazers may spot these majestic mammals at dusk and dawn. They are the largest wild land animals in England, famous for their russet

→ **Top:** Wimbleball Lake is a popular dark sky destination within Exmoor National Park (Arthur Cauty/ Shutterstock); **Bottom:** Exmoor is home to some 3,000 red deer (Nigel Stone)

coats and stags' antlers, which fall off and regrow every year. They eat a variety of food, including young shoots of heather, whortleberry, brambles, saplings, grass, acorns, fungi, berries, ivy and farm crops. In the summer, calves are usually born at woodland edges where they will lie quietly for a few days, camouflaged with dappled spots to resemble sunlight on dead bracken. Once they are strong enough, they join their mother and the rest of the herd, keeping together for at least the first year of the calf's life.

From an archaeological perspective, Exmoor has been strongly influenced by **farming** and **iron mining**, both of which have left permanent marks on the face of the land. The mining industry in particular was an important part of the local economy until most of the mines closed at the end of the 19th century. The iron ore deposits in the Brendon Hills were formed from the Morte Slates, a thick, folded sequence of Devonian-age sedimentary rocks that were notable for their mineral composition. Exmoor has also been shaped by its relationship with the sea, the northern boundary of the park formed by nearly 40km (24 miles) of spectacular coastline along the Bristol Channel.

One of the benefits of stargazing is taking the opportunity to tune into all five of our senses, including the sounds of the landscape at night. This idea inspired a soundscape project in the park, as part of the Heritage Lottery-funded Lynmouth Pavilion Project between 2013 and 2016. Sound artist Martin Prothero recorded the Exmoor seasons over the course of a year and turned them into short audible impressions of the local landscape, from the dawn chorus in spring to the roaring red deer stags in autumn, and the crunch underfoot of winter snow. You can listen to the recordings on the Exmoor National Park website under 'A Year of Sounds' (⌗ www.exmoor-nationalpark.gov.uk).

Exmoor's skies are some of the darkest in the UK, and minimal light pollution means that on a cloudless night visitors can see the Milky Way and thousands of stars with the naked eye. The Exmoor National Park team actively promote their Dark Sky Status and encourage all their visitors to look up at the night sky by hiring telescopes from their national park centres in Dulverton, Dunster and Lynmouth. Telescope hire is around £25 per night, £10 per additional night, plus a refundable deposit of £100. They also sell telescopes, as well as a range of books and other resources to help visitors get started on their stargazing journey. Their Dark Sky Friendly business accreditation scheme helps encourage local businesses to support the project further, with recipients offered dark skies training and other resources. They also host a Dark Skies Festival in October/November each year with a huge range of events, including guided stargazing sessions, night walks, stargazing retreats, talks and workshops by expert astronomers, nocturnal wildlife events, astro-themed craft sessions and night time boat adventures under the stars.

GETTING THERE Exmoor is easily accessible via the A396 road from Dunster to Tiverton. Main line train services run to Minehead, Taunton, Tiverton Parkway and Barnstaple. National Express coaches operate to Taunton, Tiverton, Minehead and Barnstaple where local connections can be picked up. Cyclists can take Sustrans National Route 3, the **West Country Way** (∅ sustrans. org.uk) that connects Land's End to Bristol via Devon, Cornwall and Somerset.

DARK SKIES HIGHLIGHTS On the border of Somerset to the north of Exmoor National Park, **Brendon Common** (Brendon EX35 6PU) offers beautiful views across the moors against the backdrop of the rushing waters of the East Lyn River. Brendon village is 2.5km (1½ miles) southeast of Lynton and 24km (15 miles) west of Minehead. **Wimbleball Lake** (page 133), 15 minutes northeast of Dulverton, is a fantastic place to spot red deer, brown long-eared bats and starling murmurations at dusk as the stars begin to appear. **Bossington Hill** (Minehead TA24 8HS) is a 15-minute drive west of Minehead, and offers spectacular views in every direction, from Dunkery Beacon in the south to the Welsh coast in the north. It is particularly breathtaking on spring nights and early mornings, when the dawn chorus erupts from blossoming thickets. The highest point in Exmoor at 519m, **Dunkery Beacon** (Minehead TA24 7AT) is a stunning, heather-covered hill 5 minutes northwest of Wheddon Cross, featuring burial mounds and an ancient cairn at its summit. On a clear day or night, visitors can see as far as Dartmoor in the south, the Mendips and Quantock Hills to the east, Wales and the Bristol Channel to the north, and north Devon and Hartland Point to the east. A 25-minute walk east from the village of Liscombe will take you to **Winsford Hill** (Dulverton TA22 9QA), a heather-strewn common with beautiful views, managed by the National Trust.

OBSERVATORIES AND ACTIVITIES While there are no public observatories in the national park itself, the next-closest facility, **Norman Lockyer Observatory** (∅ normanlockyer.com), is a 1½-hour drive away, just outside Sidmouth on the south coast. Both a historical observatory and home to an active amateur astronomical society, this has become a hub for amateur astronomy, meteorology, radio astronomy and the promotion of science education. The facility is publicly accessible during one of its frequent open evenings, and is particularly popular with families visiting the area on holiday. Exmoor National Park hosts their own **Dark Skies Festival** each autumn, with a variety of events for families and adults taking place all over the park. They have also produced their own **Dark Skies Pocket Guide** which is available as a free download from their website (∅ www.exmoor-nationalpark.gov.uk/ enjoying/stargazing), where you can also sign up for their **Dark Skies Newsletter**

for regular updates and event information. **Telescope Hire** is available from the national park centres across the park, where they also sell a range of books, telescopes and useful material.

DAYTIME ACTIVITIES For an afternoon tipple, the **Exmoor Distillery** (⊘ exmoordistillery.co.uk), a 4-minute drive south of Dulverton, is a small-batch artisan gin distillery run by local couple John and Nicola Smith. They run a number of events for visitors and tourists. For family foodies, **Quince Honey Farm** (⊘ quincehoneyfarm.co.uk), 4 minutes north of South Molton, is another family-run establishment comprising a working honey farm with guided tours, a shop selling honey products, a restaurant and a range of children's activities, including the Play Hive soft play area. The **Exmoor Owl & Wildlife Sanctuary** (⊘ exmoorowlhawkcentre.co.uk) in the village of Allerford is a lovely escape from the outside world, set in an outdoor space where all the birds are housed in free-living aviaries. Their owl flying experiences are very reasonably priced and make a great afternoon out for animal-loving adults and children, and they also offer an Adopt an Owl scheme for those wishing to donate more. In the village of Nether Stowey at the foot of the Quantock Hills, **Coleridge Cottage** (⊘ nationaltrust.org.uk/coleridge-cottage) is a treat for lovers of poetry and literary history. Run by the National Trust, this is where Samuel Taylor Coleridge lived for three years and produced some of his best known works, including *The Rime of the Ancient Mariner*. Another National Trust property, in the village of Dunster, **Dunster Castle and Watermill** (⊘ nationaltrust.org.uk/dunster-castle-and-watermill) is an ancient castle and country home with beautiful views and subtropical gardens, while **Simonsbath Sawmill** (⊘ simonsbathsawmill.org.uk), half an hour east from Barnstaple, is a fully restored sawmill and 8ha (20 acres) of riverside meadow, a rare surviving example of a once-common machine.

BRECON BEACONS NATIONAL PARK (INTERNATIONAL DARK SKY RESERVE)

Brecon Beacons National Park Visitor Centre, Libanus, Brecon, Powys LD3 8ER ✆ 01874 623366 **e** enquiries@beacons-npa.gov.uk ⊘ breconbeacons.org ♥ OS Explorer Maps OL12 & OL13.

A cluster of mountains sprinkled with Bronze Age burial mounds, Norman castles, sheep tracks, mines and quarries, the Brecon Beacons are a living snapshot of the rural history of Wales. Defining the park are the highest mountains in southern Britain and the three ranges surrounding them, and at their heart is Wales's largest expanse of **open hill common**, a 32km (20 mile) swathe of grassy moorland, heather-clad escarpments and Old Red Sandstone peaks. **Welsh mountain ponies** graze the shrub to keep it maintained and allow rarer plant species to grow. These are a hardy native breed, the descendants of pit ponies commonly used in underground mines from the mid 18th until the mid 20th century.

The framework of the landscape was shaped in the ice age, as the ice hollowed out glacial valleys and bowl-shaped hollows from the mountainsides. The most significant human impact began in the Mesolithic era, when hunter-gatherers removed and burnt the scrub to create small grassland areas. These areas encouraged grazing animals to move in, which they could then hunt and eat. By the end of the Bronze Age, most of the original forest that once covered the area had been cleared. The Celts then settled, built hill forts and fought off Roman influence, and by the 15th century industries like charcoal burning, iron forging and coal mining had established themselves around the landscape.

The name is thought to have evolved from Brycheiniog, which in turn was inspired by the legendary King Brychan who ruled this part of Wales before the Norman Conquest. The name Brecon Beacons is said to come from the ancient practice of lighting fires on the mountaintops to warn of attacks from invaders, a practice that continued into the 19th century, although for different reasons. Rather than signalling attack, they heralded celebrations like royal birthdays and

↑ On a clear night in the Brecon Beacons, you can see the Milky Way, major constellations, bright nebulas and even meteor showers (Charles Palmer/Shutterstock)

military victories. Most recently, beacons like these were lit across the country to celebrate the millennium and the Queen's Diamond Jubilee.

Although more recreational than industrial, the Brecon Beacons are still a hive of activity today. The mountains are popular for a variety of outdoor pursuits, such as mountain biking, kayaking, horseriding, gliding, rock climbing, fishing and golf. Interspersed throughout the area are market towns full of character. To the south of the Black Mountains, Crickhowell is a hotspot for hikers and outdoor lovers, while the town of Brecon at the top edge of the park is known for its famous Brecon Jazz Festival. Some 10km (6 miles) from the English border, the medieval walled town of Abergavenny is a must-visit for food lovers, while Hay-on-Wye, famous for its secondhand and antiquarian **bookshops**, hosts the much-loved annual Hay Festival of Literature and the Arts, an event that was once described by Bill Clinton as 'the Woodstock of the mind'.

If you can't wait until sunset for darkness to fall, the Brecon Beacons is also renowned for its extensive **subterranean caves**, and is home to four of the five longest limestone cave systems in Britain. They began forming over 300 million years ago, when the shells and skeletons of sea creatures formed carboniferous limestone in the shallow tropical seas of the Paleozoic era. Some of these skeletons can still be seen in the park's spectacular Lithostrotion coral fossils, which have intricately preserved internal detail. As limestone is soluble in mildly acidic water, the run-off from the peaty ground found its way into small cracks in the rock over time, which widened them over the years to create a network of fissures and tubes. A band of limestone stretches 72km (45 miles) across the national park from Blorenge in the east to Carreg Cennen in the west, and it is in this thin belt, rarely more than a mile in width, that some of the most breathtaking caves in Britain can be found.

The park has plenty of experienced and qualified cave leaders to guide visitors through the labyrinths underground, and there are also many outdoor centres and activity specialists in the area which offer caving experiences. If caving isn't your cup of tea, you can still find your way underground by visiting the Big Pit in Blaenavon, in the southeast corner of the park. This National Coal Museum is an award-winning interactive attraction, complete with an underground tour that allows visitors to experience the sights, sounds, smells and atmosphere of an authentic coal mine.

Back above ground, the national park is rich in flora and fauna, particularly crepuscular species who move around at dusk and dawn. One of the UK's largest populations of the rare, **lesser horseshoe bat** is found in the Usk Valley on the eastern side of the park. The lesser horseshoe is one of the smallest bat species in the UK, sheltering in valleys with extensive deciduous woods or dense scrub close to their roost sites. In winter they hibernate in caves, mines and other underground spaces.

The park is also home to a healthy population of **otters**, a naturally shy creature that emerges in the evenings along undisturbed riverbanks and waterways. The local rivers are breeding grounds for trout and salmon, a favourite food of the otter, and as territorial animals they can generally be found all year round along their own personal section of river, ranging from 5km to 20km. They live and breed in sheltered bankside holes called 'holts', and the fact that they exist here at all is a reflection of the UK's changing relationship with its rivers. Otters suffered a serious decline between 1950 and 1980, but their numbers have been recovering since they were made a protected species in 1981. To see if there are otters nearby, look out for signs like chunky paw prints with five toes, large fish remains, or faeces called spraints, which are said to smell like fresh hay or jasmine tea.

The Brecon Beacons National Park became an International Dark Sky Reserve in 2012, and since then has made a name for itself among amateur and professional astronomers. On a clear night, you can see the Milky Way, major constellations, bright nebulas and even meteor showers. Local accommodation providers also offer plenty of 'stay-and-gaze' options, and the scenic landscapes have inspired stunning examples of astrophotography.

GETTING THERE The Brecon Beacons National Park is within easy reach of the M4, M50 and A40. Coaches travel to Abergavenny, Cardiff, Neath and Swansea and main line train services run to Abergavenny, Merthyr Tydfil and Llandovery.

↑ One of the UK's largest populations of lesser-horseshoe bat is found in the Usk Valley
(Agami Photo Agency/Shutterstock)

DARK SKIES HIGHLIGHTS The Usk Reservoir (page 156) is a perfect spot for evening picnics under the stars, with a large flat area for setting up telescopes and an easily accessible road from Trecastle, 10 minutes to the east. The stunning ruins of Llanthony Priory (Abergavenny NP7 7NN) are one of the park's most iconic sites where visitors can enjoy pristine dark skies, 9 minutes north of Abergavenny. The priory itself is closed from 16.00 onwards but stargazers are welcome to use the car park for views over to Hatterrall Hill. Another hilltop viewpoint just south of Hay-on-Wye is Hay Bluff (Hay-on-Wye NP7 7NP), a flat-topped peak overlooking the Wye Valley with good views over Powys and Shropshire. The 13th-century castle at Carreg Cennen (Llandeilo SA19 6UA) sits on huge limestone cliffs, just 15 minutes southeast of Llandeilo, offering breathtaking views across the valley beneath some of the darkest skies in the area. At 596m, the Sugar Loaf (Abergavenny NP7 7LA) is one of the highest peaks in the heart of the Black Mountains, just north of Abergavenny. Its distinctive conical shape, reminiscent of a volcano, is what gives the mountain its name as it looks similar to an old-fashioned sugarloaf, the form in which sugar was once sold before it became cubed and granulated. Dominating the skyline, the Sugar Loaf offers wide views over the south and west while avoiding much of the nearby light pollution.

OBSERVATORIES AND ACTIVITIES A public education observatory can be found in the grounds of the Brecon Beacons Visitor Centre (⊘ breconbeacons.org) in Brecon town, first built in 2014 to facilitate astronomy in the park. The dome contains a 30cm f5 reflector telescope with a piggybacked 130mm f9 refractor telescope, all mounted on an EQ6 GOTO mount. Eyepieces, binoculars and a small library are also available for use. Visitors can enjoy lectures, observing sessions and astrophotography workshops, as well as the twice-yearly Astrocamp held in the village of Cwmdu. A new project has also been proposed to build a state-of-the-art planetarium on the site of the old Tower Colliery, the UK's oldest continuously working deep-coal mine, near Hirwaun on the southern edge of the park. The Planetariwm Wales (⊘ planetarium. wales) project seeks to establish a world-class centre for research, education and leisure, engaging students and the public with science, technology, engineering and maths through tourism. If completed, it would be Wales's first national planetarium and an innovative resource for astronomy lovers.

DAYTIME ACTIVITIES The Big Pit National Coal Museum (⊘ museum. wales/bigpit) in the centre of Blaenavon was voted Wales's Favourite National Treasure, offering a moving, informative and entertaining exploration of the lives of the miners who worked underground. Bird lovers will marvel at the

Llanddeusant Red Kite Feeding Station (redkiteswales.co.uk), a 15-minute drive southeast of Llangadog, opened in 2002 by a local partnership with support from the Brecon Beacons National Park. Their daily feeds attract red kites, buzzards, ravens and other birds of prey, and there's no need to book. In the heart of Brecon town, the **Found Gallery** (foundgallery.co.uk) is one of the leading art spaces in Wales with a vibrant exhibition programme showcasing the best in contemporary art and ceramics. For whisky lovers, **Penderyn Distillery** (penderyn.wales) is located in the historic village of Penderyn, just 3km (just under 2 miles) north of Hirwaun on the A4059. They produce award-winning single malt whiskies and spirits, as well as offering tastings, tours and masterclasses. Green-fingered visitors will be inspired by the **National Botanical Garden of Wales** (page 156), a 20-minute drive from the town of Ffairfach on the western edge of the national park. As both a visitor attraction and a centre for botanical research, the garden is home to the largest single-span glasshouse in the world, measuring 110m long by 60m wide. For a relaxing way to take in the mountain views, the heritage **Brecon Mountain Railway** (bmr.wales), with its impressively restored steam locomotives, carries passengers from Pant to Torpantau.

ELAN VALLEY ESTATE (INTERNATIONAL DARK SKY PARK)

Elan Valley Visitor Centre, Elan Valley, Rhayader, Powys LD6 5HP 01597 810880
e info@elanvalleytrust.org elanvalley.org.uk OS Explorer Map 200.

Sometimes referred to as 'the Welsh Lake District', the Elan Valley is a river valley in Powys, mid Wales covering 181km² (70 square miles) of lakes and countryside. The valley is situated in the area known as the Cambrian Mountains, home to some of the darkest skies in Europe and a hotspot for noctilucent clouds between June and late July. At its heart are the **Elan Valley Reservoirs**, a chain of manmade lakes created from damming the Elan and Claerwen rivers. The five lakes, known as Claerwen, Graig-goch, Pen-y-garreg, Garreg-ddu and Caban-coch, provide clean drinking water for the entire Birmingham area, and since their creation the estate has become a haven for wildlife and a popular destination for hikers and cyclists.

The history of the reservoirs dates to the 19th century, when Birmingham's population grew rapidly due to the Industrial Revolution. Clean water was scarce, which caused major epidemics of water-borne diseases like typhoid and cholera. The city council decided the city needed a clean water supply, and the Elan and Claerwen valleys were identified as possible solutions. Today, an average of 300 million litres of water a day can be extracted from the Elan Valley to supply Birmingham, a volume that nearly doubled when the Claerwen Dam was later completed.

The building work on the reservoirs began in 1893, when 100 occupants of the Elan Valley had to be relocated, although only the landowners received compensation. Many of the buildings were demolished, including three manor houses, 18 farms, a school and a church. A railway line was then constructed to transport the workers and building materials each day, and a village of wooden huts was purpose-built to house the workers on site. New workers spent a night in quarantine to be deloused and examined for infectious diseases before being allowed across the river to the village.

A school was provided for children under 11, after which they were expected to work. Imported alcohol and unauthorised visitors were both banned, but there was a pub for the men, a library, public hall, shop, canteen and bath house, as well as streetlighting powered by hydro-electric generators. The workers' site, known as Elan village, became totally self-sufficient, and by the end of the 19th century the population had grown to around 2,500 residents. The village can still be visited today (delousing no longer required) by heading for the Elan Valley Visitor Centre and crossing the suspension bridge.

Aside from its human heritage, the Elan Valley is rich in a variety of wildlife. The mosaic of different habitats around the estate, from wetland and upland bog to meadows, streams, mixed woodland and reservoirs, means the landscape is unique and attracts a range of species. One type of habitat found in the valley is known as *ffridd*, a word that dates back to the 14th century in Wales, but comes from the Middle English word *frith* meaning woodland or wooded countryside. *Ffridd* is a mixture of grass and heathland with bracken, scrub, rock exposures and streams, and as a habitat, it is an important component of the Welsh countryside, acting as a corridor between lowlands and uplands to help animals and plants move around.

One bird, in particular, can be seen in the spring and autumn as they migrate through to their breeding and feeding grounds. The **ring ouzel** is slightly smaller and slimmer than a blackbird, most easily recognised for the white crescent moon shape around the breast of the males. They are found mainly in steep-sided valleys, crags and gullies, and although they no longer breed in the Elan Valley, they still make an annual appearance as they pass through the area. At night, stargazers may even be lucky enough to hear them as they fly overhead on their nocturnal migration routes, the most common night call being a raucous *chrrk-chik-chik-chik*.

The area is also home to a number of nocturnal mammals that thrive in the woods and valleys. **Foxes** can be heard calling in the mating season, around autumn and winter, after which they will raise their cubs in old rabbit or badger burrows. A variety of **mustelids** are common around the estate, including badgers, otters, polecats, mink, stoats, weasels and the occasional pine marten. Badgers live in setts as family groups, while otters use the rivers and reservoirs as fishing grounds for

← Winter skies over the Craig Goch Reservoir (Allan Trow/Dark Sky Wales)

brown trout. Polecats are also found on the estate, the wild cousins of domestic ferrets, with whom they will sometimes interbreed if given the chance. Their most distinguishing feature is their facial markings, which look like a bandit's mask across the eyes, somewhat similar to a racoon's. **Bats** are another mammal found in the valley, with nine species currently recorded: common pipistrelle, soprano pipistrelle, brown long eared, Daubenton's, lesser horseshoe, natterers, Brandt's, whiskered and noctule. A bat detector is a fun and inexpensive gadget sometimes popular with stargazers, as you can detect which bats are nearby based on their sound frequencies. **Deer** are surprisingly uncommon, with only three species being recorded on the estate in recent history. Of these, there are only three red deer records and one muntjac, while the rest have been a number of roe deer sightings.

In 2015, the Elan Valley Estate became the first privately owned but publicly accessible park in the world to achieve International Dark Sky Park status. Granted the silver-tier status, it now means that just over 18,200ha (45,000 acres) of the estate are protected against light pollution for the benefit of people and wildlife. It has become a popular, peaceful destination for astronomers around the world, looking for a star-studded escape in the wild heart of Wales.

GETTING THERE
Elan Valley is situated in the county of Powys in mid Wales, and can be accessed easily from the nearby town of Rhayader. If driving from Rhayader, follow the B4518 west out of the town and the left turn for the visitor centre is signposted after 5km (3 miles). Main line train services run to Llandrindod Wells.

DARK SKIES HIGHLIGHTS
The **Claerwen Dam** (Rhayader LD6 5HF), 20 minutes southwest of Rhayader, is almost twice the size of the other dams in the Elan Valley, and offers spectacular views over the surrounding scenery. It is also within the Claerwen Nature Reserve, an expanse of mountain upland valued for its peaty and acidic soil which attracts a number of plant and animal species. Nearby, 20 minutes west of Rhayader, the **Craig Goch Dam** (Rhayader LD6 5HS) provides more stunning viewpoints across land and water at 317m above sea level. The car park at **Penrhiw-Wen** (Powys LD6 5HA) is an elevated spot with a good view of the surrounding landscape, 8 minutes northwest of Rhayader. It's also popular with hill climbers and cyclists looking for a challenge, as the incline is steep. At the northern end of the Craig Goch Reservoir, **Pont ar Elan** (page 151) offers crisp views of the Milky Way and the valley lying beneath. To the west of the Elan Valley Reservoirs, the **Teifi Pools** (Ystrad Meurig SY25 6BT) just north of Llyn Egnant provide more stunning views with a car park for good access. Llyn Teifi is one of several lakes known collectively as the Teifi Pools, situated at 455m in the Cambrian Mountains.

OBSERVATORIES AND ACTIVITIES The digital **Cambrian Mountains Dark Sky Guide** is available as a free download (⊘cambrianmountainsdarkskies. co.uk), where you can find the nine Dark Sky Discovery Sites that make up the Cambrian Mountains Astro Trail. Visitors are also encouraged to sign up to Elan Valley Estate newsletter for updates and events (⊘elanvalley.org.uk/darkskies). While there are no public observatories within the Elan Valley Estate boundary, the **Spaceguard Centre** (⊘ spaceguardcentre.com) is a 40-minute drive east of Rhayader. Also known as the National Near Earth Objects Information Centre, this observatory is the only organisation in the UK dedicated to addressing the hazard of Near Earth Objects like asteroids and comets. The observatory is privately owned but members of the public are welcome to visit on open days and see the telescopes, planetarium, robotic telescope control centre and gift shop. The organisation **Dark Sky Wales** (⊘ darkskywales.org) also runs observations and planetarium workshops as part of public education across Wales.

DAYTIME ACTIVITIES Just across the reservoir from Elan Village, **Nantgwyllt Church** (⊘elanvalley.org.uk) was built in 1898 to replace the one that was submerged by the Caban-coch Reservoir. This replacement church is well worth a visit, situated in a secluded spot by the water and home to some of the surviving furnishings and artefacts from the old church, including the oil lamps providing the only source of interior light. **Llandrindod Lake Park** (⊘ llandrindod.co.uk/attractions/b-lake), in the town of Llandrindod Wells, is a lovely spot for the summer months, with paddle boats, a café and its famous dragon fountain sculpture in the water. The **National Cycle Museum** (⊘ cyclemuseum.org.uk) in Llandrindod Wells is a charming independent museum home to over 260 cycles, including an 1818 Hobby Horse, Victorian solid-tyred machines, classic lightweight models and the latest carbon fibre designs. Also nearby, the **Red Kite Feeding Centre** (⊘ redkitefeeding.co.uk) at Gigrin Farm, half a mile east of Rhayader is a 65ha (160 acre) family-run farm where visitors can observe daily feedings and enjoy a treat in the coffee shop.

SNOWDONIA NATIONAL PARK
(INTERNATIONAL DARK SKY RESERVE)

Snowdonia National Park Information Centre, Royal Oak Stables, Betws-y-Coed, Conwy LL24 0AH ✆ 01690 710426 **e** park@snowdonia.gov.wales ⊘ snowdonia.gov.wales
📍 OS Explorer Maps OL17, OL18 & OL23.

A land awash with rusty grassland, moss-strewn rocks and turquoise pools as clear as glass, at the heart of Snowdonia National Park is **Snowdon** itself, the highest mountain in Wales at 1,085m above sea level. The name Snowdon originates from the Old English 'snow hill', while the Welsh name Yr Wyddfa means 'the tumulus', thought to refer to the folk story in which a mound of memorial stones was thrown over the giant Rhita Gawr after his defeat at the hands of King Arthur.

According to legend, Rhita had grown tired of the humans fighting over the land and, as the strongest and bravest of them all, he decided he should be in charge. One after another, he attacked and defeated the leaders of all the kingdoms, shaving off their beards and weaving them into his cloak as proof of his victory. Kings soon came from far and wide to stop him, but each was defeated until, finally, the great warrior Arthur set out with his men to Rhita's fortress in the mountains of Gwynedd. They fought on the highest peak of the highest mountain, and as the battle continued, swords were shattered, shields torn and bones broken. By the end both were wounded but, with one last burst of effort, Arthur brought his sword down into Rhita's skull and killed him. Arthur and his men piled rocks on to the fallen giant, and the place was named *Gwyddfa Rhita* – Rhita's Tomb – which changed over time to become *Yr Wyddfa*.

Snowdonia is rich in linguistic history, not only in its peaks and valleys, but also in the tracks and paths that twist up Snowdon itself. Many who have climbed the mountain will have heard of Pen-y-Pass, the most popular starting point for reaching the summit. But there is also the **Miners' Track**, which starts off wide and even before gradually becoming a much harder climb. The Miners' Track was built to serve the Britannia Copper Mine, but before that the miners had to heave the copper up the eastern side of the mountain, to be taken down to Llyn Cwellyn on the other side by a horse-drawn sledge, where it was then transported on to the town of Caernarfon to be processed and dispatched.

The history of Snowdon is intertwined with that of the Welsh **mining** industry, with the first recorded mine dating back to the 1800s, although rumours of copper mining in the region originated with the Romans. Demand for copper started to increase in the mid 18th century, when warships were built with copper bottoms to prevent worms boring into the wood. But copper extraction on Snowdon was never hugely lucrative, with many mining companies going bankrupt by the start of World War I, and the mountainside is still littered with fragments of mining history, including an abandoned barracks and the ruins of a crushing mill.

Snowdon may be the beating heart of the park, but there's more to this area than the mountains and hills. It is also home to over 320km (200 miles) of coastline and more than 35 beaches, as well as one of the most spectacular stretches of the **Wales Coast Path**. The coastal towns within the park are littered with ancient relics that reflect a longstanding relationship between the Welsh people and the sea. There is evidence that people have been living and working on these shores for as long as 5,000 years, with ancient burial chambers and settlements suggesting that people fished and sailed along the coastline. Later,

→ **Top:** Llynnau Cregennen in the shadow of Cadair Idris (stocker1970/Shutterstock); **Bottom:** Pine martens have returned to the Celtic rainforests of Dolmelynllyn in Snowdonia (Mark Medcalf/Shutterstock)

the Romans and Normans built their forts and castles in strategic locations close to the shore, where they could defend the land from their enemies. On a particularly lonely outcrop of rock, 350m above sea level, the Iron Age hill fort of Craig y Ddinas offers dramatic views over the mountains and sea between Harlech and Barmouth. It's the perfect spot for a night walk beneath some of the darkest skies on the Welsh coast, where the stars shine both above and below your head, reflected in the Irish Sea.

The stars feature regularly in the Welsh *Mabinogion* stories, a compilation of tales written in Middle Welsh and originating from ancient oral storytelling. These fables describe the lives and achievements of a group of interrelated characters, recalling their encounters between the mortal and immortal worlds. They embrace aspects of the pagan era while also conjuring up the medieval world of the Arthurian age, and in these stories the constellations are based on different legends to the better-known Greek and Roman versions. The constellation Gemini, for example, is not a pair of twins but two brothers, Gwyn and Gwyrthyr, battling for the love of Creiddylad, the most beautiful lady in the British Isles. Their rivalry is interpreted by some as the contest between summer and winter, or the light and the dark, a fitting tale for a place like Snowdonia, which is often called the 'land of contrasts' due to its varied and dynamic landscapes.

A landscape that's rich in flora and fauna, Snowdonia has also made headlines recently when it saw the return of a rare species. The native **pine marten** was once found all over the UK but by 1900, 95% of the woodland cover it relies on had been removed, and pine marten populations almost vanished from England. In 2019, after a century-long absence, the National Trust confirmed that pine martens had found their way back into the Celtic rainforests of Dolmelynllyn in Snowdonia. A project was initiated in collaboration with the National Trust rangers and Vincent Wildlife Trust to set up picnics for pine martens to encourage them to expand their range, using their favourite food of jam and eggs to draw them in. While it may be some time before visitors spot a pine marten hopping through the woods, stargazers at least have the advantage of being out at the same time as these elusive, nocturnal creatures. Look out for their scats (droppings) on the forest floor, made up of fur, feathers, bones and seeds.

In December 2015, Snowdonia National Park was the second area in Wales to be designated as an International Dark Sky Reserve, a designation that covers 18% of Wales's land area. Today, Snowdonia is one of the darkest places in Britain, particularly within its rugged, mountainous interior, and covers a thinly populated land mass of over 2,070km² (800 square miles). Whether you're in the mountains, at the side of a lake or gazing out across the sea, a clear night in Snowdonia will offer you views of the Milky Way, all the major constellations, nebulas and shooting stars.

GETTING THERE To reach Snowdonia by train, the North Wales Coast Line from Crewe to Holyhead connects you to Bangor at the northwestern edge of the park, and to Llandudno, where you can get the Conwy Valley Line down through the park as far as Blaenau Ffestiniog. By road, the park can be accessed via the M56, A55, M6, M5 and M1. Both the Explore Wales Pass and North Wales Rover ticket provide almost unlimited train and bus travel for one day.

DARK SKIES HIGHLIGHTS The **Bwlch y Groes** road (Machynlleth SY20 9AH) is the second highest public road mountain pass in Wales, linking Dinas Mawddwy and Llanuwchllyn. It has a summit altitude of 545m and excellent views across the park. A popular lakeside picnic spot today, **Llyn Geirionydd** (Llanrhychwyn LL27 0YX) is situated 15 minutes west of Llanrwst, where a derelict industrial landscape once stood. In fact, the car park lies on a waste tip near an old lead mine entrance, but you would never know by looking at such beautiful surroundings, especially the fantastic night sky views over the water. Just north of the village of Drws y Coed, near Rhyd Ddu, **Llyn y Dywarchen** (Betws-y-Coed LL41 4TR) is a popular fishing lake with a peaceful atmosphere and good views of the sky. A third lake, **Llynnau Cregennen** (Arthog LL39 1LJ), is a 10-minute drive east of Arthog, and sits about 240m above sea level beneath the slopes of the Cader Idris mountain range. Walk up the little hill above the car park for a fantastic view towards Barmouth and Cardigan Bay. Some 20 minutes east of Blaenau Ffestiniog, **Tŷ Cipar** (Betws-y-Coed LL24 0PA) is home to a former gamekeeper's house and one of the largest blanket bogs in Wales, attracting birds like the hen harrier, peregrine falcon and merlin.

OBSERVATORIES AND ACTIVITIES There are no permanent public observatories in Snowdonia, but the organisation **Discovery in the Dark Wales** (⌘ discoveryinthedark.wales) offers training and equipment to local businesses to help them spread the word about preserving the night sky. They also have a fantastic website full of resources, including a step-by-step guide to astrophotography, a library of Welsh constellation myths, tips on badger and bat watching, night walking, trail running and much more. The **North Wales Astronomy Society** hosts monthly observing events at Llanelian Community Centre on the northern edge of the park (⌘ northwalesastro.co.uk).

DAYTIME ACTIVITIES Visitors can immerse themselves in Snowdonia's industrial past by visiting the **Sygun Copper Mine** (⌘ syguncoppermine.co.uk) or the **National Slate Museum** (⌘ museum.wales/slate). The former, 5 minutes northeast of Beddgelert, is a Victorian-era copper mine offering self-guided tours on the local history of the industry. The latter, in the village of Llanberis, is situated in a former Victorian quarry with original artefacts and great activities for kids. Also in Llanberis, just across the water from the Slate Museum, the **Snowdonia Mountain Railway** (⊘ snowdonrailway.co.uk) has been carrying visitors to the summit of Snowdon for over 120 years. On a clear day, the **Hafod Eryri Visitor Centre** offers views all the way to Ireland, while the Summit Café provides excellent coffee, pasties and cakes. For adrenaline junkies, the **National White Water Centre** (⊘ nationalwhitewatercentre.co.uk) is 10 minutes north of the town of Bala. Visitors can try a range of white-water adventures on the natural rapids of the River Tryweryn, all under the guidance of local experts. For a more peaceful afternoon's activity, enjoy a cup of tea and a slice of cake in **Tŷ Hyll** (⊘ tuhwntirbont.co.uk), also known as the Ugly House, 5 minutes east of the village of Capel Curig. Far from ugly, this mysterious building is now home to an independently run tearoom and surrounded by a wildlife garden and woodland. **Dolwyddelan Castle** (⊘ cadw.gov.wales/visit/places-to-visit/dolwyddelan-castle), 7 minutes east of Blaenau Dolwyddelan, is one of a group of fortresses built to command the mountain passes, with beautiful views and an on-site exhibition for visitors to enjoy.

YORKSHIRE DALES NATIONAL PARK (INTERNATIONAL DARK SKY RESERVE)

National Park Centre, Aysgarth, North Yorkshire DL8 3TH ⊘ 01969 662910 **e** info@yorkshiredales.org.uk ⊘ yorkshiredales.org.uk ♀ OS Explorer Maps OL2, OL30, OL41, 297, 298 & 304.

They say in Yorkshire that each dale has its own character. It is a land of contrasts, of different moods and distinct landscapes. From wild and windswept moorland to tranquil wildflower meadows, to underground labyrinths, stone-built farmsteads, abandoned mines, roaring waterfalls and ancient woodlands, the Yorkshire Dales are a landscape forged between people and nature, so it is fitting that this national park has also become one of the newest International Dark Sky Reserves in the world.

The Yorkshire Dales were shaped by glaciers over thousands of years, which formed the rolling landscape of valleys, hills and moors that visitors encounter today. This structure was formed millions of years ago, when the area was home to tropical seas and giant river deltas, which in turn created the **limestone** rock that today makes up so much of the ground beneath the dales. Limestone is a hard sedimentary rock, formed when the remains of sea creatures drop to the sea floor and become compressed over time. As water has interacted with the landscape over thousands of years, features like scars, pot-holes, clints and grykes are formed, as well as creating miles of underground caves and passages beneath our feet.

The presence of limestone in the earth has shaped both the physical form of the dales and its relationship with people. Limestone results in less surface water on soil that is already thin and bare, which – combined with the poor upland weather conditions – means that it is difficult to grow crops here. As a consequence, farming in the dales has been characterised by sheep grazing on the uplands, dairy cattle fed from pasture in the valley floors, and a distinctive landscape of dry-stone walls and barns.

Because of its suitability to dairy farming, Yorkshire is home to a number of famous cheeses, including the creamy and crumbly **Wensleydale** (of *Wallace and Gromit* fame), Swaledale, made of ewe's milk, and Ribblesdale goats' milk cheeses. But the food fame doesn't end there – Yorkshire is also home to the beloved **Yorkshire pudding**, originally created as a way of using up the fat that dropped into the dripping pan by cooking a batter pudding while the joint of meat roasted. And the iconic **Yorkshire Tea** was first launched in 1977, when different blends were sold to different regions of Yorkshire depending on the softness or hardness of the water. In November 2019, it was revealed that Yorkshire Tea was the number one-selling brand of tea in the UK, taking 28% of the traditional black tea market.

But the history of the Yorkshire Dales isn't only built around food and farming.

↑ The Yorkshire Dales is one of the best destinations for looking up at the night sky (Matt Gibson/Shutterstock)

Almost every parish in Yorkshire is home to an abandoned **quarry** or two, remnants of an industry that dug limestone, sandstone, flagstone, millstone, granite and slate out of the ground. Most of these materials were either sold for construction or used to build the huge textile mills and factories which dominated the Pennine valleys from the Industrial Revolution onwards. Visitors to the dales can still find evidence of these quarries left behind in the landscape, where they have either been absorbed back into the wild, been used for landfill or filled up with water for recreational fishing.

Mining was another huge industry in the Yorkshire Dales for hundreds of years, with some coal mines dating back to the 14th century. The ruins of abandoned mines are scattered about the dales, echoes of an industrial past that has largely closed due to cheaper production abroad. These ruins, however, are beautiful in their own way, and reinforce the complex relationship between man and nature, and how the two are so intricately woven together in this unique landscape. In the village of Buckden, one story about a man known only as Buckden Bill has mystified archaeologists ever since his skeleton was found in 1964, just 365m from the exit of Buckden Gravel Mine. It is believed the man entered the mine back in 1890, but nobody knows who he was, why he was there or how he died. All that is known about him is that he seemed to be lying in a relaxed position, carrying a walking stick, wearing studded leather boots, trousers, shirt, waistcoat and a fine felt hat, and with pockets containing a clay pipe, tobacco tin, box of matches, a medicine bottle, three coins, and a funeral card for a Mr John Winskill. It is unlikely the identity of Buckden Bill will ever be resolved, but it brings to mind the question of how many other mysteries lie waiting in the caves and mines that are carved out beneath the Yorkshire soil.

Above ground, however, there is no doubt that the Yorkshire Dales is one of the best destinations for looking up at the night sky. On a clear night in the dales, visitors might see as many as 2,000 stars, and in most places it is possible to clearly see the Milky Way, as well as planets, meteors, the moon and even the International Space Station, which orbits the earth every 90 minutes. It is also a potential area for catching the northern lights when the conditions are right, which is an advantage for locals as the lights can only be predicted a few hours before they appear, so anyone looking to encounter them must be ready to drop everything and go. Most of the time, however, the dark night sky offers plenty of enchantment for the everyday astronomer and, with each hill and valley offering something different, the Yorkshire Dales are the perfect place to get lost in the dark.

GETTING THERE Main line trains stop within the national park at Horton-in-Ribblesdale, Ribblehead, Dent, Garsdale and Kirkby Stephen. The heritage

Wensleydale Railway also runs from Northallerton, and other local stations providing access to the dales include Darlington, Ilkley, Skipton, Penrith and Oxenholme. Coaches travel to nearby towns such as Lancaster, Penrith, Skipton, Leeds, Harrogate, York, Ripon, Northallerton and Darlington. The park is bordered by major trunk roads, including the M6 to the west, the A66 to the north, the A1 to the east and the A65 and A59 to the south.

DARK SKIES HIGHLIGHTS
Two of the park's information centres are designated as Dark Sky Discovery Sites. The **Hawes National Park Centre** (Hawes DL8 3NT) is housed within the Dales Countryside Museum in the centre of Hawes market town. In the daytime, the centre offers visitor information, cycle hire and a coffee shop, while the museum tells the story of the people who have lived and worked in the Yorkshire Dales for over 1,000 years. At night, it's a great spot for stargazing as the car park and surrounding area have free open access and good views of the night sky, as does the **Malham National Park Centre Car Park** (page 142) in the southern end of the park. This site has visitor information and toilet facilities, while the area outside is recommended after dark. The national park car park in **Buckden** (page 141) is another good stargazing spot, set in the hills of northern Wharfedale beneath the impressive bulk of Buckden Pike. The village is a popular stop-off point for walkers and cyclists, with plenty of places to have supper before a night beneath the stars. The **Tan Hill Inn** (page 142) in Swaledale is Britain's highest public house and a great spot for astronomers, a 17th-century inn with a welcoming fire perched on a lonely hill.

OBSERVATORIES AND ACTIVITIES
The Yorkshire Dales works with the North York Moors National Park and Nidderdale Area of Outstanding Natural Beauty (AONB) to organise their annual **Dark Skies Festival** (⌨ darkskiesnationalparks.org.uk) every February, with a range of talks, workshops and events for visitors to enjoy. Within the reserve boundary, **Lime Tree Observatory** (⌨ limetreeobservatory.com) in Grewelthorpe, near Ripon, is a publicly accessible observatory situated on a farm. It was built following the recovery of a large telescope and dome from an observatory in Kent, the telescope being a 24" reflecting telescope with a motor drive which allows observers to keep the desired object in view for long periods of time. Next to the observing room there is a small presentation room for group events. Pre-booked events are organised throughout the year, run by experienced astronomers. At the time of writing, there is also a planetarium project underway on the farm, with the plan being to convert one of the existing barns into a multi-functional space for talks, demonstrations, crafts and a theatrical planetarium.

DAYTIME ACTIVITIES White Scar Cave (whitescarcave.co.uk) in Ingleton is a spectacular natural cave system open to tourists, complete with a café and eco-friendly visitor centre. The cave contains one of the largest known chambers in Britain, known as 'The Battlefield' and measuring 90m long. In the market town of Hawes, the **Wensleydale Creamery** (wensleydale. co.uk) is a must-visit for cheese lovers. Their family experience tour includes cheese-making demonstrations and cheesy facts galore, while the creamery shop, gift shop and coffee garden round off the visit. At the top of Skipton High Street, **Skipton Castle** (skiptoncastle.co.uk) is a 900-year-old medieval castle that withstood a three-year siege during the Civil War. Visitors can see the banqueting hall, kitchen, bedchamber and privy, and climb from the depths of the dungeon to the top storey of the watchtower. For something a little different, families will love **The Forbidden Corner** (theforbiddencorner. co.uk) in the heart of Tupgill Park, half an hour east of Hawes. Home to a unique labyrinth of tunnels, chambers, follies and secret gardens, it is suitable for all ages and also serves coffee and light bites in the cafe. In Grassington village, the annual **Grassington Festival** (www.grassington-festival.org. uk) in June has been offering a lively cultural experience for 40 years, with a combination of performances, visual arts and live music. For book lovers, just outside the park boundary is the **Brontë Parsonage Museum** (bronte. org.uk) in Haworth, where the Brontë sisters wrote the now classic novels, including *Wuthering Heights* and *Jane Eyre*, that would one day bring them literary acclaim. The museum includes events and exhibitions, a library and gift shop.

NORTH YORK MOORS NATIONAL PARK (INTERNATIONAL DARK SKY RESERVE)

The Moors National Park Centre, Lodge Lane, Whitby YO21 2NB 🖉 01439 772737 **e** general@northyorkmoors.org.uk northyorkmoors.org.uk OS Explorer Maps OL26 & OL27.

"'Listen to them, the children of the night. What music they make!'" So cries Count Dracula in Bram Stoker's famous novel of the same name, referring to the wild wolves that howl outside his castle gate. The town of Whitby on the Yorkshire coast boasts plenty of attractions, but it is the **Dracula** connection that draws so many tourists in from afar. And what better story to celebrate one of the darkest places in the country, and one of the newest International Dark Sky Reserves in the world? The North York Moors' wide open skies have always made them popular with astronomers, but it wasn't until December 2020 they were officially designated an International Dark Sky Reserve. Owing to the low levels of light pollution and clear horizons, in the darkest areas of the reserve visitors can see up to 2,000 stars at any one time with the naked eye.

The seaside town of Whitby is one of the most popular destinations in the North York Moors area, known for its maritime connections to whaling and exploring, and most famously for being the inspiration for Irish writer Bram Stoker's 1897 Gothic horror novel *Dracula*. According to historians, Stoker visited the town in the summer of 1890 and was struck by its windswept headland and dramatic abbey ruins. High above the town stand the dominating remains of **Whitby Abbey**, a once-great Benedictine monastery built on the site of a much earlier building founded in AD657 by the Anglian princess and abbess Hild.

Later that year, Stoker took a walk down to the quay and entered the public library, where he found a book published in 1820 that recorded the experiences of a British consul in Bucharest. The consul mentioned a 15th-century prince called Vlad Tepes, now known more commonly as Vlad the Impaler, who was said to have impaled his enemies on wooden stakes. His people called him Dracula, meaning 'the son of the dragon'.

While staying in Whitby, Stoker would have also heard of a shipwreck five years earlier of a Russian vessel called the *Dmitry*, from Narva. The ship ran aground on Tate Hill Sands below East Cliff carrying a cargo of silver sand and, with a slightly rearranged name, Stoker used it to create the *Demeter* from Varner, the vessel that carried Dracula to Whitby with a cargo of silver sand and boxes of earth. Told in the form of letters and diaries, the beginning of Stoker's story charts the gradual disappearance of the ship's entire crew until only the captain is left, tied to the wheel as the ship runs aground. A 'large dog' then bounds from the wreck and up the church steps. Dracula has arrived...

The Yorkshire coast is also known for its history of **smuggling**, hidden tunnels and secret societies. Busy sailing ports like Whitby were often home to tax collectors and customs officials collecting money on behalf of the king. Local smugglers, who made a living carrying illegal goods in and out of the country, needed to find ways to avoid these officials, and devised a network of tunnels beneath the town to connect certain inns and taverns. Several of these tunnels are still open to visitors along Robin Hood's Bay, including one connecting the Old Smuggler and the Station Inn. Hanging on the wall outside the Old Smuggler (now a café) is a piece of ship taken from what was thought to be a French smuggling vessel, and carved with a mysterious wooden figure.

Women were particularly encouraged into the smuggling trade, as they could often get away with their crimes because the tax collectors couldn't fathom the idea that a woman would get involved in such unlawful behaviour. Housewives with a smuggling hustle on the side would go to market wearing loose-fitting clothes so they could return home with a hoard of contraband goods hidden

underneath. Entire communities of people supported the smuggling trade, with some housewives known to pour boiling water over excise men from their bedroom windows. It was also said that a bale of silk could pass from the bottom of the street to the top without leaving the houses, due to the network of carefully concealed bolt holes and tunnels.

Further inland, the Waggon and Horses inn once stood close to a bend on the Whitby to Pickering road, known as the Devil's Elbow. During the 1800s, the salt tax was the highest it had ever been, and fishermen, who needed salt to preserve their fish, worked with smugglers to source an illegal supply. According to legend, a candle would be placed in the window of the inn to warn others that there were tax officials in the pub, but one night an official snuck in undetected after hearing rumours about the inn's smuggling trade. The official left his table and made his way down to the basement to catch the culprits red-handed, but before he could make any arrests, the landlord killed him with a rock to the head. The band of men buried the corpse underneath the peat fire pit, and it was said that if the fire was ever allowed to go out, the ghost of the officer would return and seek revenge. Over time, the building became known as the Saltersgate Inn, but after falling into disrepair it was finally demolished in 2018.

There is far more to the North York Moors than smugglers, salt and Gothic horror. With its carpets of purple heather, an array of rare **moorland birds** such as red grouse, curlew and golden plover, its abundance of precious **peat bogs** and vibrant woodlands, the moors are a unique and sensitive landscape, rich in beauty and inspiration. Stargazers will find friendly locals, evocative backdrops and peaceful wild spaces, the perfect location for getting closer to the night sky.

GETTING THERE By road, the national park can be accessed via the A1(M) and A64. Main line trains run to numerous towns surrounding the national park, including York, Malton, Scarborough, Middlesbrough, Saltburn-by-the-Sea, Redcar, Whitby, Northallerton and Thirsk. Coaches also serve the region with drops at York, Thirsk, Northallerton, Scarborough and Middlesbrough.

DARK SKIES HIGHLIGHTS A popular spot for fossil hunters, **Kettleness Beach** (Kettleness YO21 3RY) is located in a remote cove just to the east of Runswick Bay, 20 minutes north up the coast from Whitby. The beach itself is difficult to access and involves scrabbling down a steep and uneven path using a rope, so visitors are advised to stick to the headland after dark for beautiful views across the sea. Another clifftop view, at 203m **Boulby Cliff** (Boulby TS13 4UR) is the highest on the east coast, and a 15-minute drive northwest up the coast from Kettleness. The wide open sea views from the top are spectacular, particularly beneath a dusky sky. Further inland, **Rievaulx**

← **Top:** Mountain biking at Sutton Bank (Steve Bell); **Bottom:** A starry sky offers a spectacular backdrop for the romantic ruins of Byland Abbey (Steve Bell)

Terrace (Helmsley YO62 5LJ) is a 6-minute drive west of Helmsley, and one of Yorkshire's finest 18th-century landscape gardens. With stunning views down over the Cistercian ruin of Rievaulx Abbey, look out for events run by the National Trust to access this property after hours. **Cod Beck Reservoir** (Osmotherley DL6 3AL), just over 2km north of Osmotherley town centre, is surrounded by picturesque woodland, and in February is a hotspot for toads who migrate along the roads at night. Leading into the village of Rosedale, **Rosedale Chimney Bank** (Pickering YO18 8SE) is a steep mountain pass that eases out on to the vast expanse of Spaunton Moor, where rare sightings of the northern lights have been reported.

OBSERVATORIES AND ACTIVITIES
The North York Moors is home to two separate Dark Skies Festivals each year. The first, the **Dark Skies Festival** (⊘ darkskiesnationalparks.org.uk) in February, hosts stargazing events, night zips, nocturnal wildlife, ghost walks, starlight runs, bike rides and children's trails. The second, the **Dark Skies Fringe Festival** in October, offers an autumnal selection of similar night sky activities. The local **Scarborough & Ryedale Astronomical Society** (⊘ scarborough-ryedale-as. org.uk) holds monthly stargazing events in Dalby Forest between October and March. **Whitby Astronomical Society** (⊘ whitby-astronomers.com) organises events on Whitby's West Cliff during the summer and in the Bruce Observatory at Whitby School during the rest of the year. Stargazing company **Hidden Horizons** (⊘hiddenhorizons.co.uk) hosts events throughout autumn and winter with access to their large telescope and immersive star dome. **Adventures for the Soul** (⊘ adventuresforthesoul.co.uk) hosts events incorporating night walks with yoga and mindfulness, while **Rewilding Adventure** (⊘ rewildingadventure.co.uk) specialises in after-dark bushcraft and outdoor activities such as moonrise viewings, dinner by campfire and moonlit meanders.

DAYTIME ACTIVITIES
The **Ryedale Folk Museum** (⊘ryedalefolkmuseum. co.uk) in the village of Hutton-le-Hole is an open-air museum exploring the heritage of the North York Moors, from the Iron Age to the 1950s, in the form of historic buildings. Their collection includes an Iron Age roundhouse, medieval crofter's cottage, Victorian dairy and washhouse, horse-drawn vehicles, Edwardian photographic studio, glass furnace and traditional craft workshops. The **Falling Foss Tea Garden** (⊘ fallingfossteagarden.co.uk), 15 minutes south of Whitby, offers freshly baked cream teas, homemade cakes and bacon butties in the heart of an ancient forest next to a stunning waterfall. In the centre of Whitby, the **Whitby Museum** (⊘ whitbymuseum.org.uk) is an

independent Victorian museum full of maritime treasures, including local fossils, model ships, Inuit bone carvings, whaling artefacts and relics of the explorer Captain Cook. **The Endeavour Experience** (⌀ hmbarkendeavour.co.uk) in Whitby is another Cook-themed attraction, one of the only full-size replicas of his world-renowned ship HMS *Endeavour*. The experience takes visitors on a voyage through time, offering a glimpse into life on board an 18th-century vessel as it sailed around the world. The **Kilburn White Horse** (⌀ visitthirsk. org.uk), 15 minutes east of Thirsk, is a limestone figure cut into the hillside in 1857, funded by a Victorian businessman who was inspired by the hill figures of southern England. During World War II, it had to be covered up to stop it being targeted by German bombers.

NORTHUMBERLAND NATIONAL PARK AND KIELDER WATER & FOREST PARK (INTERNATIONAL DARK SKY PARK)

Kielder Castle Visitor Centre, Kielder, Northumberland NE48 1ER ✆ 01434 250209 **e** info@ visitkielder.com ⌀ visitkielder.com ♥ OS Explorer Maps OL16, OL42 & OL43.

The drive up to Kielder Observatory in the southwest corner of Northumberland is a turbulent one, tucked on to a ridge overlooking the rest of Kielder Forest – the walking trails and timber plantations, full of red squirrels, bats, otters and osprey. The magic of Kielder is in its vastness, which is even more impressive when you discover that this 60,000ha (148,000 acre) park is not only manmade, but that a century ago it didn't even exist. Row upon row of sitka spruce march across the horizon, darkened by the blue-green shadow of conifer needles and interspersed with the occasional glow of oak, rowan, birch and beech. The air is still and quiet, broken only by the melancholic cry of an osprey and the distant rumble of timber trucks carrying harvested trees out of the park.

Hidden away up a forest track, the world-renowned **Kielder Observatory** is a square timber building, simply and attractively designed against the backdrop of the forest, as if it grew out of the earth on which it now stands. First opened in 2008, it was originally built to offer a unique astronomical experience in one of the best dark sky sites in Europe, where low levels of light pollution mean the stars and other cosmic phenomena are bright and easily visible to the naked eye. Visitors can enjoy stunning views across the forest from the observatory decking, where it is even possible to see bright blue noctilucent clouds caused by ice particles reflecting light from the setting sun.

Away from the observatory, the rest of Kielder is home to the largest working forest in England, as well as the biggest manmade **lake** in northern Europe. It is so large, in fact, that it contains enough water to give everyone on the planet

around 32 litres (7 gallons) of water. The lake was created in the 1970s to meet the growing demand for water to support the booming UK industrial economy, with this area chosen in particular due to the sparse population and high rainfall at twice the national average. The scheme was designed to allow the release of water into the rivers Tyne, Derwent, Wear and Tees, maintaining minimum flow levels at times of low rainfall and allowing additional flows to be released for both domestic and industrial uses. Two hydro-electric generators were also installed at the new dam to convert energy into electricity for the national grid, which means that a water release of 1,300 million litres a day can now produce enough power to illuminate a town of around 11,000 people.

One myth that originated with the reservoir is the story that there are long-lost villages lying at the bottom of it and that when the water levels fall, a church spire with a bell can be seen emerging from the lake. But while it is true that a number of houses and other buildings once stood where the lake is now situated, these buildings were flattened and taken away long before the lake was filled. This small community, however, was still forced to move out of the area, as well as losing a number of farms, houses and a school that may have been there for centuries. And the idea of a submerged church tower may have been inspired by the former village of Derwent in Derbyshire, which was drowned to create

↑ Sunset over Kielder Water (Dave Head/Shutterstock)

the Ladybower Reservoir in 1944 as a solution to increased demand for water in the East Midlands. The village was almost completely demolished, except for the church tower which the planners left standing as a memorial to the lost village. As the water levels began to rise, the spire was left poking out of the reservoir, although it was later destroyed by explosives after being deemed unsafe.

A vastly beautiful and awe-inspiring destination, rich in cultural heritage and recreational activity, there are few places like Kielder Water that can offer its visitors red squirrels, osprey, lost villages, art sculptures, hydro-electric dams, paddleboarding, stargazing and a castle, all in one place.

GETTING THERE The park can be accessed by road via the A68, A69, A7, A74(M), A1(M) or M6. The nearest stations to the park are Haltwhistle, Bardon Mill and Haydon Bridge, all of which are located on the southern edge of the park boundary.

DARK SKIES HIGHLIGHTS Some 16km (10 miles) to the northwest of Rothbury on the eastern edge of the park, **Alwinton Car Park** (page 145) is surrounded by rolling hills with good views of the night sky. In the daytime, look out for Biddlestone Chapel, all that remains of the great Biddlestone Hall after it was demolished in the 1950s. **Elf Kirk Viewpoint** (page 146) within the dark forest of Kielder Water, at the southern end of the lake to the southwest of Tower Knowe Visitor Centre, allows 24-hour overnight parking with the purchase of a £10 ticket from the Kielder Castle ticket machine. A truly peaceful spot in the heart of the woods, close to Kielder Observatory. Also in Kielder Forest in the village of Stonehaugh, an hour's drive southeast of Kielder Water, the **Stonehaugh Stargazing Pavilion** (page 147) is free to access and originally designed by students from Newcastle University as a purpose-built astronomical facility. On the southern edge of the park, just north of Greenhead, **Walltown Country Park** (page 147) is the site of an old quarry on the line of Hadrian's Wall. It's a great spot for wildlife watching as well as stargazing. **The Stell at Falstone** (page 146) is a village hall just east of Kielder Water. Look out for what appears to be a sheep pen – it's actually a great spot to sit and gaze at the skies. **Cawfields Quarry Car Park** (page 146) just north of Haltwhistle offers stunning views over Hadrian's Wall where it hangs on the edge of the sheer crags of the Whin Sill. There is a dedicated stargazing platform available to use on the picnic site.

OBSERVATORIES AND ACTIVITIES Kielder Observatory

(⊘ kielderobservatory.org) is situated just a few miles from the Scottish border, high upon Black Fell in the heart of Kielder Forest. Their educational outreach programme encourages members of the public of all ages to look up at the stars and ask questions about the universe, and the team of staff are both passionate and knowledgeable. Access is available through pre-booked events only, and the observatory is home to a number of telescopes and astronomical instruments for visitors to see. The **Battlesteads Dark Sky Observatory** (⊘ battlesteads. com/observatory) is another publicly accessible astronomical observatory in Wark on Tyne on the eastern edge of Kielder. It offers talks, activities, drop-in sessions, stargazing and courses to suit astronomers of all abilities. The **Twice Brewed Inn & Ale House** (⊘ twicebrewedinn.co.uk) in Hexham is a great place for overnight stargazing trips with cosy rooms available. Their custom-built on-site observatory, complete with sliding roof, specialist equipment and knowledgeable guides, allows visitors to learn more about the night sky – all within reach of the pub! The **Northumberland Dark Skies Festival** (⊘ northumberlandnationalpark.org.uk/northumberland-dark-skies-festival) is organised every winter with a wide range of events, from fireside chats with local astronomers to night sky guides and interactive live streams.

DAYTIME ACTIVITIES No trip to Northumberland is complete without

a visit to **Hadrian's Wall** (⊘ english-heritage.org.uk/visit/places/hadrians-wall), a UNESCO World Heritage Site stretching 117km (73 miles) from coast to coast. Originally built to guard the northwest frontier of the Roman Empire, visitors can still see the remains of the forts, towers, turrets and towns that made up the wall. The **Holy Island of Lindisfarne** (⊘ lindisfarne.org.uk) is a tidal island off the northeast coast of England, and one of the most important centres of early English Christianity. At low tide, it is possible to walk across the sands following an ancient route known as the Pilgrims' Way. In the village of Bardon Mill, just south of Hadrian's Wall, the **Roman Vindolanda Fort & Museum** (⊘ vindolanda.com) lies on the first Roman frontier in the north, known as the Stanegate Road. Families will love stepping back into the past, with one highlight being a rare collection of 2,000-year-old wooden finds in the museum, including a toy sword. The **Longstone Lighthouse** (⊘trinityhouse. co.uk/lighthouses-and-lightvessels/longstone-lighthouse) was built in 1826 on the Farne Islands off the Northumberland coast. It is best known for the 1838 wreck of the steamer *Forfarshire*, when the lighthouse keeper's daughter Grace Darling persuaded her father to risk the waves and rescue some of the survivors. In Kielder Forest, the **Kielder Salmon Centre** (⊘ visitkielder.com/visit/kielder-salmon-centre) is the largest conservation salmon hatchery in England and Wales, allowing visitors to learn more about the incredible and unique life cycle of the salmon. The centre also rears freshwater pearl mussels, one of the UK's most endangered species.

GALLOWAY FOREST PARK (INTERNATIONAL DARK SKY PARK)

Kirroughtree Forest Visitor Centre, Forest Drive, Newton Stewart DG8 7BE ☎ 01671 402994 **e** enquiries.south@forestryandland.gov.scot ⊘ forestryandland.gov.scot ♥ OS Landranger Map 77, Explorer Maps 318 & 319.

Very few people live in the 777km² (300 square miles) of forest and hills that make up Galloway Forest Park, which means light pollution is minimal and over 7,000 stars and planets can be seen with the naked eye. The area is also situated within the Galloway and Southern Ayrshire UNESCO Biosphere, an internationally recognised world-class environment for people and nature, designated because of the variety of landscapes, wildlife, cultural, heritage and learning opportunities on offer to its communities, businesses and visitors. Situated in the southwest corner of Scotland, to the west of Dumfries, the park is home to three visitor centres surrounded by rolling glens, dramatic hills, stunning forest trails, mountains and moors. Popular with walkers, cyclists, mountain bikers and families, it's a beautiful spot to soak in breathtaking mountain views and sit beneath some of the darkest night skies in the country.

Despite the tranquil landscape of the forest today, the history of Galloway is brutal and bloody. Many of the military campaigns fought in the Wars of Scottish Independence took place on Galloway soil in the late 13th and early 14th centuries. Scotland was invaded twice between the years of 1296 and 1357, both times by the English or English-supported armies. The wars became part of a great crisis for Scotland and one of the most defining times in its history, but by the end Scotland had managed to hold on to its status as an independent state.

Up on **The Merrick**, the highest mountain in southern Scotland, visitors can take in the scene of two grizzly events. First, the murder of the Covenanter Martyrs during a period of conflict known as the Killing Time. A group of Presbyterian Christians known as Covenanters were unhappy with religious changes made by the monarchy and, after fleeing into the Galloway Hills, around 100 were executed by the king's government and troops. The second was the Battle of Glen Trool in 1307, during the First War of Scottish Independence. When Robert the Bruce, of *Braveheart* fame, was crowned King of Scots after being involved in the murder of his rival John 'the Red' Comyn, a war broke out between King Robert and the English King Edward I, as well as with the Comyns and their allies. During the Battle of Glen Trool, the English were forced to ascend the Steps of Trool in single file, upon which King Robert signalled his men to push boulders down the slope on top of them, before finishing them off with swords and arrows. The English soldiers were buried at the head of the loch nearby, in a place now known as Soldier's Holm.

So much time has passed since these conflicts that the trees have grown over the battle wounds, and Galloway Forest Park is now home to dramatic ancient woodland, historic tin mines, mountain-bike trails and treetops full of native red squirrels. As the largest forest park in Britain, Galloway is a haven for **walkers** due to its fantastic selection of hiking trails for all abilities, from gentle strolls to mountain climbs. Explorers are also guaranteed to stumble upon relics of Scottish history while wandering through the hills, from ruined farming settlements like Polmaddy to ancient burial cairns like the one behind Glentrool village. The hills have also inspired a number of artists in recent years, with outdoor sculptures like the Quorum stone faces among the dry-stone sheep pens near Talnotry, or the earthwork labyrinth beside the Raiders' Road Forest Drive.

The wildlife of Galloway is already rich and varied, but it may also soon be home to one of the UK's rarest wild animals. The **Scottish wildcat** is thought to have evolved from a population of European wildcats that became isolated by the English Channel over 9,000 years ago. The largest of the wildcat family and double the size of a domestic cat, they now live a solitary existence in the remote forested moorland margins of the Scottish Western Highlands. Their numbers have sadly dwindled to around 2,000 due to the severe threat of hybridisation with feral cats,

← The Milky Way over Clatteringshaws Loch (Lewis Parry)

vulnerability to disease, deforestation and routine culling to reduce predation on game, although this has largely stopped since the species was protected in 1988 under the Wildlife & Countryside Act. They are most active at dawn and dusk, and like all cats, they have excellent hearing, retractable claws, exceptional night vision and a powerful body designed for sprinting and pouncing.

Wildcats are not only rare, but in the small pocket of places where they do still live, they are incredibly difficult to track down. They avoid humans as much as possible, although they will use areas frequented by people late at night, such as farm buildings or outhouses. Despite not liking bad weather and deep snow, they are most active in the winter months when hunger can drive them to hunt around the clock and travel widely in search of a mate. Their low numbers, elusive nature and beautiful, camouflaged markings make them incredibly difficult to spot in the wild, and many people living in the Scottish Highlands may never see one.

In 2018, conservation group Wildcat Haven launched the British Wildcat Project with a plan to reintroduce wildcats into the Scottish–English border region. If the project is successful and wildcats begin to move across the border, this would be the first time they have had a presence in England for 300 years. The first focal area is Galloway itself, where survey and research work has suggested that the mixture of natural and commercial forestry is the most suitable habitat, especially as it provides connectivity all the way across the border to Kielder Forest in Northumberland. Although deforestation has contributed to their decline over the last few centuries, this trend is now being reversed across the UK, and as a consequence the outlook is more positive for a new population of wildcats to thrive in this vibrant corner of the southern uplands.

With its beautiful forest trails, wide open mountaintops and rich cultural heritage, Galloway Forest Park is the perfect place for a stargazing trip. On moonless nights the Milky Way can be seen stretching from one horizon to the other, making this a fantastic destination for anyone looking to delve further into astronomy in the wilds of southwest Scotland.

GETTING THERE By road, the park can be accessed via the M6 and A74(M). From the south, main line trains operate from Carlisle to Dumfries, and from the north, they run from Glasgow to Stranraer via Ayr. Ferries sail from Larne/Belfast to Cairnryan, and the nearest airport is Glasgow.

DARK SKIES HIGHLIGHTS On the north side of Loch Trool, 11 minutes northeast of Glentrool, **Bruce's Stone** (Newton Stewart DG8 6SU) is a massive granite boulder commemorating Robert the Bruce's first victory over the English in the Battle of Glen Trool. It's the perfect spot for stargazing over the shimmering waters of the loch below. At **Clatteringshaws Visitor Centre** (New Galloway DG7 3SQ), 10 minutes west of New Galloway, there are beautiful views over Clatteringshaws Loch, which is a haven for waterbirds in the summer. In the rolling Galloway Hills beyond, the mighty Merrick hill can be seen on a clear day, on which the granite boulder of Bruce's Stone stands. The **Glentrool Visitor Centre** (Bargrennan DG8 6SZ), 2 minutes east of Grentrool village, is situated in the heart of the forest park, a peaceful spot by the lively waters of Loch Trool beneath Merrick hill. Look out for interpretation panels at the centre which can help visitors identify the stars. **Loch Bradan** (Tallaminnock KA19 7NT) is in one of the most secluded areas in the park, 20 minutes south of the village of Straiton off Newton Stewart Road. Some 20 minutes southeast of Loch Bradan is **Loch Doon Castle** (Craigmalloch KA6 7QE), built in the late 1200s by either Robert the Bruce or his father. The castle originally stood on an island in nearby Loch Doon, but the entire building was taken down, stone by stone, and rebuilt on its current spot in 1935 in an effort to save the castle's curtain wall from rising water levels.

OBSERVATORIES AND ACTIVITIES

The park was home to the **Scottish Dark Sky Observatory** (∂ scottishdarkskyobservatory.co.uk), a publicly accessible educational observatory with two large telescopes through which visitors could observe the night sky. The observatory featured a 20" Corrected Dall Kirkham telescope in a 5m dome and a 14" Schmidt-Cassegrain telescope for a more hands-on, open air-observing experience, as well as a presentation room, a planetarium and an elevated observation deck from which visitors could enjoy naked-eye viewing of the night sky. Sadly, in June 2021 the observatory burnt down and at the time of going to press, plans for its future remain uncertain.

DAYTIME ACTIVITIES

The **Galloway Red Deer Range** (∂ forestryandland. gov.scot/visit/forest-parks/galloway-forest-park/red-deer-range) is 15 minutes northeast of Newton Stewart, first established in 1977 to offer visitors the chance to see the park's red deer herd up close in their natural habitat. Around 25 red deer live in the range today, and the best place to spot them is in the viewing hide. In the heart of New Galloway, **CatStrand** (∂ catstrand.com) is an independent contemporary arts centre, performance and meeting space, promoting a varied music and exhibition programme with a locally sourced café on the side. For nature lovers, the **RSPB Ken-Dee Marshes Reserve** (∂ rspb. org.uk/reserves-and-events/reserves-a-z/ken-dee-marshes) is 15 minutes northwest of Castle Douglas, with a variety of wildlife to see including the red kite, pied flycatcher, redstart, white-fronted goose and willow tit.

Some 10 minutes west of Castle Douglas, **Threave Castle** (⊘ historicenvironment. scot/visit-a-place/places/threave-castle) is a treat for historians, a forbidding island fortress across the River Dee, only accessible by boat. It was built by Archibald the Grim in 1369, complete with a bell to summon the ferryman. Beyond the park boundary, families will love the **Cream o' Galloway Farm** (⊘ creamogalloway.co.uk) 20 minutes southwest of Castle Douglas. They offer tours of their working dairy farm, an adventure playground, children's rides and nature trails, as well as a shop selling ice cream and other treats.

MOFFAT (INTERNATIONAL DARK SKY COMMUNITY)

Visit Moffat, Town Hall, High St, Moffat DG10 9HF ⊘ 01683 221102 **e** info@visitmoffat. co.uk ⊘ moffatdarksky4.wixsite.com ♀ OS Explorer Map 330.

Perched in the beautiful Annandale Valley in the south of Scotland, the historic market town of Moffat is one of three International Dark Sky Communities on British soil, with a second and third being the Isle of Coll in the Hebrides and Sark in the Channel Islands. To achieve this status, Moffat successfully lobbied Dumfries and Galloway Council to make changes to their outdoor lighting policies, which resulted in a lighting plan that ended up going above and beyond the minimums set by the International Dark Sky Association. This pretty village is now a fantastic stargazing destination, showcasing an impressive number of stars from all four corners of Orion's Belt and the sky beyond.

The development of the town was based on three main industries – the **wool trade**, the **stagecoach line**, and its popularity as a **spa town**. From the 17th century onwards, Moffat began to grow from a small village into a spa town, with the sulphurous and saline waters of Moffat Water believed to have healing properties, specifically for skin conditions, gout, rheumatism and stomach complaints. During the Victorian era, the high demand for Moffat's spa water resulted in a pipe being built from the main well to a tank in what is now known as Tank Wood, and then on to a purpose-built bath house in the town centre. Numerous luxury hotels sprang up to accommodate the increasing number of visitors, including the famous **Hydropathic Hotel** built in 1878 and sadly destroyed in a fire in 1921, when Moffat's reputation as a spa town unofficially came to an end. In its heyday, the Hydropathic Hotel boasted over 300 rooms and an elegantly furnished drawing room, lounge and dining room.

Like the other spa towns of Britain, such as Bath, Harrogate and Buxton, people had been visiting Moffat to 'take the waters' for hundreds of years. It was the Romans who first brought the spa tradition to the shores of Britain, developing one of the first English spa resorts in AD43, called Aquae Sulis and now known as the city of Bath. It was here that they harnessed the city's spring waters in a

→ **Top:** Moffat's community observatory is still being built (Jim Paterson); **Bottom:** Great stargazing is possible from your own back garden in Moffat (Ian Haddow)

sophisticated bath complex, complete with a temple, and although after the fall of the Roman Empire this complex fell into disrepair, it was rebuilt in 1088 at the command of the local bishop. A medieval text notes how, by 1138, sick people from all over England 'come to wash away their infirmities in the healing waters, and the healthy gaze at the remarkable bubbling up of the hot springs'.

By the Tudor period, 'taking the waters' was met with fierce opposition by the government, as church officials saw public bathing as a sinful practice. Worried about Catholic dissidents meeting together at holy wells, King Henry VIII even banned the use of spas altogether. But by the time his daughter Elizabeth I took the throne, public baths were back in fashion and, with her seal of approval, they became trendy destinations for the middle and upper classes. Both the Georgians and Victorians continued to frequent spa resorts, many of which were catapulted to the forefront of high fashion, and some of the more notable attendees included Jane Austen, Oscar Wilde and Charles Dickens.

The spa town of Moffat became a particularly favourite haunt of the poet Robert Burns, who once engraved a pane of glass in the Black Bull pub with some locally inspired verses. Having lived much of his life in nearby Dumfries, Burns often visited Moffat, and one of the poems he carved into the glass was inspired by a beautiful but petite lady greatly admired by Burns, who rode past the pub window one morning with her portly companion. Inspired by the sight, he wrote the poem *Epigram to a Scrimpit Nature*:

> Ask why God made the Gem so small
> and why so huge the Granite?
> Because God meant mankind to set the higher value on it.

The original window can now be found in St Petersburg, Russia, after being given to Tsar Nicholas I, who visited Moffat as a young man.

Aside from its spa town heritage, Moffat was also the home of a lucrative market in the **wool** trade, which is commemorated with William Brodie's statue of a ram in the town's marketplace. Brodie was a prolific and celebrated Victorian sculptor whose most famous work is the statue of the faithful dog Greyfriars Bobby in Edinburgh, a statue which, when designated as a Category A Monument in 1977, officially became Edinburgh's smallest listed building. According to legend, when Brodie's ram statue was unveiled in Moffat, a local farmer cried, 'It has nae lugs!', referring to the ram's unexplained lack of ears. Rumour has it that Brodie was so embarrassed at his mistake that he returned to his room at the Annandale Arms Hotel, which is still open today, and hanged himself within sight of the new sculpture. Stories of him haunting the hotel corridors searching for the ram's lost 'lugs' are, however, unlikely to be accurate, as there is no truth to this tale, with Brodie dying a much more peaceful death at home, six years later.

Moffat was also an important staging post between England and Edinburgh. The **stagecoach** first appeared on England's roads in the early 16th century, so called because it travelled in stages of 16 to 24km (10 to 15 miles) before stopping at a coaching inn, where the horses would be changed and the travellers could rest. Many of the old coaching inns still exist today in one form or another, such as the Buccleuch Arms Hotel on High Street, which dates back to 1760. Some coaching inns can be recognised by the high archways that allowed coaches to pass through into the stable yard behind the inn.

Beyond the main town, the landscape surrounding Moffat is rich in wildlife, walking trails and stunning views. Just over 11km (7 miles) east of Moffat is **Grey Mare's Tail Nature Reserve**, home to the fifth highest waterfall in Britain. At 60m, it tumbles from Loch Skeen, down the deep gorge of Tail Burn and into Moffat Water in the valley below. The name is inspired by the shape of the water as it falls from the ridge; beside the burn, a walking trail leads back to Loch Skeen, the highest upland in the region, where Britain's rarest freshwater fish, the **vendace**, is flourishing. Visitors may also spot the **peregrine falcons** that nest every year, as well as **ravens**, **buzzards**, **wheatears**, **dippers**, **ring ouzels**, **merlins** and **ospreys**, which sometimes fish in Loch Skeen. A recent project to reinforce the local population of **golden eagles** in southern Scotland has also been initiated, which means there's an increased chance of seeing this magnificent bird during your visit. **Feral goats** have also roamed the Moffat Hills for hundreds of years, and quiet visitors may catch a glimpse of them on the path to Loch Skeen. During the autumn rut, the mature males will fight each other for the right to mate with the females, which is a remarkable sight to see. And further up the slopes, where the best views look out over the hills, you may even be lucky enough to spot a **mountain hare**, minky brown in the summer and snow white in the winter. These elusive mammals graze on vegetation and the bark of young trees and bushes, and when disturbed can be seen bounding across the moors in zigzag patterns, using their powerful hind legs to propel them forwards.

GETTING THERE
By road, Moffat can be accessed via the M6, A74(M), M8, M74, A702 or A701. There are frequent trains from London, Glasgow and Edinburgh to Lockerbie station, from where a bus service runs to Moffat High Street. The nearest airports are Glasgow and Edinburgh.

DARK SKIES HIGHLIGHTS
As Europe's first Dark Sky Town, the whole of Moffat is suitable for stargazing due to the adoption of special streetlighting. Some of the best spots include **Moffat Water Hall** (DG10 9LG), a rural community

centre for residents, and the car park by **Moffat Well** (DG10 9DL), a refurbished well first discovered in the 17th century and still accessible to visitors, although the water smells strongly of sulphur. The car park at **St Andrew's Church** (DG10 9ES) provides another spot to stargaze beside the beautiful church building, built in the early English Gothic style of red sandstone from the local Corncockle quarry. The **Community Nature Reserve** (DG10 9SF) is a former quarry bursting with insects, dragonflies, butterflies and bumblebees in the wildflower meadow, and with wading birds like curlew, snipe and lapwing in the winter months. The reserve closes at 20.00 throughout the year.

OBSERVATORIES AND ACTIVITIES
There are currently no public observatories in Moffat, although a **community observatory** is being built at the time of writing. The town is also surrounded by a number of facilities within driving distance, including the Trinity School Observatory in Carlisle (50 minutes south), Kielder Observatory in Northumberland (2 hours east), and the Coats Observatory and Airdrie Observatory near Glasgow (1 hour north). The **Moffat Astronomy Club** (⊘ moffatdarksky4.wixsite.com/moffatastronomy) hosts a number of events throughout the year, including talks and observing sessions.

DAYTIME ACTIVITIES
Twenty minutes northeast of Moffat is one of Scotland's favourite waterfalls known as the **Grey Mare's Tail** (⊘ nts.org.uk/visit/places/grey-mares-tail), plunging 60m from Loch Skeen into the valley below. Keep an eye out for ospreys, ring ouzels, feral goats and peregrine falcons, or search for fossils on a ranger-led guided walk. In the centre of Moffat town, the **Colvin Fountain** (⊘ visitmoffat.co.uk) was commissioned in 1875 by wealthy sheep breeder William Colvin of Craigielands and built by sculptor William Brodie. The fountain depicts a ram standing on a pile of rocks, a salute to the town's industrial heritage, although the ram's ears are missing and have been since the statue was first unveiled. Also in the town centre, the **Moffat Museum** (⊘ moffatmuseum.co.uk) opened in 1984 in an old bakehouse, and offers a fascinating insight into the town's history, from early Roman times through to the border reivers of the 13th to 17th centuries, when raiders from both sides of the English/Scottish border plundered the land and its people. The museum also explores the town's coaching history and its popularity as a spa town. For an unexpected cultural gem, head to the **Samye Ling Tibetan Centre** (⊘ samyeling.org), 40 minutes east of Moffat. The centre is a monastery and international centre of Buddhist training, but visitors are welcome to join them in the temple for meditation or a moment of reflection. They also have a café and shop, guest accommodation, courses and retreats.

TOMINTOUL AND GLENLIVET - CAIRNGORMS (INTERNATIONAL DARK SKY PARK)

Tomintoul & Glenlivet Discovery Centre & Museum, 43 The Square, Tomintoul, Ballindalloch AB37 9EX ✆ 01807 580760 **e** discovery@tgdt.org.uk ☒ cairngormsdarkskypark.org
♥ OS Explorer Maps OL50, OL51, OL52, OL53, OL54, OL55, OL56, OL57, OL58, OL59, OL60, OL61 & OL62.

The rounded, rolling landscape of Tomintoul and Glenlivet in Scotland's eastern highlands is a place of breathtaking scenery, harboured secrets, illicit industries and religious sanctuary. Roughly the shape of a diamond, the area is structured around four hill ranges, one on each corner: the Cromdales in the west, the Ladder Hills to the east, the Glen Avon foothills to the south, and Ben Rinnes to the north. It is these stunning hills, moorlands and broad open straths, shaped by a complex geological past, that provide such a special backdrop to this unique area of Scotland, and draw so many people in to gaze at the pristine night skies above. This Dark Sky Park is made up of two distinct areas: the village of Tomintoul, the highest in the highlands, and the Glenlivet Estate which surrounds it, owned by the Crown but open to the public.

Tomintoul and Glenlivet are not only characterised by their stunning landscapes; they are also known for being the source of illicit activity, particularly the illegal distillation of **whisky**. Tomintoul is on the famed Whisky Trail, which also includes Dufftown, Keith, Tomnavoulin and Marypark, places that were once hives of activity for the unlawful production of alcohol. A walk in the area will reveal relics of this illicit past, such as the **Knock Earth House**, an ancient listed monument first discovered in the 1960s by a ploughman working his field. Originally believed to be a late Bronze Age structure, this stone-lined underground chamber is now thought to have been built or adapted in the 18th century to house a whisky still, disguised by a corn-drying kiln built next to the entrance.

The **Glenlivet Distillery** has become one of the best known names in highland whisky production, and members of the public can still visit the distillery today to taste their single malt Scotch. The Livet Valley was the ideal place for their founder George Smith to learn his craft, hidden from tax officials among the hills and springs. His slowly distilled whisky became so renowned that when King George IV arrived in Scotland for a state visit in 1822 he requested a dram of Glenlivet whisky, despite it still being illegal at the time. Over time, Smith secured a licence to become the first legal distiller in the parish of Glenlivet, and the distillery was producing more than 900 litres (200 gallons) a week by the late 1830s. Later that century, Charles Dickens would write to a friend urging him to try the 'rare old Glenlivet'.

While the region has continued to thrive in whisky production and is now home to a number of distilleries, it is known for much more than a glass of Scotch.

Hidden deep in the Braes of Glenlivet, the **Scalan seminary** has become one of the most significant sites of historical interest in the area, after the persecuted Catholics of the 18th century found refuge here and ensured the survival of the Catholic faith by training over 100 priests within the seminary walls. The building is open all year for visitors to learn how the Catholic faith survived, and the circular Scalan Heritage Trail provides astonishing views over the Braes of Glenlivet and the Ladder Hills.

A land of hidden valleys and well-kept secrets, Tomintoul and Glenlivet is a fantastic destination for anyone interested in how small communities have adapted to the environment around them. Not only does this remote area have breathtaking dark skies, but it also offers easy access for stargazers, allowing everyone a chance to enjoy the night sky in the liberating tranquillity of the Scottish Highlands.

GETTING THERE Main line trains travel direct from Inverness, Glasgow, Edinburgh and London to nearby stations at Aviemore and Carrbridge, with an overnight Caledonian Sleeper service daily from London Euston. By road, the Cairngorms National Park can be accessed from the north or south by the A9. National Cycle Route 7 runs from Glasgow to Inverness, passing through the west of the park. The nearest airports are Inverness and Aberdeen.

DARK SKIES HIGHLIGHTS The car park at **Blairfindy Castle** (Ballindalloch AB37 9DE) can be found half a mile southeast of the Glenlivet Distillery, north of Tomintoul, on the site of a 16th-century ruin and Scheduled Ancient Monument. The castle was originally built as a fortified tower house before being burned to the ground by government troops following the Battle of Culloden in 1746. The castle makes a fantastic foreground subject for astrophotography. The **Field of Hope** (Ballindalloch AB37 9ET) car park just outside Tomintoul, near the junction with the A939 Lecht Road, is an accessible location with excellent all-round views of the sky, especially as the local street lights have been replaced with dark sky-friendly units. **The Carrachs** (Ballindalloch AB37 9JS) is 15 minutes east of Tomintoul and one of the few places in Scotland where the Catholic faith was kept alive during the troubled times of the 18th century. It has since become a hotspot for capturing the aurora, especially with the abandoned farm buildings, seminary and trees that make great photographs. On the eastern edge of the Cairngorms, 35 minutes east of Ballater, the **Glen Tanar Estate** (Aboyne AB34 5EU) is a spectacular spot for stargazing, with rugged heather moorland and towering Caledonian pine forests. The visitor centre is a great starting point for exploring the estate in the daylight. **Glenconglass** (Tomintoul AB37 9EP) car park is just 10 minutes north

→ The old mining building near the Well of Lecht makes a good foreground subject for photos, day or night (Jan Holm/Shutterstock)

of Tomintoul and has excellent visibility to the north, east and south horizons. From September to March, it is also another great spot for catching a glimpse of the aurora, along with stunning views of the Milky Way in autumn and early winter. The car park by the **Well of Lecht** (Ballindalloch AB37 9ES) at the foot of the Ladder Hills, 10 minutes southeast of Tomintoul, is another good stargazing spot, while the old mine building nearby makes a good foreground object for photographs of the Milky Way.

OBSERVATORIES AND ACTIVITIES

Dark Sky events take place throughout the year with the **Cairngorms Astronomy Group** (⊘ darkskies. glenlivet-cairngorms.co.uk/events), including talks, workshops and observing sessions. The group is also currently investigating the possibility of establishing an observatory in the park. For now, the closest observatory to the Park is the **Jim Savage-Lowden Observatory** in Inverness, 1½ hours' drive north of Tomintoul. Located near the site of Culloden Battlefield, this observatory is home to the **Highlands Astronomical Society** (⊘ spacegazer.com), who open regularly to the public for events and stargazing sessions.

DAYTIME ACTIVITIES

For a glimpse into royal life, **Balmoral Castle** (⊘ balmoralcastle.com) 15 minutes west of Ballater, is the Royal Family's Scottish holiday home. Closed in the winter months, throughout the rest of the year the estate welcomes visitors into the grounds and gardens, with exhibitions, wildlife safaris, golf days, salmon fishing, and a café and gift shop. For a traditional Scottish tipple 20 minutes north of Tomintoul, the **Glenlivet Distillery** (⊘ theglenlivet.com) sits in a remote and isolated valley, where the founder learnt to distil whisky away from the prying eyes of customs officers. Visitors can enjoy tasting experiences and treat themselves to a bottle from the gift shop. Nature lovers will enjoy **RSPB Loch Garten** (⊘ rspb.org.uk/reserves-and-events/reserves-a-z/loch-garten), a nature reserve 20 minutes northeast of Strathspey. The reserve boasts ancient Caledonian pine forest, sweeping moorland, dramatic mountains and beautiful wetlands, with star species being the **red squirrel**, **crested tit**, **capercaillie** and **nesting osprey**. If you're looking to learn a new skill, **Wooden Tom** (⊘ woodentom.com) is based 15 minutes south of Aviemore, and offers green woodworking courses where participants can spend a day learning the basics of ethical wood carving. No prior experience is needed and all tools and material are provided. For a taste of local history, the **Highland Folk Museum** (⊘ highlandfolk.com) is 25 minutes southwest of Aviemore. This open-air museum brings to life the existence of earlier highland communities. Visitors can see how they lived, built their homes and worked the land.

COLL (INTERNATIONAL DARK SKY COMMUNITY)

An Cridhe, Arinagour, Isle of Coll, Argyll PA78 6SY ✆ 01879 230000 **e** info@ancridhe. co.uk ⌖ visitcoll.co.uk ♥ OS Explorer Map 372.

Have you ever heard a **corncrake** calling? Sadly, it's unlikely. This once common British bird has seen such drastic declines in the last few decades that by the 1990s, the species would have gone extinct in the British Isles within ten to 20 years if conservationists hadn't stepped in. A small and secretive bird, similar to a moorhen but with beautifully flecked chestnut wings, the corncrake is far better known for its rasping call, epitomised in its scientific name *Crex crex*. Like so many bird species, the corncrake started declining in western Europe around the mid 19th century, coinciding with the mechanisation of agriculture and the earlier cutting of the hay harvest. Since the 1950s, this rate of decline has accelerated dramatically, probably because the majority of hay meadows were switched to silage production, which allowed earlier cutting dates and a loss of habitat for the corncrake. Throw in predation and road traffic, too, and the corncrake is facing an uncertain future.

Fortunately, the Isle of Coll is not only a fantastic place for stargazing, being officially recognised by the IDA (International Dark-Sky Association) as an International Dark Sky Community; it has also become a haven for corncrakes, due in part because the islanders embrace more traditional farming practices

↑ The Isle of Coll is a haven for the endangered corncrake (Ihor Hvozdetskyi/Shutterstock)

involving mowing dates and methods. Just ten years ago, the birds were almost extinct in Scotland, but Coll has become one of the most important refuges for corncrakes thanks to partnerships between the RSPB and local farmers, which has more than quadrupled the corncrake population on the island. An elusive but distinctive bird, stargazers visiting Coll may be treated to their unmistakable *crex crex* call from the hay and silage fields on spring and summer evenings, the perfect accompaniment as the day fades into night on this unique Scottish island.

The island itself sits around 9.5km (6 miles) northwest of Mull, out in the Atlantic Ocean, fringed by more than 30 beautiful beaches that are never crowded. The population numbers around 160 permanent residents, but it has also become a holiday destination for those seeking peace and quiet in the natural beauty of the Hebrides. Today, the main residents of Coll are mostly farmers or crofters raising cattle and sheep, but there is also a small fleet of lobster boats, and the land is now divided between a number of private individuals, the RSPB and a trust.

You wouldn't know it to look around at such a tranquil place, but the last few centuries of life on Coll were much more turbulent. The early history suggests that the island was inhabited first by Mesolithic hunter-gatherer camps, then Neolithic farmers, then Gael and Norse settlers, who were eventually followed by the rule of Somerled and Clan Donald's Lordship of the Isles. When this lordship was dispersed, the island was then secured by the MacLeans of Mull, with Breachacha Castle on the shore of Loch Breachacha thought to have been their official seat. Unfortunately, a gruesome battle took place in 1593 after the island was invaded by the MacLeans of Duart from Mull, and legends claim that the burn that flowed into Loch Breachacha was full of decapitated Duart heads. Since then, the burn has been named Struthan nana Ceann, which translates as the 'Stream of the Heads'.

Sadly, the 19th-century history of Coll sounds eerily familiar to many of the other Hebridean islands. By 1841, the population had risen so much that the Laird MacLean was unwilling to support the numbers, and in the years that followed, the infamous Highland Clearances, together with the potato famine, saw nearly half of Coll's people turned off the land and transported to Australia and Canada. Coll became almost deserted, and it is thanks to the community of the last few decades that the population has not only stabilised, but grown. And it is no wonder their designation as a Dark Sky Place is centered on this communal nature, as Coll is said to have some of the warmest and friendliest inhabitants of the Hebridean islands.

Thanks to the quiet and solitude of the island, it has become such a haven for wildlife that it is now both a Site of Special Scientific Interest and an RSPB nature reserve. The sandy shores are great for watching **terns** feeding on sand eels or **otters** fishing in the shallows, and in the summer the low-lying **machair** grassland is bursting with wildflowers and insects, including the incredibly rare **great yellow**

bumblebee. From spring, the wetlands are full of wading bird displays, while **skylarks** and **swallows** feed over the hay meadows where corncrakes hide in the long grass. Elsewhere, the sand dunes provide precious habitat for species like the **sand lizard**, one of the UK's rarest reptiles, the **belted beauty moth** and the extremely rare **short-necked oil beetle**, which was until recently thought to be extinct in Britain. The RSPB use low-intensity grazing with cattle and sheep to maintain these habitats for their benefit. The uplands are also home to stunning heather moorland, bog and grassland, which in turn support an array of insects and birds.

At the island edges, the lapping waters of the Atlantic Ocean are home to **basking sharks**, the biggest fish in the UK and one of only three-plankton eating sharks worldwide. With the potential to grow over 10m long and weigh up to several tons, they are the second biggest shark in the entire ocean, second only to the tropical whale shark. Up to a metre wide, their distinctive mouths are lined with a special organ called gill rakers, arranged along the gill slits and specially adapted with keratin filters to strain out plankton from the water. They also have hundreds of individual teeth, arranged in numerous rows on the upper and lower jaw, which are not used for feeding but can be involved in mating season.

Historically, basking sharks were hunted in Scotland until as recently as 1994, targeted for their big livers which contain a large amount of oil, traditionally used in lamps but also now produced for cosmetics and perfumes. The invention of synthetic alternatives has thankfully reduced this demand and the species is now protected, although they are still threatened by marine debris and microplastics, a depleted food source, global warming and the production of shark fin soup in other countries.

↑ The waters around Coll are home to basking sharks, the biggest fish in the UK (Martin Prochazkacz/Shutterstock)

Basking sharks migrate to UK shores during spring and leave again in the autumn, and are mainly found around the western isles of Scotland. Coll has become one of the best places to see basking sharks in the UK, and some wildlife excursion companies even allow visitors to swim alongside them. **Basking Shark Scotland** (⊘ baskingsharkscotland.co.uk) also organise the Coll of the Sharks Festival, involving five days of wildlife watching and events on land and at sea.

Coll is one of the best places in the UK to enjoy everything the night sky has to offer, including the chance to capture one of the most spellbinding phenomena on the planet. The **northern lights**, also known as the aurora borealis, happens when solar winds travel towards the earth and collide with our atmosphere, which causes protons and electrons to hit atmospheric particles and release energy. This energy appears as ripples, ribbons and clouds of coloured light that seem to dance through the sky. The best times of year to see the lights are autumn and winter, on a cold, clear night with limited light pollution and increased solar activity, which you can track using an app like Aurora Watch.

GETTING THERE The ferry from Oban to Coll takes just over 2½ hours and vehicle reservations are recommended. Oban is a 2½-hour drive from Glasgow, 3 hours from Edinburgh, 3 hours from Inverness and 4 hours from Aberdeen. There's also a regular direct train to Oban from Glasgow Queen Street station which takes just over 3 hours. Flights to Coll are available from Oban through Hebridean Air Services.

DARK SKIES HIGHLIGHTS As the first official Dark Sky Community in Scotland, the entire island of Coll is suitable for stargazing due to its low levels of light pollution. Coll is an RSPB nature reserve, and the car park for the **RSPB Totronald Visitor Centre** (Totronald PA78 6TB), 6 minutes north of Coll Airport, has been offered with the kind permission of the RSPB for stargazing. It lies in a slightly sheltered hollow and is surrounded by beautiful sand dunes and machair grassland. The **Cliad Football Pitch** (Arnabost PA78 6TE) on Coll Golf Course offers a large open space and an almost unobstructed 360-degree view of the sky. Just above **Arinagour village** (Arinagour PA78 6SZ) on the east coast, the elevated terrain offers spectacular views of the village and bay, as well as the night sky over the sea.

OBSERVATORIES AND ACTIVITIES There are several stay-and-gaze accommodation options on Coll, including **Coll & The Cosmos** (⊘ collbunkhouse.com/dark-skies-coll-cosmos), a stargazing weekend break specifically designed to appeal to a wide audience, with no prior knowledge of astronomy needed. The event is in collaboration with **Cosmos Planetarium**

(⌂ cosmosplanetarium.co.uk), a fully mobile, 360-degree immersive theatre experience that travels around Scotland and northern England.

DAYTIME ACTIVITIES Coll's charm lies not in museums and tour buses, but in nature, the great outdoors, watersports, exercise and the beautiful sea. Thanks to the influence of the Gulf Stream, Coll and neighbouring island Tiree are treated to more hours of annual sunlight than any other location in the British Isles, and because of their position in the windswept Atlantic, Coll is also inhospitable to the dreaded midges that tend to linger in Scotland's islands and highlands. Visitors can enjoy a round of golf, try surfing, sailing, fishing or sea kayaking, embark on a hike around the island or simply relax on the beach. Coll's beaches are quieter than those of neighbouring Tiree, and the sea is surprisingly warm due to the North Atlantic Gulf Stream. The island is also an excellent place for **birders** and **wildlife watchers**, with some of its star species being basking sharks, dolphins, otters, fulmars, skuas, terns and gannets, as well as rare species like the spotted rock-rose and sand lizard.

DAVAGH FOREST PARK AND BEAGHMORE STONE CIRCLES (INTERNATIONAL DARK SKY PARK)

OM Dark Sky Park and Observatory, 155 Davagh Rd, Omagh BT79 8JQ ✆ 028 8676 0681 **e** omdarksky@midulstercouncil.org ⌂ omdarksky.com ♥ OSNI Discoverer Map 13.

In the heart of the rolling hills and sweeping forests of Northern Ireland's Sperrin Mountains, Davagh Forest is a hub for recreational activities like hiking, biking and driving, as well as being a vibrant and wildlife-rich natural habitat. Located 80km to the west of Belfast, the Sperrin Mountains are an Area of Outstanding Natural Beauty, stretching from the western shoreline of Lough Neagh to the border of Tyrone and Donegal. Davagh is sometimes referred to as 'the forgotten forest', although perhaps it would be more accurate to call it an underrated one. As an International Dark Sky Park, Davagh Forest is a 1,500ha (3,700 acre) site managed by Forest Service Northern Ireland, set within an untouched rural landscape centered on the Beaghmore Stone Circles, a complex of early Bronze Age megalithic monuments. Thanks to the opening of the Dark Sky Observatory and Visitor Centre in 2020, the forest now offers visitors a unique opportunity to experience some of the darkest night skies in Northern Ireland.

The forest is popular with mountain bikers, hikers and drivers, especially as the Sperrin Mountains were named in National Geographic's prestigious list of the Top 101 scenic drives in the world. Despite this publicity, the area is still somewhat of a hidden gem, which means it is teeming with wildlife that might prove too elusive for more heavily visited forests. Visitors may encounter **foxes**,

sika deer, pine martens and red squirrels, as well as peregrine falcons, buzzards, sparrowhawks and the rare red grouse.

One species that has occasionally been seen is the **golden eagle**, Ireland's second largest bird of prey at almost twice the size of a common buzzard. These rare and breathtaking birds became extinct in Ireland around 1910, having been relatively common and widespread until they were shot, trapped, poisoned and robbed of eggs, before disappearing altogether from the Irish landscape. But, after a recent reintroduction project based around Donegal, the birds are making a cautious but optimistic comeback, and wandering individuals have since been observed in several upland areas throughout Ireland, including the Sperrin Mountains. In 2008, a golden eagle was even spotted flying over Belfast city centre!

The adult birds are generally dark brown when seen at a distance in flight, although on closer inspection they have a pale patch on the upper wing, barring

↑ The hi-tech OM Dark Sky Park and Observatory uses the latest technology to help visitors learn more about the night sky (OM Dark Sky Park and Observatory)

on the tail and a distinctive golden-coloured head. Like other birds of prey, they like to soar and glide on warm air currents, holding their wings in a shallow 'V' shape and nesting in traditional territories that have been used by their species for generations. It is worth looking out for them if visiting the area, as they can be seen all year round and will often display to each other on fine winter days with glamorous looping and plunging flights.

Eagles are not the only treasure found in Northern Ireland. Prospectors have been panning for **gold** across Ireland for more than 3,500 years, dating back to the late Neolithic and Bronze Age when the ancient people hammered gold into sun discs, lunulae, bracelets and torcs. This precious metal can still be found in the Sperrin Mountains today, formed in veins of white quartz through the hills, along with other minerals like iron pyrites, black magnetite and garnet. Recent plans to open new gold mines in the region have been met with firm opposition by locals and environmentalists, and it is yet unclear whether the Sperrins will stay protected, and whether the gold will remain, untouched, in the earth.

GETTING THERE The forest park is situated 80km (50 miles) west of Belfast and 24km (15 miles) northwest of Cookstown. By road, the park can be accessed via the A29, A505, A5 or A6. The observatory is signposted off the main A505 Cookstown to Omagh road. The nearest main line train stations are Londonderry, Ballymena and Portadown. The nearest airports are Belfast International, Belfast City and City of Derry.

DARK SKIES HIGHLIGHTS First discovered during peat cutting in the 1940s, the **Beaghmore Stone Circles** (Cookstown BT80 9PB), 20 minutes northwest of Cookstown, consist of seven stone rings. They are thought to be a complex of early Bronze Age megalithic features, although the name originates from *Bheitheach Mhór*, meaning big place of birch trees, suggesting the area was a woodland before being cleared by Neolithic farmers. Theories suggest the stones could be aligned with the movements of the sun, moon and stars, and today they have become popular foreground objects for local astrophotographers. In the heart of the forest, **Beleevnamore Mountain** (Omagh BT79 8JH) is known by local mountain bikers as 'The Widowmaker' due to its steep climb, but the view at the top makes it all worth it with tall forests and panoramas across the Sperrin Mountains. Elsewhere in the forest, **Boundary**

↑ Theories suggest that the seven rings of Beaghmore Stone Circles are aligned with the movements of the sun, moon and stars (JRP Studio/Shutterstock)

Rock (Omagh BT79 8JH) is another stunning viewpoint overlooking the treetops, the perfect spot for enjoying Davagh's glittering night sky.

OBSERVATORIES AND ACTIVITIES At the heart of the park is the brand-new **OM Dark Sky Observatory** (⊘ omdarksky.com), combining the latest technology to give visitors a unique opportunity to learn more about the night sky. From holographic installations to virtual reality headsets and bespoke audio-visual shows, the observatory is also home to a 14" LX600 Meade telescope. The Meade comes with StarLock, a full-time automatic integrated guider which assists with polar alignment, finding and centring the target sky object and automatically locking on to it as it moves. They also have a solar telescope which lets visitors see the sun close up, showing prominences, flares and other details from the surface of our biggest star. Group tours are available on request, and the area is also home to a number of local astronomy groups who hold observing sessions throughout the year.

DAYTIME ACTIVITIES The **Ulster American Folk Park** (⊘ nmni.com/our-museums/ulster-american-folk-park), 10 minutes north of Omagh, is an open-air history centre with costumed actors and period buildings telling the story of the Irish people who set sail for the New World in the 18th and 19th centuries. Visitors can taste samples of pioneer foods, including freshly baked soda bread and pumpkin pie, along with meeting an array of farm animals and learning about the Irish agricultural community. Some 30 minutes south of Cookstown, **The Argory** (⊘ nationaltrust.org.uk/the-argory) is a National Trust-run Irish gentry house within a stunning woodland estate. The grounds offer scenic walks, sweeping vistas, a rose garden and sundial, and there's also an adventure playground, tearoom and bookshop. The **Marble Arch Caves** (⊘ marblearchcavesgeopark.com) are an hour's drive southwest of Omagh, but well worth the visit. In one of the finest show caves in Europe and a UNESCO Global Geopark site, visitors are guided through an underworld of rivers, waterfalls, winding passages and lofty chambers. A 40–minute-drive east of the observatory, **Seamus Heaney HomePlace** (⊘ seamusheaneyhome.com) is a must-see for poetry lovers, a purpose-built arts and literary centre celebrating the life and work of the late poet and Nobel Laureate, Seamus Heaney. Heaney grew up on the edge of the Sperrin Mountains, a land that shaped his early years and became the muse for much of his memorable work. For a day out in Belfast city, an hour and a half's drive from Omagh, **Titanic Belfast** (⊘ titanicbelfast.com) will enthral the whole family as you explore the shipyard, walk the decks, travel to the depths of the ocean and uncover the true story behind the *Titanic*, in the city where it all began.

MAYO DARK SKY PARK

Ballycroy Visitor Centre, Wild Nephin National Park, Ballycroy, Westport, Co Mayo ✆ +353 (0)98 49888 **e** info@mayodarkskypark.ie ⊘ mayodarkskypark.ie ♀ OS Ireland Discovery Series Maps 32, 37, 38 & 39 & East West Mapping 'Wild Nephin'; see ad, page 196.

Nestled in the northwest corner of Ireland, between the Nephin Mountain Range and the Atlantic coastline, this International Dark Sky Park consists of around 15,000ha (37,000 acres) of protected lands across Wild Nephin National Park. Highly valued for its large expanses of peatland and diversity of species, Wild Nephin National Park (also referred to as Mayo Dark Sky Park) has now secured itself an even higher level of protection because of the pristine quality of its night sky. Owing to the low population density of Mayo, and the fact that it is largely unsuitable for agricultural use, the area has remained devoid of major cities which means its night skies are extremely dark. And being on the Atlantic coast means that the coastal edges of the park are also free of light pollution.

Mayo is distinguished as one of very few **Gold Tier** Dark Sky Parks in the world, a status that requires a complete lack of lighting on towers or buildings within the area boundary, and one that enables viewers to see the faintest possible stars in the sky. To achieve this status, an array of celestial phenomena should also be visible, such as the aurora, the Milky Way, zodiacal light, faint meteors and airglow, the natural 'glowing' in the sky as a result of sunlight interacting with the molecules in the earth's atmosphere.

At the edge of the Wild Nephin Wilderness, the Robert Lloyd Praeger Centre is named after the Irish naturalist and writer, perhaps best known for his 1937 autobiographical travelogue *The Way that I Went: An Irishman in Ireland*. Describing the landscape that would become Wild Nephin National Park, he wrote:

> The hills themselves are encircled by this vast area of trackless bog. I confess I find such a place not lonely or depressing but inspiring. You are thrown at the same time back upon yourself and forward against the mystery and majesty of nature.

His description is suited to this wild and eerie region. Around 4,000 years ago, parts of it were covered in Scots pine trees, but as the climate grew wetter and heavy rainfall washed minerals down through the soil, the land became waterlogged and mosses took over, withering the forests and forming the bogs that have come to characterise the area.

Wolves were once common here, with some theories suggesting they were probably one of the reasons so many stone forts were built around Ireland. The

→ The quality of darkness at Wild Nephin makes for excellent stargazing (Brian Wilson)

wolf once ranged across almost the entire northern hemisphere, and was so widespread in Ireland that it was nicknamed 'Wolf Land'. Even Shakespeare alludes to them in his pastoral comedy *As You Like It*, when Rosalind likens lovers' quarrels to the 'howling of Irish wolves against the moon'. It was Oliver Cromwell who brought an end to the Irish wolf, issuing the declaration:

For every bitch wolfe, six pounds; for every dogg wolfe, five pounds; for every cubb which prayeth for himself, forty shillings; for every suckling cubb, ten shillings.

It is thought that the last wolf in Ireland was killed in the late 1700s, after being hunted down in County Carlow where it had allegedly been killing sheep. Today, rewilding is the conservation buzzword that has opened up conversations about reintroducing wolves into the Irish landscape, and while it isn't on the cards just yet, there would be ecological benefits to restoring an apex predator back to the wild. The term 'trophic cascade' refers to what happens when a keystone species is removed or replaced in an ecosystem, and the trickle-down effect this can have. For wolves, their predatory behaviour could help control deer which, when left unchecked, can devastate different habitats.

It may be a while, if ever, before wolves return to the Irish landscape, but selenophiles can still get their full moon fix in this unique Dark Sky Park. Home to some of the darkest and most pristine skies in the world, a clear night in Mayo will display over 4,500 stars to the naked eye, along with planets, meteor showers and the spectacular Milky Way, as it drifts silently across the sky.

GETTING THERE Mayo Dark Sky Park is situated in the heart of the Bay Coast section of the Wild Atlantic Way, a 2,500km (1,553-mile) route along the west coast of Ireland. The visitor centre is in the village of Ballycroy, the nearest train station to which is Westport, approximately 45km (28 miles) away. By road, Ballycroy can be found on the N59 between Mulranny and Bangor Erris. The nearest airports are Sligo and Ireland West Airport Knock.

DARK SKIES HIGHLIGHTS The team at Mayo Dark Sky Park have created three signature dark sky viewing points at easily accessible locations around the park, all of which have qualified as Gold Tier quality under the IDA criteria. The first is **Ballycroy Visitor Centre** (Ballycroy F28 RX77), 15 minutes south of the town of Bangor Erris. The boardwalk and car park are open all year round and the lighting curfew in place means the quality of darkness is excellent. The **Claggan Mountain Coastal Trail** is 7 minutes north of Mulranny, and is the only coastal site within the national park. It offers panoramic views east to the mountains, south towards Claggan, and west to Achill Island. Visitors can observe the night sky from the car or walk to a more secluded spot overlooking Bellacragher Bay. The darkest and most remote site still accessible by car is the **Robert Lloyd Praeger Centre** at Letterkeen, just 20 minutes north of Newport, the gateway town to the Dark Sky Park and two classic long-distance walks: the Western Way and Bangor Trail. There is a stone bothy open 24 hours for shelter if needed, and a stunning viewpoint for visitors to enjoy. The centre is named after the Irish naturalist and writer Robert Lloyd Praeger, who once described this remote landscape as 'the very loneliest place in the country'.

OBSERVATORIES AND ACTIVITIES

Plans are under way for a world-class observatory and planetarium to be built at the park, offering visitors a daily programme of dark sky events (𝒪 mayodarkskypark.ie). For now, the annual **Mayo Dark Sky Festival** (𝒪 mayodarkskyfestival.ie), jointly hosted by the park and Friends of Mayo Dark Skies, offers talks on physics, culture, art and literature plus family-friendly science workshops, nature walks and stargazing sessions. Newport-based **Terra Firma Ireland** (𝒪 terrafirmaireland.ie; see ad, page 196) specialise in after-dark experiences including dark sky safaris and 'gastronomy and astronomy' evenings.

DAYTIME ACTIVITIES

The **National Museum of Ireland Country Life** (𝒪 museum.ie/en-ie/museums/country-life) in Castlebar is home to a fascinating collection of artefacts reflecting decades of traditional rural life in Ireland since 1850. The museum offers a programme of workshops, talks and tours and a changing programme of temporary exhibitions on historical and contemporary themes. In the town of Ballina, the **Connacht Whiskey Company** (𝒪 connachtwhiskey.com) is the perfect stop-off for a tipple. The company is known for its hand-crafted single malt pot-still Irish whiskey, distilled and barrel-aged on the banks of the River Moy, and the distillery has a visitor centre, bar and gift shop. Just west of Claggan Mountain Coastal Trail lies **Bellacragher Boat Club** (𝒪 bellacragherboatclub.ie), from where you can enjoy wildlife-watching ferry tours, boat trips to the nearby islands or explore their solar system walk (complete with planets). Astrophotography workshops are also available on request. In the village of Murrisk on the Wild Atlantic Way, the **Coffin Ship** sculpture (𝒪 mayo-ireland.ie) was commissioned by the government to commemorate the 150th anniversary of the Irish Famine. Unveiled in 1997, the bronze sculpture was created by artist John Behan, and depicts a ship with rigging made of human bones. In the vibrant town of Westport lies **Westport House** (𝒪 westporthouse.ie), one of the jewels in Mayo's crown. A 'big house' has stood on this site since the 1500s, when famous pirate queen Grace O'Malley built one of her castles here. Still in private family ownership, the estate is like something from a fairytale, with 162ha (400 acres) of mature wood, lakeland and a stunning manor house at its centre.

KERRY (INTERNATIONAL DARK SKY RESERVE)

Cools, Ballinskelligs, Co Kerry, V23 KX74 ℘ +353 (0)872 582835 **e** kerrydarkskytourism@ yahoo.ie ⦚ kerrydarkskytourism.com ♀ OS Ireland Discovery Series Maps 63, 64, 70, 71, 72, 78, 79, 83 & 84.

Known for its rugged terrain, striking mountains and windswept coastline, County Kerry in southwest Ireland has drawn astronomers to its shores for decades. This International Dark Sky Reserve is situated on the **Wild Atlantic Way**, a 2,500km (1,553-mile) route of stunning coastline with white sands and powerful waves, towering sea cliffs, vast beaches and flocks of seabirds dancing across the sky. The unique nature of this region means visitors can escape to what feels like true wilderness, with pitch-black skies and unbelievable celestial views, all while staying close to civilisation. Kerry's Dark Sky Reserve is home to as few as 4,000 residents, and runs from Kells Bay through to Caherdaniel, taking in the towns of Kells, Cahersiveen, Valentia Island, Portmagee, the Glen, Ballinskelligs, Dromid and Waterville along the way.

The people of Ireland have been captivated by the stars for thousands of years. The Neolithic inhabitants of the Iveragh Peninsula erected stone monuments to track the cycles of the sun, moon and stars, while some experts believe that ancient inscriptions in Ogham – an early medieval alphabet used to write the early Irish and Old Irish languages – found in the local area may depict celestial observations. In Dromagorteen in Kerry's **Bonane Heritage Park** (⦚ bonaneheritagepark.com), a 10m-wide stone circle is known locally as the 'Judge and Jury', and is made up of 13 stones with a central boulder burial. Experts believe it is the centrepiece of a complex astronomical calendar measuring both the lunar and solar cycles, with further monuments on the horizon marking the rising and setting of the moon on significant dates. One of the benefits of having such dark skies is being able to imagine the ancient people looking up at the same sky, and seeing the stars exactly as they did, without the influence of modern-day light pollution.

From Kerry's Dark Sky Reserve, a keen naked eye can see thousands of stars in various sizes and colours, the Milky Way and other galaxies, nebulas, star clusters, planets, satellites and shooting stars. On a moonless night, stargazers can even spot the International Space Station in orbit. In fact, a reserve like this has such

→ It's possible to see thousands of stars with the naked eye alone in Kerry (silvester kalcik/Shutterstock)

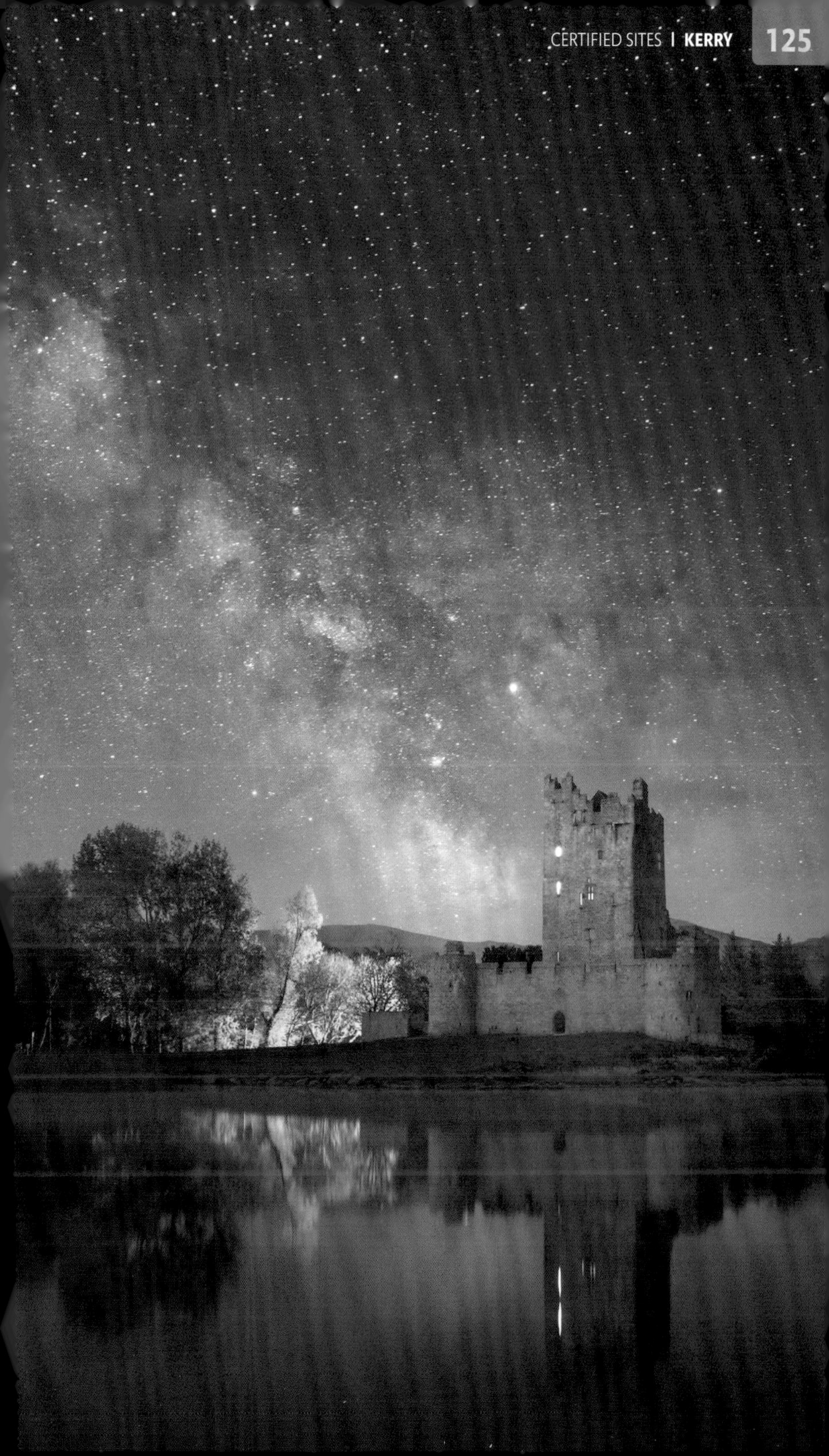

low levels of light pollution that it can be difficult to make out the constellations against the mass of other stars on display.

The **Skellig Islands** are two uninhabited, rocky islets off the southwest coast of Kerry, known as Skellig Michael and Little Skellig. Skellig Michael is known for its well-preserved early Christian monastery, which *Star Wars* fans will recognise from the final scene of *Star Wars: The Force Awakens*. Shot in July 2015, the film reimagines the monastery as an ancient Jedi temple; the undeniably cute creatures known as Porgs that appear in the scenes were only there because the island was home to so many puffins which they had to incorporate into the shots. According to one interview with creature concept designer Jake Lunt Davies, the team had to think of a way to work around these highly protected birds: 'You can't remove them,' he said. 'You physically can't get rid of them. And digitally removing them is an issue and a lot of work, so let's just roll with it, play with it… Let's have our own indigenous species.'

Although Skellig Michael is a UNESCO World Heritage Site, members of the public are allowed to visit under strict conditions. Only 180 people per day are allowed to set foot on the island – although because of its size, this can easily feel crowded – and only a handful of boats make the journey. Once landed, visitors have 2½ hours to tour the island and get back to the boat before returning to the mainland. The monastery building itself is contained within an inner and outer enclosure, situated on a sloping rock plateau at the northeastern summit of the island. Aside from the distinctive beehive-shaped stone cells, there is also a graveyard, a lime mortar church, water cisterns and over 100 stone crosses across the island. The name Skellig is derived from the Irish-language word *sceilig*, meaning a splinter of stone.

Aside from their cultural history, both Skellig Michael and Little Skellig are also at the centre of a 364ha (900 acre) **Important Bird Area**, established by BirdWatch Ireland. It is rated as of international importance for certain seabird species like **Manx shearwaters**, **storm petrels** and **puffins**, and also supports the kind of plant communities that thrive on small and remote marine islands. Storm petrels, in particular, have come to reflect how light pollution can affect the behaviour of wild species. A little bigger than a garden sparrow, the storm petrel is a black bird with a white rump that spends most of its life fluttering over the sea, feeding in flocks from shoals of fish, plankton and crustaceans. Research shows that they use the cover of darkness to avoid being attacked by skuas and gulls, only returning to their nests in the dead of night, and some studies have even shown that they use the lunar cycle as a guide. Ornithologists have then observed that when moonlight levels are low, storm petrels are attracted to artificial lighting at night, which increases their chances of injury or death, but these impacts are lessened by deliberate light reduction measures. In contrast, a study of Barau's petrels in the Indian Ocean recorded birds travelling to their mating sites over a period of time, and discovered that they actually synchronised their journeys with the full moon.

Whether on land or at sea, Kerry's International Dark Sky Reserve is a haven for both wildlife and people, a perfect getaway on the edge of the British Isles, where visitors can gaze at the glittering heavens, above the wild Atlantic Ocean.

GETTING THERE To reach Ballinskelligs, one of the gateway towns to the park, by road, follow the N70. The nearest train stations to the park are Rathmore, Killarney, Farranfore and Tralee. Visitors can fly into Kerry Airport, where there are also car-hire facilities.

DARK SKIES HIGHLIGHTS The views from **Coomanaspic Pass** (Skellig Ring, Portmagee), a 30-minute walk southwest of Portmagee, are breathtaking. From such a height at 300m (1,000ft), it is possible to see over both sides of the peninsula, marked with dramatic cliff faces that drop straight into the sea. The old watch tower at **Bray Head** (Bray Head, Valentia Island) offers stunning views of the Skelligs, Blaskets, the Dingle Sound and the Iveragh Peninsula. Long abandoned, the tower was briefly reoccupied during World War II by coastwatchers, who laid stones in the turf spelling 'EIRE' to advise passing aircraft of their location. The village of **Sneem** (Sneem, Iveragh) on the Iveragh Peninsula offers beautiful views from the bridge overlooking the river, while **Dunmore Head** (Dunquin, Dingle) on the Dingle Peninsula, one of the most westerly points in Europe, offers serene panoramas over the sea with dolphins, seabirds and wildflowers. **St Finian's Bay** (Keel, Dingle), halfway round the Skellig Ring, is popular with surfers and divers, with excellent views across the sea and sky.

OBSERVATORIES AND ACTIVITIES There are no public observatories in Kerry, although Valentia Observatory in Cahersiveen, an observatory for measuring the weather, is one of the oldest monitoring stations in the world. **Astronomy Ireland** (⊘ astronomy.ie) and **Dark Sky Ireland** (⊘ darksky.ie) are both good online resources for stargazing in the region. There are also plans for a **mobile observatory** in Kerry, which would be the first of its kind in Europe. The observatory would operate day and night in all weathers, and could be moved throughout the entire reserve as a shared resource. Contributors include University College Cork's department of physics, the European Space Agency and the Irish Astronomical Society, and it is hoped it might be completed in the next few years.

DAYTIME ACTIVITIES Skelligs Chocolate (⊘ skelligschocolate.com), 10 minutes northwest of Ballinskelligs, is the perfect spot for a treat, a charming, family-run business where visitors can watch chocolates being made, taste what's on offer, and enjoy a coffee with stunning views overlooking the Skelligs Rock. For an afternoon tipple, the **Dingle Distillery** (⊘ dingledistillery.ie) in Dingle creates artisan spirits and celebrates the tradition of independent distilling in Ireland. Their single malt whiskey is a highlight, but they also make excellent gin and vodka, while their tours offer visitors an introduction to the history of the Irish whiskey industry, the distillation process, and the sights, sounds and smells of a working distillery. Only 10 minutes northwest of Dingle town centre, the **Gallarus Oratory** (⊘ discoverireland.ie/kerry/gallarus-oratory-visitor-centre) is the best preserved early Christian church in Ireland, built between the 7th and 8th centuries using dry-stone techniques first developed by Neolithic tomb makers. According to legend, if a person climbs out of the oratory window, their soul will be cleansed, although this has proven to be impossible as the window measures approximately 18cm by 12cm. On the N71 road between Kenmare and Killarney, **Kissane Sheep Farm** (⊘ kissanesheepfarm.com) is a lovely spot for families to see newborn lambs in spring, watch sheepdog herding and shearing demonstrations. You can also enjoy the famous panorama of **Moll's Gap**, named after Moll Kissane who ran an unlicensed public house known as a *shebeen* when the mountain pass was under construction in the 1820s. For a glimpse into the past, the **Slea Head Famine Cottages** (⊘ famine-cottage.com), southwest of Ventry village, offer an enchanting and haunting experience of what it was like to live through the Irish Famine.

04 DISCOVERY SITES

Beyond the certified Reserves, Parks and Communities, there are also over two hundred Dark Sky Discovery Sites around the UK, which are classified as having low levels of light pollution, good sightlines of the sky and good public access. This list is constantly evolving as new sites are classified and light pollution levels change, but the following list provides a comprehensive selection across Britain and Ireland. For an updated list of sites, readers can visit ⊘ darkskydiscovery.org. uk or ⊘ gostargazing.co.uk, where you can also nominate other good stargazing sites in your area.

ENGLAND

CORNWALL

Bryher Community Centre Play Park Area Bryher Community Centre, Bryher, Isles of Scilly TR23 0PR ⊘ scillyaonb.org.uk ★ SQM unknown/Milky Way class ♀ OS Explorer Map 101. One of the smaller of the inhabited islands of the Isles of Scilly, this site is located in the Bryher Community Centre play park, where a lack of streetlighting means excellent views of the Milky Way. In winter, the community centre is in use and some external lights may be switched on, in which case it is recommended to come back later or try another night. Wheelchair access available but ground can be uneven. Dogs on leads welcome.

Carnewas and Bedruthan Steps Bedruthan, Padstow PL27 7UW ⊘ nationaltrust. org.uk/cornwall ★ SQM unknown/Milky Way class ♀ OS Explorer Map 106. Carnewas is a popular tourist destination on the Cornish coast, with spectacular clifftop views stretching across Bedruthan Beach. The cliffs are accessible by foot from the car park nearby, but the ground is uneven and visitors are advised to keep away from the edges, especially during stormy weather. From March to October, a steep staircase leading to the beach is open to visitors. Events are held throughout the year by the Kernow Astronomers, sometimes in partnership with the National Trust. Dogs welcome.

Garrison Playing Field St Mary's Garrison, St Mary's, Isles of Scilly TR21 0LS ⊘ scillyaonb.org. uk ★ SQM 21.2/Milky Way class ♀ OS Explorer Map 101. The site sits high above Hugh Town with frequent stargazing events held throughout winter, organised by the Isles of Scilly AONB Partnership. From Hugh Town, take the main path up to the garrison and around Star Castle, and keep following the path until you come to the playing field. The path and playing field are uneven but accessible to wheelchair users. Free parking. Dogs on leads welcome.

St Agnes Cricket Pitch Old Lane, St Agnes, Isles of Scilly TR22 0PL ⊘ scillyaonb.org.uk ★ SQM unknown/Milky Way class ♀ OS Explorer Map 101. The furthest west of all the dark sky sites in Scilly, St Agnes's small population and lack of streetlighting makes this a great spot for views of the Milky Way. The cricket pitch lies close to Periglis Beach so care should be taken at high tide and during stormy weather, particularly at night. The site is accessible to wheelchair users but it can be uneven in places. Part of this site is leased from the Duchy of Cornwall to the Isles of Scilly Wildlife Trust. Free parking. Dogs on leads welcome.

St Agnes Head Chapel Porth, St Agnes, Cornwall TR5 0NS ⊘ nationaltrust.org.uk/st-agnes-head ★ SQM unknown/Milky Way class ♀ OS Explorer Map 104. Heathland area rich with heather, gorse, birds and butterflies, overlooking the sea and managed by National Trust rangers. The site is 30 minutes' drive south of Newquay and part of the South West Coast Path. It can be reached by foot, cycle, car or bus, with plenty of signage from nearby St Agnes village. Uneven and sloping paths around the area. Parking available at Chapel Porth car park. Toilet facilities are open in the day time. Dogs welcome.

St Martin's Cricket Pitch Pool Green, St Martin's, Isles of Scilly TR25 0QL ⌂ scillyaonb. org.uk ★ SQM unknown/Milky Way class ♥ OS Explorer Map 101. From Higher Town, take the road that leads to the quay, head down the hill and turn on to the path next to the tennis courts. Continue to follow this path until you come to the cricket pitch. This site is accessible to wheelchairs, but the ground is uneven and unlit. Take care during stormy weather due to its proximity to the beach. Dogs on leads welcome.

Tresco Playing Fields Tresco & Bryher Primary School, Tresco, Isles of Scilly TR24 0QG ⌂ scillyaonb.org.uk ★ SQM unknown/Milky Way class ♥ OS Explorer Map 101. This site is based in the Tresco & Bryher Primary School playing fields at Old Grimsby on the island of Tresco, which is devoid of streetlighting and offers excellent views of the night sky. Entrance to the site is to the side of the primary school. You can also gain access by the side of the community centre and play park. Accessible to wheelchairs with some uneven ground. The site is close to Green Porth Beach, so take care during stormy weather, particularly at night, and keep to the footpaths. Dogs on leads welcome.

DEVON

Knapp Copse Local Nature Reserve

Putts Corner, Honiton EX10 0QG ⌂ eastdevon. gov.uk ★ SQM 21.42/Milky Way class ♥ OS Explorer Map 115. A mixture of woodland and meadows with spectacular views, and a great spot to listen out for nightjars in the summer months. A 10-minute drive south of Honiton, with free parking and wheelchair access. There is a height restriction barrier in place so avoid bringing larger vehicles. Wildlife and stargazing events in summer organised by Wild East Devon. Dogs welcome but please keep on leads during spring and summer due to ground-nesting birds.

Lundy Island Bideford EX39 2LY ⌂ landmarktrust.org.uk/lundyisland ★ SQM 21.26/Milky Way class ♥ OS Explorer Map 139. An unspoilt island with a small village, inn, church, castle and spectacular wildlife, including seals and seabirds. The MS *Oldenburg* is Lundy's ferry and supply ship, which takes visitors to Lundy from Ilfracombe and Bideford from the end of March until the end of October. Lundy is a no-vehicle island but cars can be parked at the ferry port. Self-catering accommodation is available to book through the Landmark Trust, who manage the island on behalf of the National Trust. Occasional stargazing events are held on the island for visitors, in particular talks and viewings of the Perseid Meteor Showers in August. No dogs allowed on the island.

Trinity Hill Local Nature Reserve Trinity Hill Rd, Axminster EX13 5SS ⌂ eastdevon.gov.uk ★ SQM 19.82/Milky Way class ♥ OS Explorer Map 116. An area of lowland heath set within conifer plantations five minutes south of Axminster town, with excellent views, open skies and a relatively unobstructed horizon. Particularly good views to the south and east. Free parking. Car park and some reserve paths accessible to wheelchairs. Wildlife and stargazing events in summer organised by Wild East Devon. Dogs welcome but please keep on leads during spring and summer due to ground nesting birds.

SOMERSET

Wimbleball Lake Lower Goodacre, Dulverton TA22 9NU ⌀ swlakestrust.org.uk/wimbleball-lake ★ SQM 21.4/Milky Way class ♀ OS Explorer Maps OL9 & 114. A popular country park and reservoir nestled in the rolling hills of Exmoor National Park. Some wheelchair-accessible paths, and mobility scooters are available to hire from the main office. Paid car parking available. Dogs on leads welcome.

BRISTOL

Durdham Down Stoke Rd, Bristol BS9 1FG ⌀ avongorge.org.uk ★ SQM unknown/Orion class ♀ OS Explorer Maps 154 & 155. An area of open limestone downland 3km (2 miles) from Bristol city centre, particularly popular with kite flyers. Busy on summer nights, there is no streetlighting on the Downs and it is recommended to visit with another person. Wheelchair accessible. For best views of the night sky, walk into the middle of the open grassland. Dogs welcome.

Leigh Woods Valley Rd, Bristol BS8 3PZ ⌀ nationaltrust.org.uk/leigh-woods ★ SQM unknown/Orion class ♀ OS Explorer Maps 154 & 155. A tranquil escape from Bristol's city centre, Leigh Woods is set against the famous Clifton Suspension Bridge. The caves and veteran trees around Avon Gorge provide valuable winter roosts for seven of the 17 UK bat species, which are best seen at dusk. The site is managed by the National Trust with free open access around the clock. Dogs on leads welcome.

Troopers Hill Malvern Rd, St George BS5 8JA ⌀ troopers-hill.org.uk ★ SQM unknown/Orion class ♀ OS Explorer Map 155. A local nature reserve in Bristol overlooking the River Avon, with a rich history in mining and quarrying. The best observation site is near the chimney on top of the hill, above the brightest of the city lights. Stargazing events organised in the winter months in conjunction with the Bristol Astronomical Society. Free and unrestricted access around the clock with wheelchair access. Dogs welcome.

Victoria Park Hill Av, Totterdown BS3 4SN ⌀ vpag.org.uk ★ SQM unknown/Orion class ♀ OS Explorer Maps 154 & 155. A 24ha (60 acre) public park on a hillside in south Bristol, just a mile from the city centre. Stargazing events organised in the winter months in conjunction with the

↑ Car-free Lundy Island is one of England's most unspoilt corners (JanDolezel/Shutterstock)

Bristol Astronomical Society. There is no on-site parking but street parking is possible and public transport runs from the city centre. Ground can be waterlogged after rain so walking boots are recommended, but wide gates and tarmac paths ensure good wheelchair access. Dogs welcome.

DORSET

Durlston Country Park Lighthouse Rd, Swanage BH19 2JL ⏾ durlston.co.uk ★ SQM 20.5/Milky Way class ♀ OS Explorer Map OL15. An astronomy centre located within 113ha (280 acres) of clifftop nature reserve on the Isle of Purbeck, with a visitor centre and renovated Victorian castle. By road, follow the brown tourist signs from Swanage, or follow the South West Coast Path on foot. Outdoor viewing point and telescope observatory are located on a paved terrace by the visitor centre. Park is open daily from sunrise to sunset, but astronomy centre times vary. Pay-and-display parking. Tramper buggies available for hire. Public events hosted throughout the year. Dogs on leads welcome outside.

ISLE OF WIGHT

Fort Victoria Country Park Car Park Fort Victoria, Yarmouth PO41 0RR ⏾ islandastronomy.co.uk ★ SQM unknown/Milky Way class ♀ OS Explorer Map OL29. A former military fort originally built in the 1850s to guard the Solent. The skyline to the south benefits from a line of trees reducing the light pollution. There is 24-hour access with free hard-surface parking and toilet facilities. Overnight camping permitted. Events organised throughout the year by the Island Planetarium, and the local Starlog Club observe each month during the new moon and last quarter. Dogs welcome.

HAMPSHIRE

Buriton Recreation Ground High St, Buriton GU31 5RX ⏾ buriton.info ★ SQM 20.65/Orion class ♀ OS Explorer Maps OL8 & OL33. A charming village set against the backdrop of the South Downs. Access the village hall behind the school to find the recreation ground which has good views of the night sky. Occasional events run in conjunction with the local Five Bells pub. Open

↑ The astronomy centre at Durlston Country Park, near Swanage (DavidYoung/Shutterstock)

access all year but visitors should take care around uneven ground and pot-holes in the car park. Dogs welcome.

Butser Hill, Queen Elizabeth Country Park Limekiln Lane, Petersfield GU32 1RT ⌂ hants.gov.uk/qecp ★ SQM 20.3/Milky Way class ♀ OS Explorer Maps OL8, OL32 & OL33. A nature reserve rich in butterflies and skylarks, Butser Hill is also one of the highest and darkest points in the South Downs National Park. Local astronomy group Hants Astro offers monthly stargazing events and the site is open 24 hours a day, all year round, for private observations. Paid car park open from dawn to dusk, but free parking along the track is available after this. Good accessibility and battery-powered wheelchairs available to hire. Dogs welcome.

Harting Down South Harting, Petersfield GU31 5PN ⌂ nationaltrust.org.uk/harting-down ★ SQM 20.7/Orion class ♀ OS Explorer Map OL8. Ancient chalk downland with scattered shrub and woodland, and panoramic views over the Weald towards the North Downs. Views to the south towards the Isle of Wight are possible by walking along the South Downs Way route a few hundred metres from the car park, just off the B2141 between South Harting and North Marden. The area is managed by the National Trust who offer

occasional stargazing events on site. A popular spot for astrophotographers. Free parking after dark. Dogs on leads welcome.

Old Winchester Hill National Nature Reserve Hayden Lane, Meonstoke SO32 3NQ ⌂ naturalengland.org.uk ★ SQM unknown/Milky Way class ♀ OS Explorer Maps OL3 & OL32. A chalk grassland nature reserve with Iron Age hillfort and Bronze Age burial mounds, situated to the east of Corhampton on the eastern side of the Meon Valley. From the top of the hill, views extend as far as Portsmouth, Southampton and, on a clear day, the Isle of Wight. The site and car park are unlit with uneven ground and steep slopes, but paths are wheelchair accessible. Open and unrestricted access with free parking. Dogs on leads welcome.

Winchester Science Centre and Planetarium Car Park Telegraph Way, Winchester SO21 1HZ ⌂ winchestersciencecentre. org ★ SQM unknown/Milky Way class ♀ OS Explorer Map OL32. Interactive learning centre just outside Winchester city centre. Private stargazing in the car park only, although the planetarium is open to visitors in the day, and evening events run throughout the year. Wide views to the east. Paid parking available or free with an annual pass. Wheelchair accessible with a slight slope. Guide dogs only on site.

↑ The views from the chalk grasslands of Old Winchester Hill stretch as far as Portsmouth and Southampton (Julian Gazzard/Shutterstock)

SUSSEX

Bignor Hill Bignor Down, Slindon RH20 1PQ ⌂ nationaltrust.org.uk/slindon-estate ★ SQM 21.2/Milky Way class ♥ OS Explorer Map OL10. A beautiful hilltop site within the Slindon Estate, with Bronze Age burial mounds and plenty of wildlife. The free car park is the best location for stargazing, with far-reaching views. To reach it, take the southbound no-through road from the village of Bignor. The car park and surrounding footpaths are wheelchair accessible, although some paths have loose chippings. Dogs on leads welcome.

Birling Gap Birling Gap Rd, Eastbourne BN20 0AB ⌂ nationaltrust.org.uk/birling-gap-and-the-seven-sisters ★ SQM 20.5/Milky Way class ♥ OS Explorer Map OL25. Part of the world-famous Seven Sisters chalk cliffs, one of the longest stretches of undeveloped coastline on the south coast. Events held by the National Trust throughout the year. Free parking in the main car park after dusk and open access at all times, all year round. There is also a public staircase from the main car park if you want to climb down to the beach. Car park surface is wheelchair accessible but the surrounding terrain is steep and uneven. Dogs welcome.

Devil's Dyke Devil's Dyke Rd, Brighton BN1 8YJ ⌂ nationaltrust.org.uk/devils-dyke ★ SQM 20.1/Orion class ♥ OS Explorer Map OL11. At over 1km long, the Dyke Valley is the longest, deepest and widest 'dry valley' in the UK. Just 8km (5 miles) north of Brighton, it can be reached on foot by following the South Downs Way. Car park is free after dusk and has good accessibility with clear views. A local astronomy group meets regularly at this site. Open access all year round for private observation. Dogs on leads welcome.

Ditchling Beacon Ditchling Rd, Brighton BN1 9QB ⌂ nationaltrust.org.uk/ditchling-beacon ★ SQM 20.3/Orion class ♥ OS Explorer Map OL11. The highest point in East Sussex, this site has 360-degree views from the summit, looking south to the sea, north across the Weald, or east to west across the South Downs. Some light pollution due to its proximity to Brighton. Car park is free after dusk, with most of the immediate area suitable for wheelchairs except the top view, which may prove challenging to some. Dogs on leads welcome.

Eames Farm Thorney Island, Emsworth PO10 8DE ⌂ conservancy.co.uk ★ SQM 19.94/Milky Way class ♥ OS Explorer Map OL8. A coastal nature reserve with grazing marsh, wetland and reedbed, located on Thorney Island in Chichester Harbour. Visitors are reminded that it is a working farm and they must keep to the paved areas by the entrance to the buildings. This outdoor space is open for stargazing at all times, and the recently refurbished building, complete with kitchen and toilet facilities, can be opened with prior agreement from the conservancy. The South Downs Astronomical Society hosts an annual observing session. Wheelchair accessible. Dogs on leads welcome outside.

Iping Common Elsted Rd, Midhurst GU29 0PB ⌂ sussexwildlifetrust.org.uk/visit/iping-stedham-commons ★ SQM 21.2/Milky Way class ♥ OS Explorer Maps OL8 & OL33. Over 40ha (100 acres) of wildlife-rich heathland managed by the Sussex Wildlife Trust. A great spot for listening to nightjars on summer evenings. Popular with astrophotographers. The best night-sky views can be found on the common, a short walk from the car park which is free but has a vehicle height barrier. Open access all year round for private observations. Dogs welcome but please keep on leads during spring and summer due to ground-nesting birds.

John Q Davis Footpath The Street, West Itchenor PO20 7AY ⌂ conservancy.co.uk ★ SQM

20.47/Milky Way class ♀ OS Explorer Map OL8. A footpath that adjoins a Public Right of Way, overlooking the foreshore at West Itchenor. The site is located 200m west of the Harbour Office, and 200m north of the public car park in West Itchenor. Open for private observations all year round. Wheelchair access from the main Itchenor Car Park. The South Downs Astronomical Society hosts an annual observing session here, in partnership with Chichester Harbour Conservancy. Dogs on leads welcome.

Maybush Copse Cot Lane, Chichester PO18 8SP ⚲ chidhamandhambrook.info/maybush-copse ★ SQM 19.88/Milky Way class ♀ OS Explorer Map OL8. Just over 3ha (8 acres) of regenerated community green space in the village of Chidham, overseen by the Friends of Maybush Copse. Open for private observations at all times. The South Downs Astronomical Society hosts an annual observing session here, in partnership with Chichester Harbour Conservancy. Wheelchair path accessible from Cot Lane entrance. Parking limited. No streetlighting. Dogs on leads welcome.

LONDON

Grove Park Community Group Garden and Nature Reserve
Baring Rd, London SE12 0DS ⚲ gpcg.org.uk ★ SQM unknown/Milky Way class ♀ OS Explorer Map 162. A community centre, large garden and 1.2ha (3 acre) nature reserve originally used by John Griffiths, who taught astronomy at the Royal Greenwich Observatory nearby. The nature reserve has free open access but the community garden is open by arrangement only. Site managed by the Grove Park Community Group in conjunction with the Baring Trust. Occasional events throughout the year. Wheelchair accessible. Dogs on leads welcome.

The Waterworks Nature Reserve Lea Bridge Rd, London E10 7NU ⚲ visitleevalley.org.uk ★ SQM unknown/Orion class ♀ OS Explorer Maps 173 & 174. A unique wildlife haven just a few kilometres from central London to the northeast. Dark Sky Discovery events are held at the nature reserve, but open access to slightly darker skies is available at the adjacent golf centre and Hackney Marsh. The site is fully accessible for wheelchair users, and there are also systems in place for the hard of hearing and visually impaired. Dogs on leads welcome.

OXFORDSHIRE

Rollright Stones Ancient Monuments
Unnamed road, Chipping Norton OX7 5QB ⚲ rollrightstones.co.uk ★ SQM unknown/Milky Way class ♀ OS Explorer Maps OL45 & 191. An ancient site of three Neolithic and Bronze Age monuments on the borders of Oxfordshire and Warwickshire. Clear views from the east to the southwest from the stone circle, or cross the road with caution for good views west to east. In regular use by Chipping Norton Amateur Astronomy Group for public and private events. Free access after dusk for private observations. Wheelchair accessible. Dogs on leads welcome, except in the stone circle.

South Park Headington Hill, Oxford OX4 1NG ⚲ scienceoxford.com ★ SQM 19.6/Orion class ♀ OS Explorer Map 180. A popular park in the city centre with good visibility across the historic Oxford spires, towers and beyond. Free open access at all times with stargazing events hosted by Science Oxford. For the greatest visibility, head to the centre of the lower area, best accessed via the gates on Morrell Avenue or Headington Hill. Fairly even ground but no streetlighting and a small drainage ditch around the lower edge of the park. Dogs welcome.

WARWICKSHIRE

Aunt Phoebe's Recreation Ground A3400, Long Compton CV36 5WA ⟨⟩ cnaag.com ★ SQM unknown/Milky Way class ♀ OS Explorer Maps OL45 & 191. A large, flat recreation area in the centre of the village of Long Compton, on the southern border of the county, approximately 10km (6 miles) north of Chipping Norton. Events held throughout the year in conjunction with Chipping Norton Amateur Astronomy Group. Free, open access all year round, with a car park for private observations. No lighting but flat, well-drained ground ensures accessibility for wheelchair users. Dogs welcome.

WORCESTERSHIRE

Mill Pond Hollybed Common, Malvern WR13 6DB ⟨⟩ malvernhillsaonb.org.uk ★ SQM 21.1/ Milky Way class ♀ OS Explorer Map 190. A large meadow nature reserve a few minutes' drive south from Malvern with an old orchard and grazing cattle. Paid car parking available. Level ground around the pond with hard-surfaced tracks and car park area. Be aware of open water at night. Dogs on leads welcome.

HEREFORDSHIRE

Mathon Church Car Park Mathon Rd, Malvern WR13 5PW ⟨⟩ malvernhillsaonb.org. uk ★ SQM 21.1/Milky Way class ♀ OS Explorer Map 190. A quiet car park behind St John the Baptist Church in Mathon, a rural village just to the west of Malvern, away from brightly lit areas. Open access with prior agreement from the Old School House adjacent to the church. Wheelchair accessible. Visitors are asked to vacate the site by midnight. No dogs.

SHROPSHIRE

Carding Mill Valley Bur Way, Church Stretton SY6 6JG ⟨⟩ nationaltrust.org.uk/ carding-mill-valley-and-the-long-mynd ★ SQM unknown/Milky Way class ♀ OS Explorer Map 217. A National Trust space with car park, tearoom and toilets situated in the Shropshire Hills AONB. The car park is free between dusk and dawn. Stargazing events run throughout the year with the National Trust and local astronomers. Uneven terrain outside the car park area with low vegetation and steep slopes. Dogs on leads welcome.

Cross Dyke Car Park Bur Way, Church Stretton SY6 6JG ⟨⟩ nationaltrust.org.uk/ carding-mill-valley-and-the-long-mynd ★ SQM unknown/Milky Way class ♀ OS Explorer Map 217. A National Trust-owned car park situated on the Long Mynd, a heath and moorland plateau that forms part of the Shropshire Hills AONB. Open access land all year round for private observations. Stargazing events run throughout the year with the National Trust. Uneven terrain outside the car park area with low vegetation and steep slopes. Dogs on leads welcome.

Pole Cottage Bur Way, Church Stretton SY6 6JG ⟨⟩ nationaltrust.org.uk/carding-mill-valley-and-the-long-mynd ★ SQM unknown/ Milky Way class ♀ OS Explorer Map 217. A National Trust-owned car park situated on the Long Mynd, part of the Shropshire Hills AONB. Excellent horizon all round. Stargazing events run occasionally with the National Trust and local astronomers. Open access land. Uneven hard surface in car park. Dogs on leads welcome.

Shooting Box Car Park Ratlinghope Rd, Church Stretton SY6 6JG ⟨⟩ nationaltrust.org.uk/ carding-mill-valley-and-the-long-mynd ★ SQM unknown/Milky Way class ♀ OS Explorer Map 217. A National Trust-owned car park set among heath and moorland, part of the Shropshire Hills AONB. Excellent horizon visibility, especially westwards, with occasional artificial light from remote farms and traffic. Stargazing events run throughout the year with the National Trust and local astronomers. Open access land. Uneven hard surface in car park. Dogs on leads welcome.

WEST MIDLANDS

Barr Beacon Beacon Rd, Walsall WS9 0PQ ⊘ go.walsall.gov.uk ★ SQM unknown/Orion class ♀ OS Explorer Map 220. A nature reserve rich in wildlife, with 360-degree views of the surrounding landscape. One of the highest points in the West Midlands. Events held throughout the year in association with the Walsall Astronomical Society. Site is open 24 hours but the car park closes at night unless events are scheduled. Wheelchair accessible. Dogs welcome.

CAMBRIDGESHIRE

The Bog Oak Car Park New Decoy, Great Fen, Peterborough PE7 3PW ⊘ greatfen.org.uk/new-decoy ★ SQM 20.20/Milky Way class ♀ OS Explorer Map 227. Part of the Great Fen, a vast, flat landscape and habitat restoration project, this site is situated just outside the village of Holme. Excellent views in all directions. The site has free open access all year round with good wheelchair access. Dogs welcome.

Ramsey Heights Countryside Classroom Chapel Rd, Huntingdon PE26 2RS ⊘ greatfen.org.uk/ramsey-heights ★ SQM 20.33/Milky Way class ♀ OS Explorer Map 227. Open grassy space beside an educational facility run by the local Wildlife Trust, just outside the village of Holme. The viewing area has some low trees to the east and south, but still offers good sight lines. Accessible paths, either short grass or hard surfaces leading to the viewing point. Site is also partly a car park so be aware of moving vehicles. Dogs welcome.

SUFFOLK

Haw Wood Farm Caravan Park
Haw Wood Farm, Saxmundham IP17 3QT ⊘ hawwoodfarm.co.uk ★ SQM 21.75/Milky Way class ♀ OS Explorer Map 231. Campsite surrounded by newly planted woodland and wildflower meadows in the Suffolk countryside, just off the A12 north of Saxmundham. Uninterrupted 360-degree views. Spring and autumn star parties organised by the local astronomy group. The site is level and has surfaced vehicular access to all parts. Dogs on leads welcome.

Suffolk Coast National Nature Reserve, Walberswick Lodge Rd, Southwold IP18 6UZ ⊘ explorewalberswick.co.uk ★ SQM unknown/Milky Way class ♀ OS Explorer Map 231. Public car park overlooking Suffolk Coast National Nature Reserve with very little light pollution. Open access all year round. Car park is short grass and tarmac, but no pavement or lighting on the road leading to it. Dogs on leads welcome.

Westleton Common Mill St, Saxmundham IP17 3BD ⊘ westleton.onesuffolk.net ★ SQM 20.65/Milky Way class ♀ OS Explorer Map 231. Open coastal heathland some 10km (6 miles) northeast of Saxmundham rich in wildlife, and a site of national importance for the silver-studded blue butterfly. Good visibility on all sides. Local astronomy group holds regular observing sessions on the common. Viewing area is concrete hard standing and accessible by wheelchair via a gravel path from the parking area. Free open access all year round. Dogs welcome.

NORFOLK

Barrow Common Common Lane, King's Lynn PE31 8DB ⊘ norfolkcoastaonb.org.uk ★ SQM 21.23/Milky Way class ♀ OS Explorer

Map 250. A large undulating common around 10km (6 miles) east of Hunstanton, forming a mosaic of acid grassland, gorse, hawthorn, bracken scrub, woodland, a disused sand quarry and old chalk pit workings. Excellent sight lines and a spectacular 180-degree view of the north horizon. Events organised on site by local astronomy groups. Free open access all year round for private observations. Wheelchair accessible. Dogs welcome.

Great Ellingham Recreation Ground Watton Rd, Attleborough NR17 1HZ ⏣ brecklandastro.org.uk ★ SQM 21.0/Milky Way class ♀ OS Explorer Map 237. An observatory and outdoor astropad in the village of Great Ellingham. The observatory has a 20" computer-controlled telescope, built and maintained by the local Breckland Astronomical Society. Outdoor site accessible all year round. Observatory group visits by arrangement. Events and star parties hosted throughout the year. No dogs.

Kelling Heath Holiday Park Sports Field Sandy Hill Lane, Holt NR25 7HW ⏣ kellingheath.co.uk ★ SQM 21.23/Milky Way class ♀ OS Explorer Map 252. A holiday park in a beautiful woodland and heathland setting away from artificial lighting, situated on the north Norfolk coastline between the market towns of Sheringham and Holt. Events held on site, including popular twice-yearly star parties. Site is surrounded by trees but has good sky views. Free open access and parking at any time. Good wheelchair access. Dogs on leads welcome.

RSPB Titchwell Marsh Nature Reserve Main Rd, King's Lynn PE31 8BB ⏣ rspb.org.uk/reserves-and-events/reserves-a-z/titchwell-marsh ★ SQM 21.26/Milky Way class ♀ OS Explorer Map 250. A few minutes' drive east of Hunstanton, the reserve has a sandy beach with a boardwalk, lagoon nature reserve and visitor centre, popular with birders. Local astronomy groups run occasional public events in collaboration with the RSPB. Free open access and parking available. Car parks and paths are wheelchair accessible. Visitors are reminded to avoid disturbance to wildlife. Dogs on leads welcome on the West Bank path and around the visitor centre, but not elsewhere on the reserve.

Wiveton Downs SSSI Langham Rd, Holt NR25 7JP ⏣ norfolkcoastaonb.org.uk ★ SQM 21.26/Milky Way class ♀ OS Explorer Map 251. An elevated heathland site of geological interest, set within the sloping glacial valley of the River Glaven. Occasional events on site. Free open access with a wheelchair-accessible gravel car park. Visitors are reminded to watch out for rabbit holes in the grass. Dogs on leads welcome.

DERBYSHIRE

Surprise View Grindleford, Hope Valley S32 1DA ⏣ peakdistrict.gov.uk/darkskies ★ SQM 20.4/Milky Way class ♀ OS Explorer Map OL1. Car park on the outskirts of Hathersage with a panoramic view of the surrounding Hope Valley. Private observers should use the rear car park if they are setting up telescopes or other equipment. The site is fully accessible to wheelchairs but visitors are advised that there are no lights and the car park opens on to the busy A6187 road, so please bring a torch and be mindful of moving vehicles. Dogs on leads welcome.

LANCASHIRE

Beacon Fell Visitor Centre Beacon Fell Rd, Preston PR3 2EW ⏣ forestofbowland.com/stargazing ★ SQM unknown/Milky Way class ♀ OS Explorer Map OL41. A country park around 10km (6 miles) north of Preston with extensive conifer woodlands, moorland and a high summit with open views. Events run throughout the year by local astronomy groups and the Forest of Bowland. Multiple viewing locations in car parks and at summit trig point with no sightline restrictions. Wheelchair accessible but be advised there is no lighting in car parks or on tracks. Dogs welcome.

Clerk Laithe Lodge Slaidburn Rd, Clitheroe BB7 3EB ⌂ clerklaithe.co.uk ★ SQM unknown/ Milky Way class ♀ OS Explorer Map OL41. A guest house and restaurant in the Forest of Bowland, near the banks of the River Hodder. Location of the lodge means there is very little light pollution and stargazing facilities are available for residents on request. Free open access and hard-surface car park, paths and patio areas. Wheelchair access to lodge and toilet. No dogs.

Crook O'Lune Picnic Site Low Rd, Halton LA2 6PA ⌂ forestofbowland.com/star-gazing ★ SQM unknown/Orion class ♀ OS Explorer Map OL41. A popular and attractive spot where the River Lune curves through tree-lined banks. Open views to the north and east horizon over the Lune Valley, but views to the south and west limited by adjacent trees. Open access car park with café. All access via paved paths with no steps. Access to the river by ramp. Events run throughout the year by local astronomy groups and the Forest of Bowland. Dogs welcome.

Gisburn Forest Hub Dale Head, Slaidburn BB7 4TS ⌂ forestryengland.uk/gisburn-forest-and-stocks ★ SQM unknown/Milky Way class ♀ OS Explorer Map OL41. A working forest managed by Forestry England with beautiful views, mountain-bike trails and footpaths. Events run throughout the year by local astronomy groups and the Forest of Bowland. Free open access and level paths for wheelchair users. Dogs welcome.

Parsley Hay A515, Buxton SK17 0DG ⌂ peakdistrict.gov.uk/darkskies ★ SQM unknown/Milky Way class ♀ OS Explorer Map OL24. A tiny cluster of houses a short drive south of Buxton which evolved with the laying of the Cromford and High Peak railway line. Open access all year round. Car park is wheelchair accessible with panoramic views. Dogs welcome.

Minninglow Car Park Mouldridge Lane, Matlock DE4 2PN ⌂ peakdistrict.gov.uk/ darkskies ★ SQM unknown/Milky Way class ♀ OS Explorer Map OL24. Car park beside the High Peak Trail west of Matlock with panoramic views and good accessibility. Visitors are advised to watch out for rough, wet and muddy ground underfoot. Dogs welcome.

Slaidburn Visitor Car Park B6478, Clitheroe BB7 3ES ⌂ forestofbowland.com/ star-gazing ★ SQM unknown/Milky Way class ♀ OS Explorer Map OL41. An open car park to the east of the village of Slaidburn in the Ribble Valley. Open views from the village car park, low hedges and bushes screen the few street lights giving excellent views. Events run throughout the year by local astronomy groups and the Forest of Bowland. Free open access and paved areas for wheelchair users. Dogs on leads welcome.

YORKSHIRE

Buckden National Park Car Park Buckden Wood Lane, Skipton BD23 5JA ⌂ yorkshiredales. org.uk ★ SQM unknown/Milky Way class ♀ OS Explorer Map OL30. Car park on the edge of the village of Buckden within the Yorkshire Dales National Park. Free parking for stargazers between dusk and dawn, even if car park instructions say otherwise. Wheelchair accessible with toilet facilities. Dogs on leads welcome.

Dales Countryside Museum Car Park Station Yard, Burtersett Rd, Hawes DL8 3NT ⌂ www.dalescountrysidemuseum.org.uk ★ SQM unknown/Milky Way class ♀ OS Explorer Map

OL2, OL19 & OL30. Local museum telling the story of the people who have lived and worked in the Yorkshire Dales for the last 1,000 years. For the best views, drive down to the bottom end of the car park. Occasional events run by the Yorkshire Dales National Park. Free open access with mostly level ground. Free parking for stargazers between dusk and dawn, even if car park instructions say otherwise. No dogs.

Fewston Reservoir Blubberhouses, Otley LS21 2NY ⊘ yorkshirewater.com/things-to-do/fewston-walk ★ SQM 20.94/Milky Way class ♀ OS Explorer Map 297. Located in the south of the Nidderdale Area of Outstanding Natural Beauty, Fewston Reservoir offers a number of relaxing paths along the side of the water and through the woods. Recommended viewing point at car park, which is wheelchair accessible. Visitors are reminded to be careful round the water's edge. Full open access. Dogs welcome.

Malham National Park Centre Car Park Chapel Gate, Malham BD23 4DA ⊘ yorkshiredales. org.uk/places/malham_national_park_centre ★ SQM unknown/Milky Way class ♀ OS Explorer Map OL2. The gateway to Malham National Park, where visitors can watch peregrine falcons at Malham Cove, see impressive Gordale Scar or visit the waterfall at Janet's Foss. Free parking from dusk until dawn. Car park is level tarmac and toilet facilities are available. Dogs welcome.

The Moors National Park Centre, Danby Lodge Lane, Danby YO21 2NB ⊘ northyorkmoors.org.uk/visiting/see-and-do/the-moors-national-park-centre ★ SQM unknown/Milky Way class ♀ OS Explorer Maps OL26 & OL27. Visitor centre, café and toilets on the outskirts of the moorland village of Danby, at the heart of the North York Moors. Occasional events with local astronomy groups, as well as other science-themed family events throughout the year. Open access and free parking after dusk. Wheelchair-accessible site. Dogs welcome except in Crow Wood.

Scarborough & Ryedale Astronomical Society Observatories Dalby Forest Drive, Pickering YO18 7LT ⊘ forestryengland. uk/dalby-forest ★ SQM unknown/Milky Way class ♀ OS Explorer Map OL27. Dalby Forest is a 3,440ha (8,500 acre) forest situated within the boundaries of the North York Moors National Park. Observatories are based outside the Forestry England Visitor Centre. Public observing events take place each month between October and March. Group bookings also available on request. Wheelchair accessible and toilet facilities available. Dogs welcome outside.

Scar House Reservoir Unnamed road, Pateley Bridge HG3 5SW ⊘ yorkshirewater.com/things-to-do/scar-house-walk ★ SQM 21.42/Milky Way class ♀ OS Explorer Map OL30 & 298. A reservoir at the head of Nidderdale, set in a tranquil and isolated moorland. Visitors are advised to stay clear of the water's edge and take care in icy conditions. Wheelchair access is available along one side of the reservoir and over the dam. Dogs welcome.

Sutton Bank National Park Centre High St, Sutton Bank YO7 2EH ⊘ northyorkmoors.org. uk/visiting/see-and-do/sutton-bank-national-park-centre ★ SQM unknown/Milky Way class ♀ OS Explorer Map OL26. A high point on the Hambleton Hills with extensive views over the Vale of York and the Vale of Mowbray. Occasional events with telescopes and advice provided by York Astronomical Society. Free open access but 24-hour parking charges. All footpaths around the centre are wheelchair accessible and there is a disabled toilet on site. Dogs welcome.

Tan Hill Inn Tan Hill, Swaledale DL11 6ED ⊘ tanhillinn.com ★ SQM unknown/Milky Way

class ♀ OS Explorer Maps OL19 & OL30. A unique and historic inn dating back to the 17th century and Britain's highest public house at 528m above sea level. Events organised throughout the year as part of the North Pennines AONB Partnership programme. Open access and free parking all night. The car park is level but some rough stones in places, and there is also a level, grassy area for viewing. Dogs on leads welcome.

Thruscross Reservoir Thruscross, Harrogate HG3 4BB ⚲ yorkshirewater.com/things-to-do/thruscross-reservoir ★ SQM 21.08/Milky Way class ♀ OS Explorer Map 297. Tranquil reservoir off the A59 a short drive west from Harrogate encircled by a 7km (4½ mile) walking path, with picnic spots and ruins of an old mill. Free parking available but be aware of vehicle height restrictions. Recommended viewing point at car park, which is wheelchair accessible. Visitors are reminded to be careful round the water's edge. Full open access. Dogs welcome.

Toft Gate Lime Kiln Car Park Greenhow Hill HG3 5JL ⚲ nidderdaleaonb.org.uk/toft-gate-lime-kiln ★ SQM unknown/Milky Way class ♀ OS Explorer Maps OL2 & 298. Situated just west

of Pateley Bridge are the remains of a lime kiln dating back to the 1860s, a picturesque reminder of Nidderdale's industrial heritage. Good views from the picnic area adjacent to the ruined kiln, and even better from nearby Coldstones Cut. Free open access all year round. Wheelchair-accessible paths. No lighting on site. Dogs welcome.

University of York Astrocampus
Heslington Ln, York YO10 5DD ⚲ astrocampus.york.ac.uk ★ SQM unknown/Orion class ♀ OS Explorer Map 290. Two observatories and an information centre on the University of York campus, part of the Department of Physics. Star parties and other events hosted on site by the university. Site is secure and well-lit, patrolled by security 24 hours a day. Free open access to the public by arrangement. Free parking on site after dusk. Site is accessible except the first floor of the main observatory. No dogs.

CUMBRIA

Allan Bank, Grasmere Allan Bank, Ambleside LA22 9QB ⚲ nationaltrust.org.uk/allan-bank-and-grasmere ★ SQM unknown/Milky Way class ♀ OS Explorer Map OL7. A National Trust

↑ The University of York Astrocampus is home to two observatories (James Lees)

property overlooking the Grasmere Valley and woodland grounds. Access only during evening events. No parking available on site but pay-and-display public car parks in Grasmere. Limited wheelchair accessibility. Dogs on leads welcome.

Clesketts, Geltsdale Stagsike Cottages, Brampton CA8 2PN ⟁ rspb.org.uk/reserves-and-events/reserves-a-z/geltsdale ★ SQM unknown/Milky Way class ♀ OS Explorer Maps OL43 & 315. A remote and rugged nature reserve in north Cumbria encompassing two hill farms, with rare upland birds like black grouse, curlew and hen harrier. Events organised throughout the year as part of the North Pennines AONB Partnership programme. Free parking. Limited accessibility but viewing is possible from a parked car. Dogs on leads welcome.

Cow Green Reservoir B6277, Langdon Beck DL12 0HX ⟁ visitcumbria.com/evnp/cow-green-reservoir ★ SQM unknown/Milky Way class ♀ OS Explorer Map OL31. A 3km- (2 mile) long reservoir rich in flora and fauna, including rare alpine plants like the Teesdale violet. Events organised throughout the year as part of the North Pennines AONB Partnership programme. Free parking. Open access all year. Wheelchair accessible but the road down to the reservoir is steep. Visitors are advised to wear appropriate clothing as the site is very exposed. Dogs welcome.

Low Gillerthwaite Field Centre Ennerdale, Cleator CA23 3AX ⟁ lgfc.org.uk ★ SQM 23.6/Milky Way class ♀ OS Explorer Maps OL4 & 303. Adapted from traditional Lakeland 17th-century farm buildings, the field centre in west Cumbria's Ennerdale Valley is surrounded by mountains, valleys and fells. Events take place throughout the year. Free open access to pedestrians and cyclists. Vehicular access by arrangement with the warden. Wheelchair users have full access around the centre, although some

assistance may be required to access the meadow. Dogs on leads welcome.

DURHAM

Balderhead Reservoir Balderhead Rd, Barnard Castle DL12 9UX ⟁ watersideparksuk.com/park/balderhead ★ SQM unknown/Milky Way class ♀ OS Explorer Map OL31. A popular fishing destination some 10km (6 miles) west of Barnard Castle, with good views across the reservoir. Events organised throughout the year as part of the North Pennines AONB Partnership programme. Visitors are reminded to beware of deep water. Open all year round with good access. Free parking. Dogs on leads welcome.

Bowlees Visitor Centre B6277, Newbiggin DL12 0XE ⟁ northpennines.org.uk/bowlees-visitor-centre ★ SQM unknown/Orion class ♀ OS Explorer Map OL31. Visitor centre 3km (1.8 miles) northwest of Middleton-in-Teesdale; café, shop and gateway to the North Pennines AONB landscape. Events organised throughout the year as part of the North Pennines AONB Partnership programme. Car park free or voluntary charge, with a wheelchair-accessible tarmac surface, although access to viewing area may be limited during bad weather. Dogs on leads welcome outside visitor centre.

Burnhope Reservoir A689, Bishop Auckland DL13 1BN ⟁ www.northpennines.org.uk ★ SQM unknown/Milky Way class ♀ OS Explorer Map OL31. One of the smaller reservoirs in the area and a great spot for nocturnal wildlife. Events organised throughout the year as part of the North Pennines AONB Partnership programme. Visitors are reminded to beware of deep water. Open all year round with good access. Free parking. Dogs on leads welcome.

Hamsterley Forest Visitor Centre Car Park Bedburn Rd, Hamsterley DL13 3NL ⟁ forestryengland.uk/hamsterley-forest ★ SQM unknown/Milky Way class ♀ OS Explorer Map OL31. Picturesque woodlands situated to the north of Barnard Castle along the sides of a stunning sheltered valley. Events organised throughout the year as part of the North Pennines AONB Partnership programme. Visitors are reminded to beware of deep water. Open all year round with good access. Free parking. Dogs on leads welcome.

Parkhead Station Parkhead Station House, Bishop Auckland DL13 2ES ⌂ parkheadstation. co.uk ★ SQM unknown/Milky Way class ♀ OS Explorer Map 307. A former station site turned bed and breakfast on Durham County Council's Waskerley Way Railway Path. Events organised throughout the year as part of the North Pennines AONB Partnership programme. The viewing area is close to the Waskerley Way, which may have some bicycle traffic. Surrounding moorland is wet and boggy in places, and the path is a little uneven but generally accessible. No dogs.

Pow Hill Country Park Pow Hill, Consett DH8 9NU ⌂ durham.gov.uk ★ SQM unknown/ Milky Way class ♀ OS Explorer Map 307. A Durham County Council Country Park on the banks of Derwent Reservoir near Edmundbyers. Events organised throughout the year as part of the North Pennines AONB Partnership programme. Free car park is open all day but may be closed in severe weather. Visitors are advised to take care around deep water. Path is relatively flat and accessible. Two disabled bays available and a hard-surface path runs to the viewing point. Dogs on leads welcome.

Selset Reservoir B6276, Barnard Castle DL12 0PR ⌂ watersideparksuk.com/park/selset ★ SQM unknown/Milky Way class ♀ OS Explorer Map OL31. A trout-fishing destination just to the southwest of Middleton-in-Teesdale, surrounded by the beautiful scenery of the North Pennine

grouse moors. Events organised throughout the year as part of the North Pennines AONB Partnership programme. Visitors are reminded to beware of deep water. Open all year round with good access. Free parking. Dogs on leads welcome.

NORTHUMBERLAND
Allen Banks Bardon Mill, Hexham NE47 7BP ⌂ nationaltrust.org.uk/allen-banks-and-staward-gorge ★ SQM unknown/Milky Way class ♀ OS Explorer Map OL43. At around 10km (6 miles) east of Haltwhistle is this sheltered car park at Allen Banks, one of the largest areas of ancient woodland in Northumberland. Events organised throughout the year as part of the North Pennines AONB Partnership programme. Free open access. Car park is free after dusk with level surfaces. Accessible toilets available on site. Dogs on leads welcome.

Allendale Golf Course High Studdon, Allendale NE47 9DH ⌂ allendale-golf.com ★ SQM unknown/Milky Way class ♀ OS Explorer Map OL43. A golf course in the north of the North Pennines AONB, on a west-facing hillside with excellent views over the East Allen Valley. Events organised throughout the year as part of the North Pennines AONB Partnership programme. Free open access to the car park but no access to facilities except during events. Access to the fairway is not permitted. Car park is hardstanding but on a slight slope. No dogs.

Alwinton Car Park Alwinton, Morpeth NE65 7BQ ⌂ northumberlandnationalpark.org.uk/places-to-visit/coquetdale/alwinton ★ SQM 21.50/Milky Way class ♀ OS Explorer Map OL16. A pretty village situated where the River Alwin joins the River Coquet. Events hosted throughout the year at the nearby Rose & Thistle Inn. Site accessible at all times. Free parking and accessible toilets open at all times. Dogs on leads welcome.

Battlesteads Observatory Hexham Rd, Wark NE48 3LS ⌖ battlesteads.com/observatory ★ SQM 21.13/Milky Way class ♀ OS Explorer Map OL43. A public astronomical observatory on the edge of Kielder Water. Events held throughout the year, including astronomy for beginners, cosmology, astrophotography and stargazing. Site is open and free. Observatory is open every night. Fully accessible. No dogs.

Cawfields Quarry Car Park Pennine Way, Haltwhistle NE49 9PJ ⌖ northumberlandnationalpark.org.uk/places-to-visit/hadrians-wall/cawfields ★ SQM 21.16/Milky Way class ♀ OS Explorer Map OL43. Viewing point where Hadrian's Wall hangs on the edge of the sheer crags of the Whin Sill. Car park is level with good access to lakeside. Please take care around deep water. CCTV is on site for vehicle security. Car park open 24 hours with parking charges during the day. Star- and solar-gazing events hosted with Northumberland National Park and the local astronomy group. Dogs on leads welcome.

Elf Kirk Viewpoint Whickhope, Hexham NE48 1AA ⌖ visitkielder.com/great-outdoors/elf-kirk-viewpoint ★ SQM 21.09/Milky Way class ♀ OS Explorer Map OL42. One of the most iconic viewpoints in Kielder with stunning views across the park. Free open site with small car park which is wheelchair accessible. Security patrols visit the car park throughout the night. Dogs welcome.

Elsdon Village Hall and Village Green B6341, Elsdon NE19 1AA ⌖ northumberlandnationalpark.org.uk ★ SQM 21.27/Milky Way class ♀ OS Explorer Map OL42. An ancient village with a village green and medieval church. Indoor astronomical activities will be hosted at the village hall, by arrangement. The village green is accessible day and night. Wheelchair accessible. Dogs on leads welcome outside.

Falstone Village Hall and The Stell Falstone NE48 1AA ⌖ falstone.org/village-hall ★ SQM 21.45/Milky Way class ♀ OS Explorer Map OL42. Village hall just to the east of Kielder Water with excellent views of the night sky. Public stargazing events hosted throughout the year. Free open access. Most of the site within the vicinity of the village hall is wheelchair accessible. No dogs.

Hawkhope Car Park Falstone, Kielder NE48 1BB ⌖ visitkielder.com ★ SQM 21.45/Milky Way class ♀ OS Explorer Map OL42. Car park with excellent views located at the gateway to Kielder Water and Forest Park, on the banks of Kielder Water. Free parking between dusk and dawn for stargazing. Wheelchair accessible. Dogs on leads welcome outside.

Ingram Village Hall Ingram, Alnwick NE66 4LU ⌖ northumberlandnationalpark.org.uk ★ SQM 21.49/Milky Way class ♀ OS Explorer Maps 332 & OL16. A village in the beautiful and remote Breamish Valley of the Cheviot Hills. Events hosted by the village hall throughout the year across various local sites. Free open access. Free parking and toilets nearby. Dogs on leads welcome outside.

Kielder Castle Kielder Castle, Kielder NE48 1ER ⌖ visitkielder.com/visit/kielder-castle-visitor-centre ★ SQM 22.02/Milky Way class ♀ OS Explorer Map OL42. A former hunting lodge turned visitor centre in the heart of Kielder Forest. Events hosted throughout the year. Free parking between dusk and dawn. Disabled, level parking available in the grounds. Dogs on leads welcome outside.

Kielder Observatory Black Fell, Kielder NE48 1EJ ⌖ kielderobservatory.org ★ SQM unknown/Milky Way class ♀ OS Explorer Map OL42. The darkest site in Europe that has an observatory, with four telescopes, a classroom for events and viewing deck for free public observing.

Full calendar of events hosted throughout the year. Free open access if events are on, otherwise a 45-minute walk from the nearest car park. Alternatively, a key is available from Kielder Village to enable drive up. No dogs.

Kirknewton Village Hall B6351, Kirknewton NE71 6XF ⟁ kirknewton-northumberland.com/village-hall ★ SQM 21.13/Milky Way class ♥ OS Explorer Maps 339 & OL16. A village on the most northerly edge of Northumberland National Park, within the valley of Glendale. Star- and solar-gazing events hosted throughout the year. Car park and toilets open at all times. Ground is level and wheelchair accessible. Dogs on leads welcome outside.

Stonehaugh Stargazing Pavilion and Community Hall Unnamed road, Stonehaugh NE48 3DZ ⟁ www.stonehaugh.com ★ SQM 21.03/Milky Way class ♥ OS Explorer Map OL43. A purpose-built venue for stargazers in the heart of a peaceful forestry village. Events are hosted throughout the year. Pavilion is accessible 24 hours a day, although the surrounding terrain is on a slight incline. No dogs.

Tarset Village Hall Lanehead, Hexham NE48 1NT ⟁ tarset.co.uk/community/villagehall.cfm ★ SQM 21.54/Milky Way class ♥ OS Explorer Map OL42. A community space in the pretty hamlet of Lanehead. Public star- and solar-gazing events are hosted throughout the year. Free open access. Village hall and car park are both level and wheelchair accessible. No dogs.

Tower Knowe Visitor Centre Tower Knowe, Kielder NE48 1BX ⟁ visitkielder.com/visit/tower-knowe-visitor-centre ★ SQM 21.45/Milky Way class ♥ OS Explorer Map OL42. A visitor centre located at the gateway to Kielder Water. Events hosted throughout the year, including stargazing, utilising all areas of the site for dark sky observations. Indoor space is also available. Free parking between dusk and dawn for stargazing. Wheelchair accessible. Dogs on leads welcome outside.

Walltown Country Park Car Park Pennine Way, Brampton CA8 7HF ⟁ northumberlandnationalpark.org.uk/places-to-visit/hadrians-wall/walltown ★ SQM 21.13/Milky Way class ♥ OS Explorer Map OL43. An old quarry and wildlife haven off the A69 northeast of Greenhead, on the line of Hadrian's Wall. Star- and solar-gazing events hosted throughout the year. Uneven terrain away from the paths. Free car park accessible 24 hours. Wheelchair accessible. Dogs on leads welcome.

SCOTLAND

MIDLOTHIAN

Newbattle Abbey College Newbattle Rd, Dalkeith EH22 3LL ⟁ newbattleabbeycollege.ac.uk ★ SQM unknown/Orion class ♥ OS Explorer Maps 345 & 350. Adult learning college within a historic heritage site outside Edinburgh. The college's good distance from the city centre means it escapes some of the brighter sources of light pollution, as well as being away from tall buildings which can obstruct views. Wheelchair accessible. No dogs.

FIFE

Dunfermline Public Park St Margaret's Drive, Dunfermline KY12 7HT ⟁ visitdunfermline.com ★ SQM unknown/Orion class ♥ OS Explorer Map 367. A pleasant park in the centre of Dunfermline with low-level lighting. Free open access. The site is on a hillside, although diagonal paths are available to reduce the incline. The park has tarmac paths throughout with best disabled access via the Carnegie Hall car park. Dogs welcome.

ARGYLL AND BUTE

Balevullin Car Park Balevullin, Isle of Tiree PA77 6XD ⟳ isleoftiree.com ★ SQM unknown/ Milky Way class ♀ OS Explorer Map 372. A stunning and unique location on the Isle of Tiree, looking out over a beautiful bay and beach. Free open access car park, but no overnight parking permitted. Generally accessible but off-road wheelchairs are available on the island for muddy seasons. Dogs on leads welcome.

ABERDEENSHIRE

Glen Tanar Aboyne AB34 5EU ⟳ glentanar. co.uk ★ SQM 21.7/Milky Way class ♀ OS Explorer Maps OL54 & OL59. Just over 10,000ha (25,000 acres) of Caledonian pine forest, heather-clad hills and farmland, situated in Royal Deeside. Events and group visits hosted on site. Visitor centre, toilets and car park accessible. Parking charges apply. Dogs on leads welcome.

MORAY

The Acorn Centre Inverharroch, Lower Cabrach AB54 4EU ⟳ cabrachtrust.org ★ SQM unknown/Milky Way class ♀ OS Explorer Map OL62. An old school building in one of the most remote areas of Scotland, set against wild mountainous terrain and unspoilt views. Potential to spot the aurora in this area. Events and gatherings offered throughout the year, and the building can be leased for private stargazing. Free open access and wheelchair accessible site. Dogs on leads welcome outside.

The Carrachs Chapeltown, Ballindalloch AB37 9JS ⟳ cairngormsdarkskypark.org ★ SQM 21.7/ Milky Way class ♀ OS Explorer Maps OL58 & OL62. A rural car park in the Braes of Glenlivet on the Glenlivet Estate in the Cairngorms National Park. Chances of aurora sightings in this area. Stargazing events hosted by the Tomintoul & Glenlivet Dark

Skies Project and the Glenlivet Estate ranger service. Site is wheelchair accessible with a small parking area. Dogs on leads welcome.

Glenlivet Blairfindy Car Park B9136, Ballindalloch AB37 9DJ ⟳ cairngormsdarkskypark.org ★ SQM 21.7/Milky Way class ♀ OS Explorer Map OL61. A rural site on the Glenlivet Estate in the Cairngorms National Park. Aurora sightings possible in this area. Events hosted by the Tomintoul & Glenlivet Dark Skies Project and the Glenlivet Estate ranger service. Wheelchair accessible site with a limited parking area. Dogs on leads welcome.

Tomintoul Field of Hope Main St, Tomintoul AB37 9EX ⟳ cairngormsdarkskypark.org ★ SQM 21.7/Milky Way class ♀ OS Explorer Maps OL58 & OL61. A car park just outside Tomintoul on the Glenlivet Estate in the Cairngorms National Park. Potential to spot the aurora in this area. Events hosted by the Tomintoul & Glenlivet Dark Skies Project and the Glenlivet Estate ranger service. Accessible site with a small parking area. Dogs on leads welcome.

HIGHLAND

Abriachan Community Forest Great Glen Way, Inverness IV3 8LB ⟳ abriachan.org. uk ★ SQM unknown/Milky Way class ♀ OS Explorer Map 416. An area of forest and open hill ground around 10km (6 miles) north of the village of Drumnadrochit, set high above the western shore of Loch Ness. Good views due to elevated position and distance from urban light pollution. Occasional events hosted by Abriachan Community Trust and Highland Astronomy Tours. Free open access but visitors should monitor the weather in case of high wind or snow. Wheelchair accessible. Dogs welcome.

Camas na Sgianadin Broadford, Isle of Skye IV49 9AL ⟳ isleofskye.com ★ SQM unknown/

Milky Way class ♥ OS Explorer Map 412. A coastal car park just off the main road between Dunan and Broadford, with trees providing cover from the lights of passing cars. The site and forest track are sloping but wheelchair accessible. Free open access. Dogs on leads welcome.

Castlehill Heritage Centre Harbour Rd, Castletown KW14 8TG ⊘ castletownheritage. co.uk ★ SQM 22/Milky Way class ♥ OS Explorer Map 451. Heritage centre with large car park in the historic village of Castletown. Regular events and observing sessions hosted by Caithness Astronomy Group. Free open access to car park but the heritage centre and courtyard are only open during events. Wheelchair accessible. No dogs.

Clan Donald Centre Armadale Castle, Isle of Skye IV45 8RS ⊘ armadalecastle.com ★ SQM unknown/Milky Way class ♥ OS Explorer Map 412. The front lawn, back lawn and steadings of the Clan Donald Centre in the grounds of the romantic ruins of Armadale Castle. The rest of the estate is only accessible during daylight opening hours. Flat gravel path and lawn area is wheelchair accessible. No dogs.

Corran Point A861, Fort William PH33 7AA ⊘ westhighlandpeninsulas.com ★ SQM 21.32/ Milky Way class ♥ OS Explorer Maps 384 & 391. A fenced-off area between the seashore and the 19th-century Corran Lighthouse. Good views in all directions with some light pollution to the north. Be aware of changing tides. Free open access. Wheelchair accessible. Dogs welcome.

Glencanisp Estate Lochinver, Sutherland IV27 4LW ⊘ visitscotland.com ★ SQM unknown/Milky Way class ♥ OS Explorer Map 442. The wildlife-rich grounds of Glencanisp Lodge, by the side of Loch Druim Suardalain. Situated far from artificial light sources. Occasional events. Free open access. Wheelchair accessible. Dogs on leads welcome.

Glen Nevis Visitor Centre Glen Nevis, Fort William PH33 6PF ⊘ ben-nevis.com/visitor-center/visitor-center.php ★ SQM unknown/Milky Way class ♥ OS Explorer Map 399. Visitor centre near Ben Nevis mountain with a shop, toilets and useful information. Free open access all year round outside the centre. Wheelchair accessible. Dogs on leads welcome outside.

Kinloch Forest A851, Isle of Skye IV43 8RA ⊘ forestryandland.gov.scot/visit/kinloch ★ SQM unknown/Milky Way class ♥ OS Explorer Map 412. A restored native woodland rich in wildlife and with dramatic views over the Sound of Sleat towards the Knoydart Mountains. Free open access and a firm surface for wheelchair users. Dogs welcome.

Knockbreck Primary School Car Park Dunvegan, Isle of Skye IV55 8GP ⊘ visit-waternish.co.uk ★ SQM unknown/Milky Way class ♥ OS Explorer Map 407. A car park opposite the school with 360-degree views. School has security lighting on until 19.00. Free open access. Wheelchair accessible. Dogs on leads welcome.

Kylerhea Unnamed road, Isle of Skye IV42 8NH ⊘ forestryandland.gov.scot/visit/kylerhea ★ SQM unknown/Milky Way class ♥ OS Explorer Map 413. A peaceful spot on the Sound of Sleat, great for watching otters and other marine mammals. A flat area with a slope. Free open access all year round. Dogs on leads welcome.

Leitir Easaidh All Abilities Car Park A837, Lairg IV27 4HB ⊘ walkhighlands.co.uk/ ullapool/leitir-easaidh.shtml ★ SQM unknown/ Milky Way class ♥ OS Explorer Map 442. The car park for the Assynt All Abilities path, situated by the stunning waters of Loch Assynt. Situated far from artificial light sources. Free open access. Car park and walking path are fully wheelchair accessible. Dogs welcome.

Resipole Farm Holiday Park Loch Sunart, Acharacle PH36 4HX ⌂ resipole.co.uk ★ SQM 21.34/Milky Way class ♀ OS Explorer Map 390. A pleasant holiday park on the shores of Loch Sunart in the ancient crofting village of Acharacle. The designated viewing area gives a good line of sight in all directions, although there are hills to the north. Free open access. Hard-surface paths leading to the edge of a grassy viewing area. Dogs on leads welcome.

RSPB Forsinard Flows Flows Field Centre, Forsinard KW13 6YT ⌂ rspb.org.uk/reserves-and-events/reserves-a-z/forsinard-flows ★ SQM 21.3/ Milky Way class ♀ OS Explorer Map 449. Lookout tower on a nature reserve off the A897, north of Helmsdale, offering unique views of the night sky over the peatlands. Potential site for viewing the aurora. Annual Dark Skies event hosted with Caithness Astronomy Group. Free open access. Wheelchair-accessible site except the top of the tower. Dogs on leads welcome.

Sallachan Beach Sallachan Loop Rd, Fort William PH33 7AB ⌂ westhighlandpeninsulas. com ★ SQM 21.5/Milky Way class ♀ OS Explorer Maps 384 & 391. A remote, grassy area next to the River Gour on the shores of Loch Linnhe, with gated access to Sallachan Beach. Good viewing opportunities in all directions. Free open access. Wheelchair accessible. Dogs welcome.

Stein Jetty Car Park Stein, Isle of Skye IV55 8GA ⌂ visit-waternish.co.uk ★ SQM unknown/ Milky Way class ♀ OS Explorer Map 407. A coastal car park with access to the jetty, shoreline and a field to the south. Fairly good views with some interference from surrounding hills. Visitors are reminded that the jetty has no lighting or coastguards so please be aware of slippery surfaces and open water. Wheelchair accessible. Dogs welcome.

Trumpan Car Park Trumpan Loop Rd, Isle of Skye IV55 8GW ⌂ visit-waternish.co.uk ★ SQM unknown/Milky Way class ♀ OS Explorer Map 407. A car park with 360-degree views and no artificial lighting with a seated viewing area on site. Good views of the northern skies. Free open access. Wheelchair accessible. Dogs on leads welcome.

Walking & Wildlife Adventures Office Grounds B8021, Gairloch IV21 2EA ⌂ walkandwild.com ★ SQM unknown/Milky Way class ♀ OS Explorer Map 434. Gardens of the house and office overlooking the Isle of Skye across the water. Good views to the west and

↑ Forsinard Flows is a great site for spotting both deer and the northern lights (SuperStock)

south with no streetlighting for at least 16km (10 miles) in any direction. Track and gardens are level with good wheelchair access. Parking closer to site is available on request. Please call ahead to notify of group visits of 6 or more people. No dogs.

WALES

ANGLESEY

Glan Morfa Lodge and Wildlife Experience B4421, Gaerwen LL60 6LY ⌖ holidaycottages-anglesey.com ★ SQM unknown/Milky Way class ♀ OS Explorer Map 263. A visitor centre and patio area at Glan Morfa Lodge in the south of Anglesey, in an Area of Outstanding Natural Beauty. Free open access up to midnight. Groups of six or more should contact in advance. Wheelchair accessible. Dogs on leads welcome.

POWYS

Brecon Beacons Visitor Centre Glan Tarrell, Libanus LD3 8ER ⌖ breconbeacons. org ★ SQM 21.4/Orion class ♀ OS Explorer Map OL12. Information centre with tearoom, gift shop and outdoor play area. Also known locally as the Mountain Centre. Events hosted throughout the year by Dark Sky Wales and the Cardiff Astronomical Society. Good views to the south and east from the lawn and clear, unobstructed views to the north and west behind the centre on the road next to the common land. Free open access. Wheelchair accessible. Dogs on leads welcome.

Crai Village A4067, Libanus LD3 8YP ⌖ breconbeacons.org ★ SQM 21.47/Milky Way class ♀ OS Explorer Map OL12. A picturesque village with unhindered views of all horizons and minimal light pollution. A local farmer has kindly provided access to his field next to the local church, which is signposted for visitors. Please close the gate on entry and exit. Wheelchair accessible but beware of mud. No dogs.

Pont ar Elan Elan Valley, Rhayader ⌖ elanvalley.org.uk ★ SQM 21.88/Milky Way class ♀ OS Explorer Map 200 (SN 902 715). Bridge over the River Elan just before the Craig Goch Reservoir. Free open access. Wheelchair accessible but visitors are warned the site can become icy in winter. Dogs welcome.

Star Inn Car Park Unnamed road, Dylife ⌖ starinndylife.co.uk ★ SQM 21.93/Milky Way class ♀ OS Explorer Map 215 (SN 863 940). Excellent dark sky site next to the aptly named Star Inn pub, which was sadly closed at the time of going to press. Free open access. Wheelchair accessible but visitors are warned the site can become icy in winter. Dogs on leads welcome.

CEREDIGION

Coed Y Bont Abbey Rd, Pontrhydfendigaid ⌖ naturalresources.wales/coedybont ★ SQM 21.85/Milky Way class ♀ OS Explorer Map 187 (SN 737 659). A community woodland on the edge of Pontrhydfendigaid village, made up of two adjoining woods, the native broadleaf Coed Dolgoed and the ancient woodland Coed Cnwch. Good views in most directions, although some trees obstruct views to the west. Free open access. Wheelchair accessible but the site can become icy in the winter months. Dogs welcome.

Dolgoch Hostel Dolgoch, Tregaron ⌖ elenydd-hostels.co.uk/en/our/dolgoch-hostel ★ SQM 20.8/Milky Way class ♀ OS Explorer Map 187 (SN 805 562). A pretty old stone farmhouse on the eastern border of Ceredigion, with good views of the night sky. Telescopes can be erected in the car park and at the front and rear of the

buildings. All observation areas have minimal light pollution. Free open access. Wheelchair accessible. No dogs.

Hafod Arch, near Devil's Bridge B4574, Aberystwyth ⌖ naturalresources.wales/thearch ★ SQM 21.92/Milky Way class ♀ OS Explorer Map 213 (SN 765 755). A car park and picnic area named after the old gateway arch to the Hafod Estate, which still stands on the side of the road by the Devil's Bridge. Part of the Hafod Estate, a wooded and landscaped area in the Ystwyth Valley. Free open access. Wheelchair accessible but the site can become icy in the winter months. Dogs welcome.

Llanerchaeron A482, Aberaeron ⌖ nationaltrust.org.uk/llanerchaeron ★ SQM unknown/Milky Way class ♀ OS Explorer Maps 198 & 199 (SN 480 602). An elegant Georgian villa set in the wooded Aeron Valley, including a farm, walled gardens and lake. Managed by the National Trust. Free parking from dusk until dawn. Open access. Wheelchair accessible. Dogs on leads are welcome in the woodland and parkland walks but not on the property.

Penbryn Sarnau, Cardigan SA44 6QL ⌖ nationaltrust.org.uk/penbryn ★ SQM unknown/Milky Way class ♀ OS Explorer Map 198. A beautifully secluded sandy cove hidden down leafy lanes and lined with flower-covered banks. Free parking from dusk until dawn. There is a steep climb down to the beach and back up to the car park. The walk along the woodland footpath has several steep steps and moderately rough terrain, and the beach is over 1.5km (1 mile) long, depending on the tide. Free open access. Wheelchair users can be dropped off directly at the beach. Dogs are welcome on the beach between October and April.

Ty'n Cornel Hostel Drovers Rd, Tregaron ⌖ elenydd-hostels.co.uk/en/our/tyn-cornel

★ SQM 20.9/Milky Way class ♀ OS Explorer Map 187 (SN 750 534). A former farmhouse in the stunning Cambrian Mountains, at the head of the Doethie Valley. Telescopes can be erected in the car park or patio area. Good views in all directions with minimal light pollution. Free open access to outside areas. Wheelchair accessible. No dogs.

PEMBROKESHIRE
Broadhaven South Car Park
Pembrokeshire Coast Path, Bosherston SA71 5DH ⌖ pembrokeshirecoast.wales ★ SQM unknown/Milky Way class ♀ OS Explorer Map OL36. A wide bay backed by sand dunes with lily ponds, boulders and caves to explore. The cliff top offers stunning 360-degree views of the sea and night sky above. Managed by the National Trust. Visitors are advised to be aware of cliff edges. Free open access. Cliff top is wheelchair accessible. Dogs welcome.

Garn Fawr National Trust Car Park Trefasser Cross, Goodwick SA64 0JJ ⌖ nationaltrust.org.uk/strumble-head-to-cardigan/trails/garn-fawr-viewpoint-walk ★ SQM 21.50/Milky Way class ♀ OS Explorer Map OL35. Viewpoint to the west of Fishguard on a high point of hard volcanic rock with good views of the sky and minimal light pollution. Excellent views to the south with some distant lights that have little impact. Free open access. Wheelchair accessible. Dogs on leads welcome.

Kete National Trust Car Park
St Ann's Head, Haverfordwest SA62 3RR ⌖ discoveryinthedark.wales/pembrokeshire ★ SQM 21.46/Milky Way class ♀ OS Explorer Map OL36. A large car park with good visibility in all directions, especially to the west and southeast overlooking the sea. Some flashes from the lighthouse but this does not cause a significant problem. Free open access. Wheelchair accessible. Dogs welcome.

← **Top:** The dramatic gateway arch at the entrance to Hafod Estate (Dafydd Wyn Morgan/Cambrian Mountains Initiative); **Bottom:** Conti's café at Llanerchaeron (Dafydd Wyn Morgan/Cambrian Mountains Initiative)

Martins Haven National Trust Car Park Pembrokeshire Coast Path, Haverfordwest SA62 3BJ ⌂ visitpembrokeshire.com/explore-pembrokeshire/beaches/martins-haven ★ SQM 21.65/Milky Way class ♥ OS Explorer Map OL36. A small pebble beach used as the embarkation point for the Skomer Island boats, known for good diving spots and seal watching. Free open access. Car park is wheelchair accessible but the rest of the site has some steep slopes and rough terrain. Dogs welcome but please be aware of cattle and ponies within the deer park nearby.

Newgale Sands Beach Welsh Rd, Haverfordwest SA62 6AS ⌂ visitpembrokeshire.com/explore-pembrokeshire/beaches/newgale ★ SQM 21.08/Milky Way class ♥ OS Explorer Maps OL35 & OL36. Over 3km (2 miles) of pebble-backed sand, popular with families, surfers and dog walkers. A clear, unobstructed view of most of the sky. The best location is on the beach just by the Pebbles car park but, for less able users, the car park also offers good views. Visitors are advised to take care around the shingle bank and to monitor the tides carefully. Free parking between dusk and dawn. Dogs welcome all year except the centre third of the beach, which is free of dogs between May and September.

Poppit Sands Beach Car Park B4546, St Dogmaels SA43 3LR ⌂ visitpembrokeshire.com/explore-pembrokeshire/beaches/poppit-sands ★ SQM 21.27/Milky Way class ♥ OS Explorer Maps OL35 & 198. A sandy beach backed by dunes at the mouth of the Teifi Estuary, with possible views of bottlenose dolphins, harbour porpoises and seals. Excellent views in all directions. Visitors should be aware of tide times and strong currents. Car park is free between dusk and dawn. Free open access. Wheelchair accessible with a viewing platform at the end of the boardwalk. Dogs welcome October to April.

↑ Newgale Sands is a popular beach with families and surfers (jennyt/Shutterstock)

Skrinkle Haven Car Park
Pembrokeshire Coast Path, Tenby SA72 6DY
⟨⟩ pembrokeshirecoast.wales ★ SQM 21.04/
Milky Way class ♀ OS Explorer Map OL36. A small
bay encircled by high cliffs, with a wide expanse
of soft, golden sand when the tide is low. Good
views of the southern and northern skies. The
beach itself is not wheelchair accessible as visitors
will need to make their way down some steep
steps, but the car park and picnic area at the top
of the pathway offers good views over the bay
and out to sea. Visitors are advised to be aware of
high, unlit cliff tops with unguarded edges. Free
open access. Dogs welcome.

Sychpant Picnic Site Cwm Gwaun,
Fishguard SA65 9UA ⟨⟩ pembrokeshirecoast.
wales ★ SQM 21.40/Milky Way class ♀ OS
Explorer Map OL35. A beautiful and rugged
moorland area with wooded slopes and
waterfalls, noted for its abundance of high

brown fritillary butterflies. Good views with
little light pollution in a valley location. Visitors
are advised to be aware of small ponds and
rivers throughout the area. Some views are
restricted at lower levels, but views to the
southwest are greatly improved by crossing the
footbridge over the stream. Free open access.
Car park and picnic area wheelchair accessible.
Dogs on leads welcome.

CARMARTHENSHIRE
Llanllwni Mountain Picnic Site Llanllwni,
Pencader ⟨⟩ discovercarmarthenshire.com
★ SQM 21.80/Milky Way class ♀ OS Explorer
Map 186 (SN 507 389). An area of common land
around 20km (12 miles) northeast of Carmarthen
town, with grazing ponies and birds of prey,
popular with walkers, cyclists and horse-riders.
There are 360-degree views of the night sky with
some light pollution on the horizon. Free open

access. Wheelchair users will need to remain on the paved area of the site. Visitors are advised the site can be icy in the winter months. Dogs welcome.

Llyn Brianne Car Park A483, Llandovery ✐ discovercarmarthenshire.com ★ SQM 22.12/Milky Way class ♀ OS Explorer Map 187 (SN 793 484). A manmade reservoir in the headwaters of the River Tywi. Excellent conditions with unobstructed panoramic views of the night sky. Free open access. Wheelchair accessible but the site can be icy in the winter, and the surfaces are a little uneven in places. Dogs welcome.

National Botanical Garden of Wales Middleton Hall, Llanarthne SA32 8HN ✐ botanicgarden.wales ★ SQM unknown/Milky Way class ♀ OS Explorer Maps 178 & 186. An inspiring attraction featuring themed gardens with over 8,000 plants from all over the globe, the world's largest single-span glasshouse, a tropical butterfly house, play areas, nature reserve, café and coffee shop, all set within a beautiful Regency landscape. Access only via regular events held on site, including observing sessions, talks and telescope advice clinics in the Great Glasshouse. Wheelchair accessible. No dogs except on 'Doggy Days' every Monday and Friday, when they are allowed on a lead in the garden.

Usk Reservoir Car Park Llywel, Brecon ✐ breconbeacons.org ★ SQM 21.90/Milky Way class ♀ OS Explorer Maps 187 & OL12 (SN 834 287). A beautiful and peaceful 113ha (280 acre) reservoir set among forest and moorland, popular for trout fishing. One of the darkest places in Brecon Beacons National Park, with flat areas for telescopes. Occasional events run by the local community, students from the University of South Wales and local astronomical societies. Free open access. Wheelchair accessible. Dogs welcome.

SWANSEA
Gerazim Chapel Heol y Mynydd, Cwmcerdinen SA5 7PX ✐ visitwales.com ★ SQM unknown/Milky Way class ♀ OS Explorer Maps 165 & 178. Around 20km (12 miles) north of Swansea is this hilltop chapel, built in 1811 with unobstructed views towards all horizons. The chapel has been recently auctioned and it remains unclear whether the building itself is open to the public, however, the surrounding area is public access and the chapel makes an interesting foreground subject for astrophotography. Visitors should be aware of the roads in winter as they are not gritted. Wheelchair accessible. Dogs on leads welcome.

NEATH PORT TALBOT
Glyncorrwg Ponds Ynyscorrwg Park, Port Talbot SA13 3EA ✐ www.afanforestpark.co.uk ★ SQM unknown/Milky Way class ♀ OS Explorer Map 166. Set within 3,600ha (9,000 acres) of the Afan Forest Park with walking and biking trails, trout fishing and canoeing. Unobstructed views of the night sky. Occasional events throughout the year. Free open access. Wheelchair accessible. Dogs welcome.

RHONDDA CYNON TAF
Barry Sidings Countryside Park Trehafod, Pontypridd CF37 2PP ✐ www.rctcbc.gov.uk ★ SQM unknown/Orion class ♀ OS Explorer Map 166. A country park surrounded by mountains, with bike hire, walking trails, adventure playground and green open spaces. Good southerly views but limited towards the western and eastern horizons. Free open access. Wheelchair accessible. Dogs welcome.

Bwlch Mountain Lay-by Bwlch-Y-Clawdd Rd, Treorchy CF42 6LL ✐ darkskywales.org ★ SQM unknown/Milky Way class ♀ OS Explorer

Map 166. A lay-by on top of Bwlch Mountain, southwest of Treorchy, with uninterrupted views to the south, east and west. The site is often frequented by local astronomy groups who are usually happy for guests to join them observing. Visitors are advised to be aware of large drops and close proximity of the mountain road. Free open access. Wheelchair accessible but the gravel surface can be slightly more difficult to negotiate. Dogs welcome.

Daerwynno Outdoor Centre St Gwynno Forest, Pontypridd CF37 3PH ⬧ daerwynno.org ★ SQM unknown/Milky Way class ♀ OS Explorer Map 166. An outdoor activities centre based in a stone-built farmhouse and surrounded by the St Gwynno Forest. Wide panoramas with mostly unobscured views. Free open access. Generally suitable for wheelchair users but access to the site is a 400m distance over uneven ground. No dogs.

Dare Valley Country Park Dare Rd, Aberdare CF44 7PT ⬧ darevalleycountrypark. co.uk ★ SQM unknown/Orion class ♀ OS Explorer Map 166. A public park comprising just over 200ha (500 acres) of woodland, pasture and moorland mountainside with a visitor centre, walking trails, café and campsite. A large parking area in which to observe the night sky with good, mostly unobstructed horizon views. Free open access all year round. Wheelchair accessible. Dogs welcome.

Garn Eiddel Car Park A4233, Treorchy CF43 4EA ⬧ darkskywales.org ★ SQM unknown/Milky Way class ♀ OS Explorer Map 166. A car park on top of Maerdy Mountain just southwest of Aberdare, with beautiful panoramic views. Slight light pollution to the south. The site is often frequented by local astronomy groups who are usually happy for guests to join them observing. Visitors are advised to be aware of large drops and close proximity of the mountain road. Free

open access. Wheelchair accessible but the gravel surface can be slightly more difficult to negotiate. Dogs welcome.

Hendre Mynydd Car Park A4061, Treorchy CF42 5RY ⬧ darkskywales.org ★ SQM unknown/Milky Way class ♀ OS Explorer Map 166. A car park on top of Rhigos Mountain, to the west of Aberdare, with uninterrupted views to the south, east and west. The site is often frequented by local astronomy groups who are usually happy for guests to join them observing. Visitors are advised to be aware of large drops and close proximity of the mountain road. Free open access. Wheelchair accessible but the gravel surface can be slightly more difficult to negotiate. Dogs welcome.

Red Lion Pub Penderyn Church Rd, Aberdare CF44 9JR ⬧ redlionpenderyn.com ★ SQM unknown/Milky Way class ♀ OS Explorer Map OL12. A traditional 12th-century drover's inn perched high on a hill, with beautiful views over the village of Penderyn and the Brecon Beacons National Park. Spectacular views of the night sky, while the large pub car park provides an open area for viewing. Free open access. Wheelchair accessible but the gravel surface can be slightly more difficult to negotiate. Dogs on leads welcome.

CAERPHILLY

Parc Penallta Penallta Rd, Ystrad Mynach CF82 7GN ⬧ greenspacescaerphilly.co.uk/parc-penallta ★ SQM unknown/Milky Way class ♀ OS Explorer Map 166. Some 15km (9 miles) south of Merthyr Tydfil, off the A470, the site of one of the largest figurative earth sculptures in the country, *Sultan the Pit Pony*, which is carved from a former coal tip. For the best viewpoint in the park, head to the High Point Observatory for 360-degree panoramic views. Free open access. Wheelchair accessible. Dogs welcome.

Rose and Crown Public House

Eglwysilan Rd, Pontypridd CF83 4JG ⌂ visitcaerphilly.com/the-rose-and-crown ★ SQM unknown/Orion class ♀ OS Explorer Map 166. A country pub overlooking the Taff and Aber valleys with locally sourced food and a beer garden. In good weather, views extend to the Severn Estuary. Some light pollution from the pub. Free open access to outside areas. Wheelchair accessible. No dogs.

MERTHYR TYDFIL

Plas Dolygaer Pontsticill, Merthyr Tydfil CF48 2UR ⌂ darkskywales.org ★ SQM 21.46/Milky Way class ♀ OS Explorer Map OL12. A group accommodation centre on the southern edge of Brecon Beacons National Park. Not directly overlooked by any streetlighting. Occasional events held throughout the year. Free open access to outside areas. Centre, paths and ramps are all wheelchair accessible. No dogs.

ISLE OF MAN

Axnfell Plantation Ballacollister Rd, Laxey IM4 7JU ⌂ manxnationalheritage.im ★ SQM unknown/Milky Way class ♀ OS Landranger Map 95. A plantation forest of Japanese larch and sitka spruce near Laxey on the steep north-facing slopes of Glen Roy. Potential site for views of the aurora. Occasional events hosted by the Isle of Man Astronomical Society. Free open access. Wheelchair accessible. Dogs welcome.

Ballanette Nature Reserve Ballannette Park, Baldrine IM4 6AJ ⌂ visitisleofman. com ★ SQM unknown/Milky Way class ♀ OS Landranger Map 95. Peaceful nature reserve in Baldrine with stunning northerly views. Uninterrupted horizon to the north and east. Potential site for views of the aurora. Occasional events hosted by the landowner, AstroManx or the Isle of Man Astronomical Society. Free open access. Wheelchair accessible. Dogs on leads welcome.

Ballaugh Beach Car Park Coast Rd, Ballaugh IM7 2EA ⌂ visitisleofman.com ★ SQM unknown/Milky Way class ♀ OS Landranger Map 95. A sand and shale beach on the exposed northwest of the island, popular with wind- and kitesurfers. Potential site for views of the aurora. Occasional events hosted by AstroManx or the Isle of Man Astronomical Society. Free open access. Wheelchair accessible. Dogs welcome.

Ballure Reservoir Car Park A18, Ramsey IM7 1AB ⌂ visitisleofman.com ★ SQM unknown/ Milky Way class ♀ OS Landranger Map 95. A small reservoir just south of Ramsey, stocked with rainbow trout and popular with anglers. Potential site for views of the aurora. Occasional events hosted by AstroManx or the Isle of Man Astronomical Society. Free open access. Wheelchair accessible. Dogs welcome.

Clypse Kerrowdhoo Reservoir Car Park Clypse Moar Rd, Hilberry IM4 5BG ⌂ visitisleofman.com ★ SQM unknown/Milky Way class ♀ OS Landranger Map 95. A scenic reservoir on the eastern side of the island between Douglas and Laxey, surrounded by countryside with good views to the north, east and south of the island. Occasional events hosted by AstroManx or the Isle of Man Astronomical Society. Free open access. Wheelchair accessible. Dogs welcome.

Conrhenny Car Park Begoade Rd, Onchan IM4 6AX ⌂ visitisleofman.com ★ SQM unknown/ Milky Way class ♀ OS Landranger Map 95. A plantation with unspoilt panoramic views over Douglas Bay. Occasional events hosted by AstroManx or the Isle of Man Astronomical Society. Free open access. Wheelchair accessible. Dogs welcome.

Cregneash Village Howe Rd, Cregneash IM9 5PX ⌁ visitisleofman.com ★ SQM unknown/ Milky Way class ♀ OS Landranger Map 95. A picnic area in front of the Creg y Shee café on the southern tip of the island. Good views in all directions. Occasional events hosted by the site owner, AstroManx or the Isle of Man Astronomical Society. Free open access. Wheelchair accessible. Dogs on leads welcome.

Footpath at the Rear of Peel Castle West Quay, Peel IM5 1TB ⌁ visitisleofman.com ★ SQM unknown/Milky Way class ♀ OS Landranger Map 95. A footpath on the seaward side of an 11th-century castle originally built by Vikings. Occasional events hosted by the landowner, AstroManx or the Isle of Man Astronomical Society. Free open access. Footpath has steps but the first part is flat, approximately 45m from the best viewing spot. Dogs welcome.

Fort Island Fort Island Rd, Derbyhaven IM8 1AA ⌁ manxnationalheritage.im ★ SQM unknown/Milky Way class ♀ OS Landranger Map 95. An island in Malew parish noted for its attractive ruins, also known as St Michael's Isle. Occasional events run by the Isle of Man Astronomical Society. Clear horizon from the northeast to the southwest. Free open access. Wheelchair accessible. Dogs on leads welcome.

Glen Mooar Beach Car Park A4, Ballig IM6 1HP ⌁ visitisleofman.com ★ SQM unknown/ Milky Way class ♀ OS Landranger Map 95. A large car park with a stream to the south and the sea to the left. Good views of the whole sky with horizon views from the west to north. Occasional events hosted by AstroManx or the Isle of Man Astronomical Society. Free open access. Wheelchair accessible. Dogs welcome.

Glen Wyllin Beach Car Park Bayr Ny Balleira, Kirk Michael IM6 1EE ⌁ visitisleofman. com ★ SQM unknown/Milky Way class ♀ OS Landranger Map 95. A long strip of sand, shingle and rock coastline around 10km (6 miles) north

↑ Peel Castle was originally built by the Vikings (SuperStock)

of Peel, stretching for kilometres to the north and south from the beach car park. Uninterrupted horizon views from the northeast to southwest. Occasional events hosted by AstroManx or the Isle of Man Astronomical Society. Free open access. Wheelchair accessible. Dogs welcome.

Mount Murray Golf Club Mount Murray Rd, Santon IM4 2HT ⌂ comishotelandgolfresort. com ★ SQM unknown/Milky Way class ♥ OS Landranger Map 95. Golf club car park and area adjacent to the 1st tee, situated around 5km (3 miles) southwest of Douglas. Occasional events hosted by the golf club, AstroManx or the Isle of Man Astronomical Society. Driving range lights turned off at 21.00. Free open access. Wheelchair accessible. No dogs.

Niarbyl Café Car Park Niarbyl Rd, Bayr Niarbyl IM5 3BR ⌂ manxnationalheritage. im ★ SQM unknown/Milky Way class ♥ OS Landranger Map 95. A large car park on the southwest coast of the island, south of Peel, with minimal light pollution and an uninterrupted horizon view from south to north. Occasional events hosted by the Isle of Man Astronomical Society. Free open access. Wheelchair accessible. No dogs.

Northern End of Mooragh Park Park Rd, Ramsey IM8 3AP ⌂ visitisleofman. com ★ SQM unknown/Milky Way class ♥ OS Landranger Map 95. Popular park and boating lake with tennis courts and children's play area. Some streetlighting to the south in Ramsey. Occasional events hosted by AstroManx or the Isle of Man Astronomical Society. Free open access. Wheelchair accessible. No dogs.

Onchan Pleasure Park Onchan Park, Onchan IM3 1HU ⌂ visitisleofman.com ★ SQM unknown/Milky Way class ♥ OS Landranger Map 95. A popular leisure attraction with a boating lake, crazy golf and large play park. Occasional

events hosted by AstroManx or the Isle of Man Astronomical Society. Excellent views over the sea to the south and east. Free open access. Wheelchair accessible. No dogs.

Port Lewaigue Car Park/Port e Vullen Car Park Maughold Rd, Port e Vullen IM7 1AW ⌂ visitisleofman.com ★ SQM unknown/Milky Way class ♥ OS Landranger Map 95. A small settlement on the rugged east coast of the island. Uninterrupted views over the northern horizon as well as the west and east. Occasional events hosted by the landowner, AstroManx or the Isle of Man Astronomical Society. Free open access. Wheelchair accessible. Dogs welcome.

Port Soderick Brooghs, Little Ness Car Park Port Soderick Glen Rad, Douglas IM1 5PT ⌂ manxnationalheritage.im ★ SQM unknown/Milky Way class ♥ OS Landranger Map 95. A flat coastal site behind Port Soderick just to the southwest of Douglas, which is known for its abandoned pleasure grounds and beach. Uninterrupted views from the northeast to southwest. Occasional events hosted by the Isle of Man Astronomical Society. Visitors are advised to be aware of the unfenced cliff edge approximately 20m away. Free open access. Wheelchair users can access site by car only. Dogs welcome.

Port Soderick Upper Car Park Marine Drive, Douglas IM1 5PT ⌂ visitisleofman. com ★ SQM unknown/Milky Way class ♥ OS Landranger Map 95. A small hamlet to the south of Douglas, known for its abandoned pleasure grounds and beach. Good views of the whole sky, especially from the northwest to south. Occasional events hosted by AstroManx or the Isle of Man Astronomical Society. Free open access. Wheelchair accessible. Dogs welcome.

Poulsom Park, Castletown Victoria Rd, Castletown IM9 1EN ⌂ visitisleofman. com ★ SQM unknown/Milky Way class ♥ OS

Landranger Map 95. A play park in the heart of Castletown, nestled between the train station and the Silverburn River. Occasional events hosted by the site owner, AstroManx or the Isle of Man Astronomical Society. Dark skies to the west and north. Some streetlighting to the south and east but generally obscured by trees. Free open access. Wheelchair accessible. Dogs on leads welcome.

Rushen Abbey Car Park Mill Rd, Ballasalla IM9 3DB ⌂ visitisleofman.com ★ SQM unknown/Milky Way class ♀ OS Landranger Map 95. A former abbey located around 3km (2 miles) from Castle Rushen, an important political site on the island in medieval times. Some streetlighting obscured by trees but otherwise good views in all directions. Occasional events hosted by AstroManx or the Isle of Man Astronomical Society. Free open access. Wheelchair accessible. Dogs on leads welcome.

The Sloc Car Park A36, Colby IM9 4BX ⌂ visitisleofman.com ★ SQM unknown/Milky Way class ♀ OS Landranger Map 95. A popular site among local astronomers, in the south of the island, with panoramic views over the south and northwest and very little light pollution. Occasional events hosted by AstroManx or the Isle of Man Astronomical Society. Free open access. Wheelchair accessible. Dogs on leads welcome.

Smeale Coastal Area A10, Ramsey IM7 3EH ⌂ manxnationalheritage.im ★ SQM unknown/Milky Way class ♀ OS Landranger Map 95. Situated in the north of the island, one of the island's darkest sites with almost zero light pollution. Uninterrupted horizon views from southwest to northeast. Potential site for views of the aurora. Occasional events hosted by the Isle of Man Astronomical Society. Free open access. Wheelchair users can access the site by car. Dogs welcome.

Sound Restaurant Car Park Sound Rd, Cregneash IM9 5PZ ⌂ thesound.im ★ SQM unknown/Milky Way class ♀ OS Landranger Map 95. A car park at the southern tip of the island with uninterrupted views to the south, northeast and northwest. Occasional events hosted by the Isle of Man Astronomical Society. Free open access. Wheelchair accessible. Visitors are warned of the cliff edge approximately 50m away. Dogs on leads welcome.

Sulby Reservoir Car Park A14, Sulby IM7 2BE ⌂ manxnationalheritage.im ★ SQM unknown/Milky Way class ♀ OS Landranger Map 95. The island's largest and deepest reservoir, situated in the shadow of its highest peak, Snaefell. Extremely low light pollution levels and excellent visibility all round. Occasional events hosted by the Isle of Man Astronomical Society. Free open access. Wheelchair users can access the site by car. Dogs welcome.

Tynwald Mills Overflow Car Park Poortown Rd, Ballig IM4 3AD ⌂ tynwaldmills. com ★ SQM unknown/Milky Way class ♀ OS Landranger Map 95. Dark car park around 3km (2 miles) southeast of Peel, near a shopping centre surrounded by fences and trees. Good sky views. Occasional events hosted by the landowner, AstroManx or the Isle of Man Astronomical Society. Free open access. Wheelchair accessible. No dogs.

West Baldwin Reservoir Car Park West Baldwin Rd, Braddan IM4 5EU ⌂ visitisleofman. com ★ SQM unknown/Milky Way class ♀ OS Landranger Map 95. A reservoir on the site of an old village, the remains of which can be seen when the water is low. Good views to the south, east and west. Occasional events hosted by AstroManx or the Isle of Man Astronomical Society. Free open access. Wheelchair accessible. Dogs welcome.

NORTHERN IRELAND

COUNTY ANTRIM

Altarichard Forest Car Park

Altarichard Rd, Magherahoney BT53 8YJ
⌖ discovernorthernireland.com ★ SQM
unknown/Milky Way class ♀ OSNI Discoverer Map
5. Magnificent panoramic views of Rathlin Island
and beyond. Car park and picnic area on site. Free
open access. Car park is wheelchair accessible.
No dogs.

Carrick-a-Rede Whitepark Rd, Ballintoy BT54

6LS ⌖ nationaltrust.org.uk/carrick-a-rede ★ SQM
unknown/Milky Way class ♀ OSNI Discoverer Map
5. A rope bridge first erected by salmon fishermen
in 1755, connecting the cliffs across the Atlantic
Ocean and now managed by the National Trust.
Occasional events hosted on site. Free open
access. Wheelchair accessible. Dogs on leads
welcome, but not to cross the bridge.

Divis and the Black Mountain Car

Park Divis Rd, Belfast BT17 0NG ⌖ nationaltrust.
org.uk/divis-and-the-black-mountain ★ SQM
unknown/Milky Way class ♀ OSNI Discover Map
15. A mountain in the heart of the Belfast Hills
with a rich archaeological landscape and a host of
wildlife. Managed by the National Trust. Free open
access. Wheelchair accessible. Dogs welcome.

Killylane Reservoir Shanes

Hill Rd, Kilwaughter BT42 4RE
⌖ discovernorthernireland.com ★ SQM
unknown/Milky Way class ♀ OSNI Discoverer
Map 9. A reservoir popular with anglers and local
astronomy groups, with excellent views of the
night sky. Free open access. This location is not
wheelchair accessible but there is a tarmac car
park close to the water. No dogs.

Murlough Bay Car Park Murlough Rd,

Ballycastle BT54 6RG ⌖ nationaltrust.org.uk/
murlough-national-nature-reserve ★ SQM
unknown/Milky Way class ♀ OSNI Discoverer
Map 5. A fragile 6,000-year-old sand dune system
with woodland and dune heath, home to over
720 species of butterflies and moths. Free open
access. Car park is wheelchair accessible. Dogs on
leads welcome.

↑ You'll find wonderful scenery and great sky views in spades at Spelga Reservoir (Shailpik Biswas/Shutterstock)

COUNTY LONDONDERRY

Benone Strand Benone Av, Limavady BT49 0LQ ♂ discovernorthernireland.com ★ SQM unknown/Milky Way class ♀ OSNI Discoverer Map 4. Around 12km (7 miles) of golden sand and a magnificent mountain backdrop with high cliffs and stunning views across to Donegal. The nearby Mussenden Temple makes an interesting foreground subject for astrophotography. Free open access. Specialist beach equipment available to book for visitors with limited mobility. Dogs welcome October to May.

COUNTY ARMAGH

Oxford Island National Nature Reserve Oxford Island, Craigavon BT66 6NJ ♂ oxfordisland. com ★ SQM unknown/Milky Way class ♀ OSNI Discoverer Map 20. Located on the southeastern shores of Lough Neagh, a wildlife haven with reed beds and ponds, forests and wildflower meadows. Occasional events held throughout the year. Free open access to pedestrians at all times. Wheelchair accessible. No dogs.

COUNTY DOWN

Spelga Reservoir South Car Park Kilkeel Rd, Newry BT34 5XL ♂ discovernorthernireland. com ★ SQM unknown/Milky Way class ♀ OSNI Discoverer Map 21. A remote car park around 10km (6 miles) east of Newry, near the south shore of Spelga Reservoir, with beautiful scenery and good sky views. Free open access. Car park is wheelchair accessible. No dogs.

FEEDBACK REQUEST AND UPDATES WEBSITE

At Bradt Guides we're aware that guidebooks start to go out of date on the day they're published – and that you, our readers, are out there in the field doing research of your own. You'll find out before us when a fine new family-run hotel opens or a favourite restaurant changes hands and goes downhill. So why not write and tell us about your experiences? Contact us on ☎ 01753 893444 or **e** info@bradtguides.com. We will forward emails to the author who may post updates on the Bradt website at ♂ bradtguides.com/updates. Alternatively, you can add a review of the book to ♂ bradtguides.com or Amazon.

APPENDIX 1

WHAT TO SPOT IN THE NIGHT SKY

From treetop owls to galaxies far, far away, the sky in the northern hemisphere at night is full of bright and beautiful objects. This list provides a good selection for astronomers of all abilities, and no telescopes are needed to get started as many of these objects can be seen with the naked eye.

MOONS AND PLANETS

MOON The brightest celestial object in the earth's sky after the sun, the moon orbits our planet approximately every 27 days. The changing phase of the moon continuously reveals different details on its surface, as sunlight casts shadows across it.

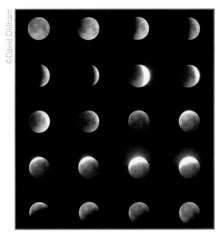

LUNAR ECLIPSE A lunar eclipse occurs when the moon moves into the earth's shadow. It can occur only when the sun, earth and moon are very closely aligned, with the earth between the other two, and only on the night of a full moon.

MERCURY The smallest and closest planet to the sun in our Solar System, Mercury is only slightly larger than our moon. One Mercurian day would feel like 59 earth days, although it only takes 88 earth days to orbit the sun. Mercury is difficult to spot due to its proximity to the sun; however, it can be seen during periods of 'greatest elongation' when it appears furthest from the sun as viewed from earth.

VENUS Named after the Roman goddess of love and beauty, Venus is the brightest natural object in the earth's night sky after the moon. Its dense carbon dioxide atmosphere reflects sunlight, making it easily visible after sunset or before sunrise (hence its nickname of 'the morning star').

MARS One of the most explored bodies in our Solar System, Mars is a very dynamic planet with its own seasons, polar ice caps, canyons and extinct volcanoes. Thanks to robotic explorers, scientists believe Mars was a wetter, warmer place billions of years ago, with a much thicker atmosphere.

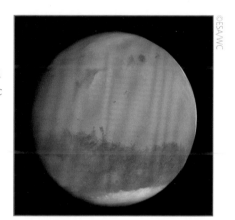

JUPITER The largest planet in our Solar System. The surface of Jupiter is home to the iconic Great Red Spot, which is believed to be a giant storm, bigger than our own planet, that has been raging for hundreds of years. Observing it using even very small binoculars will reveal up to four of Jupiter's largest moons as pin-points of light either side of the planet.

↑ The constellations of the northern hemisphere (pshava/Shutterstock)

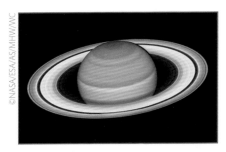

©NASA/ESA/AS/MHWWC

SATURN A gas giant made mostly of hydrogen and helium, Saturn is orbited by over 60 moons. Its famous rings are made of billions of particles of ice and rock which range in size from that of a grain of sugar to a two-storey house.

STARS AND CONSTELLATIONS

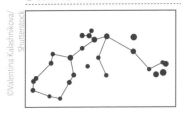

©Valentina Kalashnikova/Shutterstock

AQUARIUS Also known as the Water Bearer, Aquarius is one of the constellations of the Zodiac. Its brightest star is a rare yellow supergiant called Beta Aquarii or Sadalsuud.

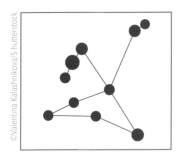

©Valentina Kalashnikova/Shutterstock

AQUILA A constellation on the celestial equator. Its name originates from the Latin for 'eagle', representing the bird that carried Jupiter's thunderbolts in Roman mythology.

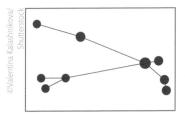

©Valentina Kalashnikova/Shutterstock

ARIES Depicted as a ram, Aries is a relatively dim constellation and features only four bright stars – Hamal, Sheratan, Mesarthim and 41 Arietis.

BOÖTES According to Egyptian mythology, Boötes was a guardian goddess who took the form of a hippopotamus and kept the pole stars under control. It is best seen in the springtime, rising in the northeast after sunset. Look for the bright red/orange star, Arcturus, and a shape of stars forming the pattern of a kite.

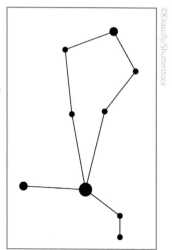

CAMELOPARDALIS This giraffe-shaped constellation is circumpolar, which means it is visible all night as it rotates around the north celestial pole. However, the stars that form this constellation are faint, meaning it can only be seen from dark sky locations.

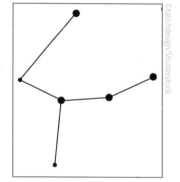

CANCER The Crab constellation is the dimmest of the 13 constellations of the Zodiac. The stars that make up this constellation are difficult to see; however, from dark sky locations you might catch a glimpse of the open cluster known as the Beehive (Messier 44) as a faint patch of light in the sky.

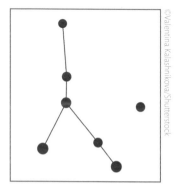

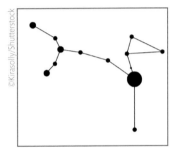

©Krasolly/Shutterstock

CANIS MAJOR The constellation containing Sirius (the Dog Star, and the brightest star in the night sky – Sirius means 'glowing' or 'scorching' in Greek) and the larger of the two hunting dogs belonging to Orion, the smaller being Canis Minor.

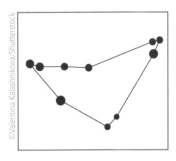

©Valentina Kalashnikova/Shutterstock

CAPRICORNUS An arrow-shaped constellation of the Zodiac taking the form of a sea goat. The Tropic of Capricorn – the place where the sun appears overhead at noon on the winter solstice – originally passed right through its namesake constellation, but the line has since shifted to pass through Sagittarius instead.

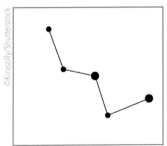

©Krasolly/Shutterstock

CASSIOPEIA A large constellation in the northern sky, named after a vain and boastful queen from Greek mythology. Appearing like a giant W in the sky, the second V in the W is often used by astronomers to form an arrow which points towards the Andromeda galaxy.

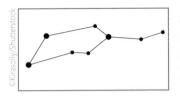

©Krasolly/Shutterstock

CETUS Also known as the Whale, the constellation Cetus was a sea monster in Greek mythology, thought to have inspired Herman Melville's nautical novel *Moby-Dick*.

CYGNUS The Swan is one of the most recognisable constellations of the northern hemisphere, featuring a prominent asterism known as the Northern Cross. Locate this pattern of stars from dark sky sites and you will see the Milky Way passing right through it.

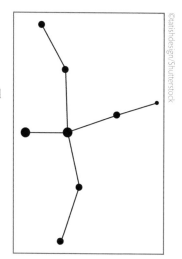

DELPHINUS In Greek mythology, the Dolphin was the messenger of the sea god Poseidon. It is one of the smaller officially recognised constellations in the night sky.

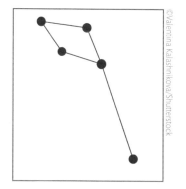

DRACO The Dragon constellation is based on the Roman myth of a giant titan who fought with the Olympian gods in a decade-long battle.

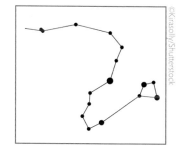

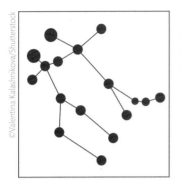

GEMINI The name of this constellation is Latin for 'twins', and its two brightest stars are named after Castor and Pollux, a pair of twin half-brothers from Greek mythology.

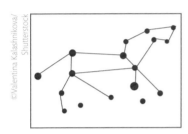

LEO Another Zodiac constellation, named after the Nemean lion killed by Hercules as one of his 12 Labours. Look for a pattern of stars that appears as a backwards question mark in the sky, an asterism known as the 'Sickle of Leo'.

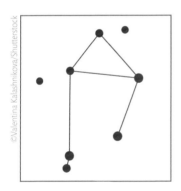

LIBRA Named after the Latin for weighing scales, this is the only constellation in the Zodiac to represent an inanimate object.

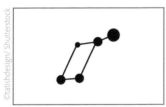

LYRA A small constellation in the shape of a harp, representing the lyre belonging to Orpheus, an ancient Greek figure who could charm any living thing with his music. Its brightest star is Vega; as the earth's axis shifts over a 26,000-year cycle, our perception of north changes and so does the North Star. Several thousand years ago, Vega was the North Star. It will reclaim that title again in around 12,000 years.

ORION A prominent constellation on the celestial equator and visible throughout the world. It is named after a hunter in Greek mythology. Its best-known star is Betelgeuse (pronounced 'Beetlejuice'), a dying, red supergiant star; when it finally explodes, astronomers believe it will be visible in the daytime for weeks. The constellation is also where you'll find Rigel, a blue supergiant star slightly dimmer than Betelgeuse. The name is thought to originate from the Arabic for 'the left leg of the giant'.

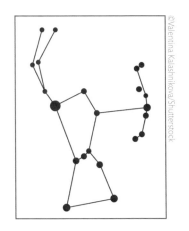

PEGASUS The Winged Horse constellation most easily recognised by the Square of Pegasus, a major asterism made up of four stars of nearly equal brightness.

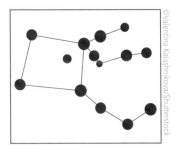

PISCES The brightest star in this constellation is a bright giant known as Eta Piscium or Kullat Nunu. It is 294 light years from earth and 316 times more luminous than the sun.

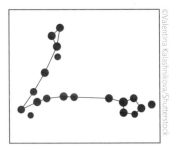

SAGITTARIUS The constellation Sagittarius is at the centre of the Milky Way Galaxy. It is the largest constellation in the southern hemisphere, although only its 'Teapot' asterism gets high enough above the southern horizon to be seen from the UK.

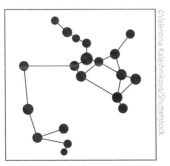

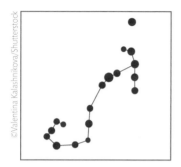

SCORPIUS In Greek mythology, the constellation Scorpius was identified with the scorpion that killed Orion the hunter. The name can be literally translated as 'the creature with the burning sting'. The brightest object in the constellation is Antares, a red supergiant sometimes referred to as 'the heart of the scorpion'.

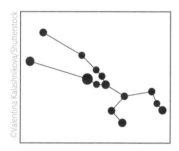

TAURUS The Bull is one of the oldest documented constellations, with descriptions of Taurus going as far back as the early Bronze Age. It is famous for its red giant star, Aldebaran, as well as a star cluster known as the Pleiades.

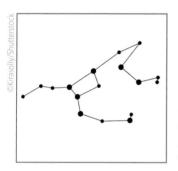

URSA MAJOR Known as the Great Bear, Ursa Major is the largest constellation in the northern hemisphere. Its seven brightest stars form a saucepan-shaped asterism called the Plough or the Big Dipper, one of the most recognisable shapes in the sky. The last two stars of the saucepan, Merak and Dubhe, are nicknamed the 'pointers' as they can be used to find the pole star.

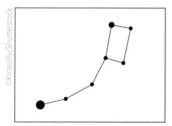

URSA MINOR Like its bigger sibling, the tail of the Little Bear also looks like a saucepan, hence the alternative name of the Little Dipper. Its brightest star is Polaris, or the North Star, which is the closest star to the north celestial pole. To find it, draw a line from the two outermost stars in the 'bowl' of the Plough.

VIRGO The constellation Virgo, the Maiden, can be seen in spring and summer in the northern hemisphere and in autumn and winter in the southern hemisphere. The constellation includes an asterism called 'the Bowl of Virgo': a region of the sky densely populated with distant galaxies.

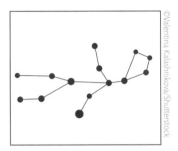

BINARY STARS

A pair of stars orbiting a common center of mass. To the naked eye, they usually appear as one point of light until examined more closely using a telescope. One of the finest examples of a binary star is Almach in the Andromeda constellation, formed of a bright blue star and an orange companion. Pictured: Albireo.

GALAXIES, STAR CLUSTERS AND NEBULAE

MILKY WAY A barred spiral galaxy made up of several hundred billion stars, as well as our own Solar System. It looks like a splash of milk spilled across the sky, but if you could see it from the top, you would see a central bulge surrounded by four large spiral arms that wrap around it.

ANDROMEDA GALAXY (MESSIER 31) The Milky Way's closest neighbour, and the most distant object in our sky visible to the naked eye. In a few billion years, it is likely that Andromeda will merge with the Milky Way, but by that time the sun will have swollen into a red giant and swallowed the earth.

TRIANGULUM GALAXY
(MESSIER 33) About half the size of the Milky Way, the Triangulum Galaxy is around 3 million light years from the earth and, like Andromeda, is also on a collision course with our own galaxy.

CIGAR GALAXY
(MESSIER 82) The closest starburst galaxy to earth, the centre of this galaxy is 100 times more luminous than the Milky Way.

BODE'S GALAXY
(MESSIER 81) This is one of the brightest galaxies visible from earth, located in the constellation Ursa Major, with an active galactic nucleus containing a supermassive black hole.

NEEDLE GALAXY
(NGC 4565) Named after its narrow profile, this edge-on spiral galaxy lies 30 to 50 million light years away in the constellation Coma Berenices.

WHIRLPOOL GALAXY
(MESSIER 51A) The graceful, winding arms of this spiral galaxy are star formation factories, compressing hydrogen gas to create clusters of new stars.

SUNFLOWER GALAXY (MESSIER 63)

A spiral galaxy located in the northern constellation Canes Venatici. The name is inspired by its bright yellow central disc and a number of short spiral arm segments dotted with starburst regions and dust lanes.

PHANTOM GALAXY (MESSIER 74)

A spiral galaxy located in the constellation Pisces. Small telescopes will reveal a bright nucleus surrounded by a hazy halo, while larger telescopes will show the galaxy's spiral arms.

SOMBRERO GALAXY (MESSIER 104)

A majestic, unbarred spiral galaxy located in the constellation Virgo. It is visible in binoculars and small telescopes, but only appears as a small patch of light. The name originates from the galactic bulge and the dust lane that crosses in front of it.

PLEIADES (MESSIER 45)

A group of more than 800 stars within the constellation Taurus, dominated by hot blue stars that have formed within the last 100 million years. To find the Pleiades, draw a line using the three stars in Orion's belt and then follow it upward, past his bow, until you find what looks like a smaller, hazier version of the Plough.

HYADES (CALDWELL 41)

The closest star cluster to our sun, the Hyades were formed around 625 million years ago and sit within the constellation Taurus. The brightest star is Alderbaran, reddish in colour and known as the 'eye of the bull'.

THE DOUBLE CLUSTER (CALDWELL 14) A pair of star

clusters within the constellation Perseus, both visible to the naked eye.

BEEHIVE CLUSTER (MESSIER 44) An open star

cluster in the constellation Cancer, appearing as a blurry patch of light to the naked eye.

BUTTERFLY CLUSTER (MESSIER 6) A bright, open star

cluster in the constellation Scorpius, described by the astronomer who named it as a butterfly with open wings.

WILD DUCK CLUSTER
(MESSIER 11) A rich, compact

star cluster in the constellation
Scutum in the southern sky.
Through binoculars, it appears as a
diamond-shaped patch, while the
brighter stars form a V-shape like a
flock of flying ducks.

PTOLEMY CLUSTER
(MESSIER 7) A bright, open star

cluster in the constellation Scorpius,
easily visible to the naked eye but
best seen through binoculars.

HERCULES
GLOBULAR CLUSTER
(MESSIER 13) One of the

brightest and best-known globular
clusters in the northern sky.
With clear skies and no light
pollution, this cluster can be seen
without binoculars.

KING COBRA CLUSTER
(MESSIER 67) An open star

cluster in the northern constellation
Cancer, it can be found roughly
halfway and slightly above the
imaginary line connecting the stars
Regulus in Leo and Procyon in
Canis Minor.

ORION NEBULA (MESSIER 42)
One of the brightest nebulae in the sky and a prominent asterism in the winter sky. It is visible to the naked eye and located just below the constellation Orion's Belt.

CRAB NEBULA (MESSIER 1)
An expanding supernova remnant and pulsar wind nebula, located in the northern constellation Taurus.

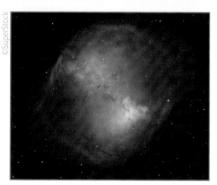

DUMBBELL NEBULA (MESSIER 27)
A planetary nebula in the constellation Vulpecula, large in size, quite bright, and visible through binoculars and small telescopes.

EAGLE NEBULA
(MESSIER 16) A star-forming nebula in the constellation Serpens, it is best known for the Pillars of Creation region, three large pillars of gas famously photographed by the Hubble Telescope in 1995.

RING NEBULA
(MESSIER 57) A planetary nebula found just south of Vega, the brightest star in the constellation Lyra and one of the stars that form the prominent asterism the Summer Triangle.

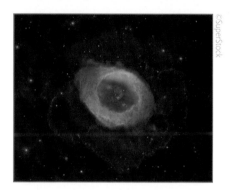

LAGOON NEBULA
(MESSIER 8) A large, bright nebula in the constellation Sagittarius, named after the lagoon-shaped band of dust to the left of the cluster's centre.

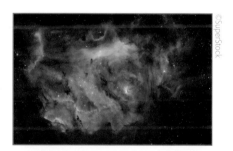

OWL NEBULA
(MESSIER 97) A planetary nebula in Ursa Major, named after its appearance in larger telescopes which reveal two dark patches that look like the eyes of an owl.

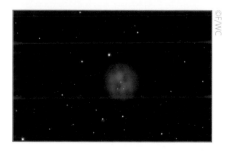

COMETS AND METEORS

COMET A cosmic snowball of frozen gas, rock and dust that orbits the sun. When it travels through our atmosphere, it heats up and releases dust and gas, which form a giant glowing head larger than most planets. Comets are informally known as shooting stars. Pictured here: Neowise.

PERSEIDS One of the highlights of the meteor shower calendar due to its high hourly rate and bright meteors originating from the Swift-Tuttle comet. The average speed for a Perseid meteor is 58km (36 miles) per second.

GEMINIDS One of the best and most reliable annual showers with rates of approximately 120 meteors per hour. They are bright, fast and yellow in colour.

OTHER COMETS AND METEORS Harder to photograph, but also features of our night sky are the following comets and meteors. **Quadrantids** are known for their bright fireball meteors and are named after a now-defunct constellation, the Quadrant, from which they appear to radiate. **Lyrids** are one of the oldest known meteor showers, the first recorded sighting of which dates back to ancient Chinese documentation. **Eta Aquariids** are the meteor shower made from space debris originating from Halley's Comet, the only naked-eye comet that can appear twice in a human lifetime. Meanwhile, **Alpha Capricornids** are a shower of slow, yellow fireballs, thought to have been created around 3,500 to 5,000 years ago, when half of the parent body disintegrated and fell into dust. These are very difficult to see, appearing as they do in July when the skies are less dark. **Draconids** are one of the less active meteor showers in recent years, although in 1933 and 1946 they produced some of the most exciting displays of the century. **Orionids** originate from the constellation Orion, just to the north of its brightest star Betelgeuse. In moonless skies, viewers may see up to 15 meteors per hour. An annual meteor shower associated with the comet Encke, **Taurids** don't offer huge numbers of shooting stars, but the ones that do appear may be bright, spectacular fireballs. **Leonids** – a bright and colourful shower – have fast meteors travelling up to over 70km (44 miles) per second. **Ursids** are a sparse shower producing around five meteors per hour at its peak. Ursids appear to radiate from near the star Beta Ursae Minoris within the constellation Ursa Minor.

ATMOSPHERIC PHENOMENA

NORTHERN LIGHTS
A natural light display in high-latitude regions of the sky, resulting from disturbances in the magnetosphere caused by solar wind. Also known as the aurora borealis, they appear in the night sky as glowing ribbons and curtains of green, blue, pink, and violet.

NOCTILUCENT CLOUDS
Shining, cloud-like phenomena in the upper atmosphere of earth's sky. Only visible during astronomical twilight, they are made up of frozen ice crystals high up in the air, reflecting the light from the sun after it has set beyond the horizon.

MANMADE OBJECTS

©Neill Sanders

INTERNATIONAL SPACE STATION (ISS) A multi-nation construction project and the largest single structure humans have ever sent into space. It has four gyroscopes which allow it to change altitude, and several sets of thrusters that allow it to rotate. The ISS circles the globe every 90 minutes at a speed of around 28,000km/h (17,500mph); in one day, it travels about the distance it would take to go from earth to the moon and back.

©Daniel Monk/Kielder Observatory

SATELLITES A satellite is the name given to any moon, planet or machine that orbits a planet or star. It is more commonly used to refer to a machine that is launched into space and moves around the earth or another cosmic body. Satellites don't have exterior lights, but you can still spot them at the beginning and end of the night as sunlight is reflected off their solar panels.

©Poket Idol/Shutterstock

DRONE Also known as an Unmanned Aerial Vehicle (UAV), a drone is an unpiloted aircraft or spacecraft. In recent years they have become popular among hobbyists, and at night they are usually fitted with anti-collision lights.

WILDLIFE

©Sandra Standbridge/Shutterstock

BARN OWL A distinctive and widely distributed bird with a heart-shaped face, buff back feathers and bright white underparts. They are often heard before they are seen, earning them their folk name 'screech owl'.

TAWNY OWL A reddish-brown owl with a rounded body and paler underparts. Tawny owls are famous for their *twit-twoo* calls, but these are actually the calls of two separate birds. The female lets out a harsh *keewik* call, and the male responds with a softer *huhuhuhooo*.

COMMON PIPISTRELLE BAT Our smallest and most common bat, they have reddish-brown coats and blackish-brown ears.

DAUBENTON'S BAT Sometimes referred to as the 'water bat', this species is usually seen flying over wetlands at twilight, skimming the water's surface for insect prey.

NOCTULE BAT The UK's largest bat, this species roosts in the trees and can be seen flying over the canopy in search of insects.

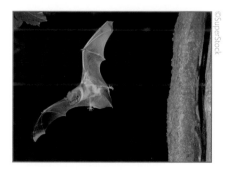

NIGHTJAR A crepuscular bird species found on UK heathlands in the summer months. They are best encountered at dusk and dawn, when they emit their famous churring song, rising and falling as they turn their heads.

REDWING Redwings migrate to the UK every autumn from the Scandinavian coast. They travel at night, and can be heard by listening out for their soft *seep seep seep* call as they pass overhead through the night sky.

STARLING Starling murmurations appear just before dusk during the winter months, when huge groups twist, turn and swirl across the sky in beautiful shape-shifting clouds.

CINNABAR MOTH A striking red species flying mainly at night, particularly around well-drained, rabbit-grazed grassland.

ELEPHANT HAWKMOTH

A pink and olive-green species best seen flying at dusk, feeding on plants like honeysuckle and other tubular, nectar-rich flowers.

SCARLET TIGER MOTH

With its metallic green-black colouring, whitish-yellow spots and red hindwings, this species is usually seen in the early evening and at night in wetland and coastal habitats.

SILVER Y MOTH   Our most

common migrant moth, this crepuscular species is easily identified by the distinctive metallic 'Y' on each forewing.

SEND US YOUR SNAPS

We'd love to follow your adventures using our *Dark Skies* guide – why not tag us in your photos and stories on Twitter (🐦 BradtGuides) and Instagram (📷 bradtguides)?

APPENDIX 2

FURTHER INFORMATION

BOOKS

Beall, Abigail *The Art of Urban Astronomy: A Guide to Stargazing Wherever You Are* Trapeze, 2019. An inspiring guidebook for city-dwellers looking to escape the urban bustle by reconnecting with the stars. Packed full of star charts, facts and useful information to get started with backyard astronomy.

Bell, Jim *The Hubble Legacy: 30 Years of Discoveries and Images* Sterling, 2020. A collection of the most stunning imagery captured by the Hubble Space Telescope, and a reminder of what the universe looks like up close.

Chapman, Emma *First Light: Switching on Stars at the Dawn of Time* Bloomsbury Sigma, 2020. A fascinating account of the first billion years of the universe's existence when the chaos of the Big Bang began to create galaxies, black holes and stars.

DeGrasse Tyson, Neil *Astrophysics for People in a Hurry: Essays on the Universe and Our Place Within It* W W Norton, 2017. A succinct and sparkling collection of essays on the big universal questions, from quantum mechanics to the search for extraterrestrial life.

Freistetter, Florian *A History of the Universe in 100 Stars* Quercus, 2021. Part compendium, part astronomer's memoir, the author takes us through the past and future of the cosmos, telling the stories of those who have tried to decipher the stars.

Ganeri, Anita *Star Stories: Constellation Tales from Around the World* Running Press, 2019. A book for the kids' bedtime, this beautiful collection brings together constellation stories from ancient Greece to North America, Egypt, China, India and the South Pacific.

Hawking, Stephen *A Brief History of Time: From the Big Bang to Black Holes* Bantam, 2011. The internationally acclaimed masterpiece from one of the world's greatest minds, this is essential reading for anyone delving into the mysteries of the universe.

Kerss, Tom *Moongazing: Beginner's Guide to Exploring the Moon* Collins, 2018. An in-depth guide exploring lunar maps, history, geology, exploration, origin and orbit.

Marchant, Jo *The Human Cosmos: A Secret History of the Stars* Canongate, 2020. A beautiful journey through the human relationship with the night sky, how we have lost that connection, and how rediscovering it could vastly improve our wellbeing.

Murdin, Paul *The Secret Lives of Planets: A User's Guide to the Solar System* Hodder, 2020. An enchanting tour of our solar system, the planets we share it with, and where we fit in.

STAR CHARTS

Dunlop, Storm and Wil Tirion *Night Sky Almanac: A Stargazer's Guide* Collins Astronomy, 2020

Henbest, Nigel and Heather Couper *Philips Stargazing Month-by-Month Guide to the Night Sky in Britain & Ireland* Philips (annual)

APPS

APOD Viewer Fun facts and beautiful photography from outer space.

Aurora Alert Predicts potential displays of the northern lights nearby.

ISS Detector and **ISS Spotter** Alerts you when the ISS is due to pass overhead.

Luminos Detailed maps and photographs from the stars and planets.

Meteor Shower Calendar A list of upcoming meteor showers and peak dates.

SkyView and **Google Skymap** Point your camera at the sky and see a labelled map of the cosmos above you.

WEBSITES

⊘ **astronomynow.com** The online hub of the UK's bestselling astronomy magazine.

⊘ **darkskydiscovery.org.uk** Stargazing locations around the UK with an interactive map.

⊘ **gostargazing.co.uk** The best stargazing locations and events in the UK; see ad, inside-back cover.

⊘ **nasa.gov** News and updates from the frontline of space exploration, as well as the fantastic Image of the Day feature from satellites and telescopes around the world.

⊘ **skyandtelescope.org/observing/sky-at-a-glance** A weekly digest of the night sky with simple maps and current celestial events.

DOCUMENTARIES
No televisual journey into space is complete without smiley physicist Brian Cox, and his 2019 series *The Planets* is a great introduction to the history of our solar system. For those interested in space exploration history, *Mission Control: The Unsung Heroes of Apollo* pays homage to the mission control staff who put a man on the moon, while *Challenger: The Final Flight* focuses on the fatal crash of NASA's Space Shuttle *Challenger* in 1986. *The Last Man on the Moon* also explores the Apollo missions but from a more human perspective, looking at the pressure an astronaut's lifestyle can put on their family and home life. Despite the dramatic title, *NOVA: Blackhole Apocalypse* is a well-produced and entertaining documentary about the history

and science of black holes, while ***Death Dive to Saturn*** takes us on a voyage to Saturn in the steps of the Cassini space probe, tasked to navigate a tightrope path between the planet and its rings to collect data. For something a little different, ***The Mars Generation*** follows a group of young space enthusiasts at Space Camp in Alabama, and for a more light-hearted – yet fascinating – watch, ***Behind the Curve*** takes us behind the scenes of the Flat Earth Society and their controversial beliefs.

PODCASTS For general space-themed content, the BBC offers a range of podcasts including *5 Live Science* and *In Our Time,* or check out *Cool Space News* for updates on the latest projects at NASA's Mission Control, hosted by US space writer and journalist Rod Pyle. The NASA Johnson Space Center in Texas also hosts the excellent *Houston We Have a Podcast,* and the team behind the European Southern Observatory cover the latest discoveries in space science on their series *ESOcast.* The European Space Agency also hosts an official behind-the-scenes podcast on space exploration, *ESA Explores.* The Hubble Space Telescope's *HubbleCast* explains some of the fundamentals of astronomy and cosmology, while the *Royal Observatory Greenwich* podcast offers monthly stargazing guides and interviews with space scientists. The *Interplanetary Podcast* covers all things astrophysics, spaceflight and cosmology, with a great selection of interviewees; for a more academic-focused discussion, try *The Supermassive Podcast* with journalist Izzie Clarke and astrophysicist Dr Becky Smethurst, who discuss the latest astronomy research in their monthly podcast for the Royal Astronomical Society.

ORGANISATIONS For amateur astronomers, the **British Astronomical Association** is widely recognised as one of the world's leading non-professional groups. Since its inception over 125 years ago, the BAA has empowered its members to contribute scientifically valuable observations, often in collaboration with professionals. They also help beginners to get started with equipment, workshops and useful information (⊘britastro.org).

For those interested in the more professional side of astronomy, the **Royal Astronomical Society** promotes the study of astronomy and geophysics, including solar physics, planetary and space sciences, geophysics and the 'new astronomies' like astroparticle physics and astrobiology. They also publish research journals, organise scientific meetings, provide grants, support outreach, award prizes and lobby government (⊘ras.ac.uk).

The **Royal Observatory** in London is part of the Royal Museums Greenwich, and makes a great day out for anyone interested in the history of astronomy, time and navigation. You can stand at the Prime Meridian of the world with one foot in the west and one in the east, or get up close and personal with the stars in one of their planetarium shows, led by expert astronomers. There are also plenty of useful educational resources on their website (⊘ rmg.co.uk/royal-observatory), particularly for younger astronomers. Members of the public are encouraged to look up their local astronomy society or club using the **Federation of Astronomical Societies** website (⊘ fedastro.org.uk). The **Society for Popular Astronomy** (⊘ popastro.com) is another excellent resource for beginner stargazers.

INDEX

Numbers in **bold** relate to major entries.

INDEX OF ADVERTISERS

THE BRADT STORY

In the beginning

It all began in 1974 on an Amazon river barge. During an 18-month trip through South America, two adventurous young backpackers – Hilary Bradt and her then husband, George – decided to write about the hiking trails they had discovered through the Andes. *Backpacking Along Ancient Ways in Peru and Bolivia* included the very first descriptions of the Inca Trail. It was the start of a colourful journey to becoming one of the best-loved travel publishers in the world; you can read the full story on our website (bradtguides. com/ourstory).

Getting there first

Hilary quickly gained a reputation for being a true travel pioneer, and in the 1980s she started to focus on guides to places overlooked by other publishers. The Bradt Guides list became a roll call of guidebook 'firsts'. We published the first guide to Madagascar, followed by Mauritius, Czechoslovakia and Vietnam. The 1990s saw the beginning of our extensive coverage of Africa: Tanzania, Uganda, South Africa, and Eritrea. Later, post-conflict guides became a feature: Rwanda, Mozambique, Angola, and Sierra Leone, as well as the first standalone guides to the Baltic States following the fall of the Iron Curtain, and the first post-war guides to Bosnia, Kosovo and Albania.

Comprehensive – and with a conscience

Today, we are the world's largest independently owned travel publisher, with more than 200 titles. However, our ethos remains unchanged. Hilary is still keenly involved, and **we still get there first**: two-thirds of Bradt guides have no direct competition.

But we don't just get there first. Our guides are also known for being **more comprehensive** than any other series. We avoid templates and tick-lists. Each guide is a one-of-a-kind expression of an expert author's interests, knowledge and enthusiasm for telling it how it really is.

And a commitment to wildlife, conservation and respect for local communities has always been at the heart of our books. Bradt Guides was **championing sustainable travel** before any other guidebook publisher. We even have a series dedicated to Slow Travel in the UK, award-winning books that explore the country with a passion and depth you'll find nowhere else.

Thank you!

We can only do what we do because of the support of readers like you – people who value less-obvious experiences, less-visited places and a more thoughtful approach to travel. Those who, like us, take travel seriously.

Bradt GUIDES

TRAVEL TAKEN SERIOUSLY

IDA
MAYO INTERNATIONAL DARK SKY PARK

Páirceanna Náisiúnta na hÉireann
National Parks of Ireland

An Roinn Tithíochta,
Rialtais Áitiúil agus Oidhreachta
Department of Housing,
Local Government and Heritage